The Education
of Teachers

The Education of Teachers

A Look Ahead

Kenneth R. Howey
William E. Gardner

Longman

New York & London

THE EDUCATION OF TEACHERS: A Look Ahead

Longman Inc., 1560 Broadway, New York, N.Y. 10036
Associated companies, branches, and representatives
throughout the world.

Copyright © 1983 by Longman Inc.

Developmental Editor: Nicole Benevento
Editorial and Design Supervisor: Frances Althaus
Production Supervisor: Ferne Kawahara
Manufacturing Supervisor: Marion Hess
Cover Design: Dan Serrano

Library of Congress Cataloging in Publication Data

Main entry under title:

The Education of teachers.
  Bibliography: p.
  Includes index.
  Contents: Teacher education / Kenneth R. Howey—
Methodological considerations in future research
and development in teacher education / Del
Schalock—The need for theoretical frameworks
in educating teachers / Norman A. Sprinthall and
Lois Theis-Sprinthall—[etc.]
  1. Teachers—Training of—Addresses, essays,
lectures. I. Howey, Kenneth R. II. Gardner,
William E.
LB1715.E325   370'.7'1   81-20841

ISBN 0-582-28354-X   AACR2

Manufactured in the United States of America

Contents

Acknowledgments

The following material has been reprinted by permission, as noted:

"A Summary of the Major Characteristics of Each of the Four Information-Gathering Techniques," from EVALUATION: A PRACTICAL GUIDE FOR TEACHERS by Terry D. TenBrink. Copyright © 1974 by the McGraw-Hill Book Company. Used with the permission of McGraw-Hill Book Company.

"Cycle and Phase Arrangement for TPEP," in "Western Kentucky University Follow-up Evaluation of Teacher Education Graduates" by R.D. Adams. From TEACHER EDUCATION PROGRAM EVALUATION AND FOLLOW-UP STUDIES: A COLLECTION OF CURRENT EFFORTS, S.M. Hord and G.E. Hall (eds.). Copyright © 1979 by The Research and Development Center for Teacher Education, University of Texas at Austin. Reprinted by permission of Shirley M. Hord.

"An Overview of Research in Teacher Education" by Richard L. Turner. From TEACHER EDUCATION, Kevin Ryan (ed.), 74th Yearbook (part 2) of the National Society for the Study of Education, 1975. Reprinted by permission of the N.S.S.E.

Tables and Figures

TABLES

FIGURES

Introduction

Kenneth R. Howey
William E. Gardner

This book has a threefold purpose. First, it provides a review of research and development related to the education of teachers. While the manuscript is hardly inclusive of the myriad activities undertaken over time to improve teacher education, it is comprehensive in that it does critically review inquiry which has been undertaken into all phases of teacher education: initial teacher preparation, induction into the profession (the first years of teaching), and inservice teacher education. Second, it discusses salient issues and problems related to teacher education and the efforts undertaken to study and improve it. Thus, sociopolitical and legal-economic as well as conceptual and methodological concerns are addressed. Third, it identifies specific areas where further research and development appear most warranted if we are to better understand and improve upon the critical process of educating teachers.

The talents of several scholars are drawn upon in an effort to address teacher education in each of its phases and from multiple perspectives. Each of the distinguished contributors brings a rich history of involvement in teacher education. They have studied their own efforts to educate teachers and those of others as well. They are acutely aware of the difficulties involved in conducting research and development concerned with teacher education. Their recommendations for the future are tempered by the reality of their past efforts and their insights into the complex of economic and political factors which shape current practice.

The book is ordered basically according to the phases through which a teacher proceeds. In the chapter following this introduction, Kenneth Howey, one of the coeditors, provides an overview of normative policy and practice in each of the three major phases of teacher education. He begins by examining a number of evolving conditions in our society which have the potential for altering the nature of schooling and hence the functions of teachers. Research into teacher education is obviously related to role-expectations for teachers and what constitutes effectiveness in these roles. He reminds the reader at the outset that an enlightened discussion of research and development in teacher education must consider probable changes in what teachers will be asked to do.

He acknowledges that many present policies and practices will remain largely as they are and that there is much to be learned about current teacher education efforts as well. Drawing upon extensive survey research, he identifies what appear to be some of the more obvious limitations in contemporary teacher education efforts. He begins by reviewing common concerns in initial teacher education, notes the limited attention to the needs of the beginning teacher, and reports the perceptions of experienced teachers relative to their continuing education. In each of these instances he identifies general areas which appear most in need of further experimentation, understanding, or improvement.

This overview chapter concludes with a brief discussion of what is known about those who select teaching as a vocation. While the data base here is admittedly fragmentary, it does raise concerns about how teachers are selected and admitted to teacher education programs and eventually teaching positions. Acknowledging that there are evident limitations in terms of studies of teacher characteristics, well-conceived chains of inquiry are called for which would examine the interaction between specific teacher traits and (1) success in different types of learning or teacher training conditions, (2) accommodation to basically different teaching roles and responsibilities, and (3) specific teacher behaviors which have in turn been associated with desired pupil outcomes.

In Chapter 2, the noted methodologist and teacher educator, Del Schalock, reminds us that large-scale, long-term, well-funded research efforts in teacher education are simply nonexistent. He suggests that major advances in teacher education are not likely to be made until research on the costs and benefits of natural and/or planned program variation are undertaken. He calls for lines of inquiry with sufficient replication of studies in order that confidence can be assigned to observed effects. Schalock provides multiple examples of the various types of program improvement studies that are needed, and reviews the advantages and limitations of each approach for the reader. He calls for diverse and multi-faceted forms of research which demand equally diverse methodology.

The basic position in Schalock's chapter is that not only has research but our *methodological capability* as well been severely constrained to date. He maintains that the methodological problems which confront researchers in teacher education are considerably more complex than once thought and, thus, research on substantive issues will have to be paralleled by advances in methodology. He concludes his chapter with an insightful discussion of needed adaptations in conventional educational research methods to the study of teacher education and suggests how future studies may well differ markedly from past ones. He emphasizes that a major need in future research is to engage in both hypothesis-formulation and hypothesis-testing studies coordinated at multiple sites where there are ongoing teacher preparation programs. His chapter is interspersed with numerous examples from his own research and is especially instructive in terms of offering specific examples of how teacher education programs might be studied in the future.

In Chapter 3, Norman Sprinthall and Lois Theis-Sprinthall address a critical yet largely ignored area, that of theoretical frameworks for guiding the education of teachers. These scholars draw upon their experiences in both developmental psychology and teacher education and review emerging theoretical perspectives and research findings specifically related to cognitive development in adults. The studies they examine have repeatedly demonstrated that cognitive-developmental stages predict differential functioning for adults in general, and for teachers specifically. Thus, a key concern is whether more complex stages of adult development associated with indices of teaching effectiveness can, in fact, be promoted. They examine this central question of how developmental growth might be stimulated by reviewing selected research studies in some depth. These provocative findings suggest that cognitive development can be fostered and the empirically supported principles for doing this can provide a badly needed theoretical framework for teacher education. They conclude their chapter by suggesting how these principles can be put into practice and also suggest directions for future research and development.

In Chapter 4, attention is given specifically to preservice teacher education. Martin Haberman examines research concerned with student teaching, commonly perceived as the most critical aspect of beginning teacher education. He reviews the history of the clinical or student-teaching phase of the beginning teacher's education, noting that almost all studies of student teaching have failed to take into account the host of sociological and organizational behaviors which affect the student teacher. Similarly, he points out the emphasis in this critical phase of teacher education on practicing techniques rather than experimenting in a professional laboratory context. He maintains that the former orientation has also shaped the little systematic research and development that has occurred into student teaching.

Haberman cautions us about the current trend toward more school-based experiences for the future teacher. He suggests that this advocacy be accompanied by very careful consideration of just what those experiences should be. He suggests that economic and political conditions dictate that a price will inevitably be paid for making future teachers more "relevant" to school practice in terms of a trade-off of other important learning experiences. He concludes his chapter by suggesting future lines of inquiry with an emphasis on acquiring a better understanding of just how future teachers are influenced in their behavior.

In Chapter 5, James Cooper moves the focus from studies of student teaching to an examination of how all key aspects of initial teacher education might be evaluated. His recommendations are germane to many in-service program designs as well. This leader in teacher education evaluation selects from the work of a consortium of eight institutions of higher education engaged in longitudinal program evaluation. He examines the pros and cons of different evaluation designs and specific methods of data collection. He also speaks to such important management strategies as how to involve faculty and how to present data in understandable and usable terms. Since the major goal of evaluation is to make judgments, he reviews some of the essential judgments which evaluation of teacher education programs should address. Specific examples of program evaluation from the eight teacher preparation institutions are shared. He concludes his chapter with a discussion of where further research and development is needed with an emphasis on those variables which should be considered in any systematic and comprehensive evaluation scheme.

In Chapter 6, the focus shifts from preservice teacher education to research concerned with the critical transition of changing from learning to teach to teaching others to learn. Two pioneers in research into the beginning teacher's life share their insights into this period. John M. Johnston and Kevin Ryan examine both the research and nonresearch literature concerned with the beginning teacher. They note limitations of much of this research yet conclude that much of what has been learned to this point in time unfortunately is not put into practice. They underscore the need for research which will provide a more complete picture of the complex events in the lives of beginning teachers. Like Haberman, they note that we have but the barest understanding of the important socialization process for the beginner and they share specific ideas in terms of how a more fine-grained portrait of these teachers might be obtained. They provide thoughtful guidelines for how the education or induction of the beginning teacher might better proceed, and they also outline an agenda for future research into the process of beginning to teach.

Chapter 7 moves more fully into an examination of the inservice phase of teacher education. Sam Yarger, with his wide background of research and development into teacher education, and his colleague Gary Galluzzo, take a critical look at research in the area of inservice teacher education. They acknowledge at the outset the lack of precision in key terms in the literature of inservice teacher education and the concomitant problems this presents in attempting to study and improve it. The authors first provide what they believe to be necessary definitions for communicating effectively with the reader and go on to identify five basic types of research. What is especially helpful, however, is their analysis of the extent to which each of these basic types of research is able to help answer four fundamental questions about continuing teacher education: what exists, what is appropriate, what is feasible, and, finally, what is effective?

They next share multiple examples of each major type of research and note where major gaps exist. They build upon what *is* known as well as what is *not* known in outlining an agenda for future research on inservice teacher education. Their recommendations for future research and development are comprehensive and ordered within the framework they have developed for specifying the critical questions which must be answered and the variety of data which can be collected to answer them.

In the final chapter, William Gardner, Dean of the College of Education at the University of Minnesota, critically examines several common themes and salient issues which appear in the book. He brings to this task the perspective of one who has major managerial responsibilities and combines this with broad experiences in interinstitutional and organizational negotiations concerned with teacher education. He notes the influence of several external mediating factors in shaping current and future directions in teacher education. He weighs the probable efficacy of various recommendations for the education of teachers against other strategies such as changes in the recruitment and selection process or a reshaping of the responsibilities of various teachers. This concluding chapter provides the reader an insightful discussion of related changes which will have to occur as well if research and development in teacher education is to proceed in a more ideal manner in the future.

1

Teacher Education: An Overview

Kenneth R. Howey

University of Minnesota

This book is concerned with research and development related to the education of teachers. It brings together different dimensions of the existing knowledge base and suggests future directions for how it can be improved as well. The questions of how best to prepare good teachers and sustain their effectiveness are directly related to the question of what is expected of teachers—what is it exactly that a teacher does. This latter question is not as easy to answer as it appears, even if the mission of schools and the functions of teachers were largely unchanging in nature. They obviously are not. The remaining two decades of this century foreshadow a number of conditions which could alter the nature of schooling and the roles of teachers. Thus, an enlightened discussion of research and development in teacher education must consider what might cause permutations in the teacher role.

I would argue that there are four possible interrelated conditions which would certainly affect teacher education. In an effort to illustrate how various teaching roles might be altered, these conditions are briefly reviewed here: an unstable economy, heightened social unrest, demands for broadened educational services, and potential responses by those within the education professions who will be asked to do more with less.

There is hardly consensus among economists and other fiscal experts about the immediate, let alone the longer-range, prospects for the economy. However, many are pessimistic about conditions in the foreseeable future and no easy solutions to current economic problems are evident. The extent of our dependency on external sources for certain forms of energy for the immediate future, alone, suggests that there will be economic instability in the years ahead. Without doubt, this instability will have an effect upon publicly supported schools and those who work in them. Government revenues may well be diminished, and monies currently targeted for education may well be redirected in order to meet other evolving needs. Tax monies levied and earmarked for the support of schools will likely receive intensified scrutiny.

Diminished resources are obviously related to teacher salaries. For example, while throughout the decade of 1970s salaries of teachers rose annually, in many situations they did not keep pace with the rate of inflation.

Given these projections one can anticipate an increasingly militant posture by teachers in contract negotiations. At the same time, teacher demands for adequate compensation and desirable working conditions will more and more be related to the degree to which they are able to meet a multiplicity of educational demands. More evidence of the ability of schools to respond to a broad range of goals will be requested. There is likely to be increased and continued tension in the years ahead. As some of society's more persistent problems resurface and affect more people—especially people somewhat previously insular to these problems —demands for assistance in combating these problems will be directed at the schools. The types of problems which gave rise to curriculum development in sex education, drug education, moral education, and multicultural education are still with us. The debate over what functions the school ought to and reasonably can assume will likely be sharpened in the future.

It is also likely that we will have a situation where more *new* teachers will face these pressures since a larger number of beginning teachers will be entering the profession in the years ahead. There is also the likelihood that many experienced teachers will continue to leave teaching to seek alternative careers. Certainly reports of teacher dissatisfaction with work conditions are widespread. The National Education Association in their 1980–81 survey indicated that only 21.8 percent of teachers certainly would and only another 24.6 probably would choose teaching as a career if they had the choice to make over again. Thus it is possible that we may have a largely bimodal teaching force by the late 1980s made up of relatively large numbers of inexperienced teachers on the one hand and relatively mature and quite experienced teachers on the other. The number of middle-aged, experienced teachers is likely to be relatively small because of the protracted period of time in the 1970s when fewer beginning teachers entered the profession, and because many others who did enter will have sought alternative careers at an age when they still perceived themselves as marketable. This is especially likely if the conditions of expanded and intensified demands, weakened salaries, and diminished working conditions do evolve.

What are the implications of this brief scenario which portrays unstable economic conditions and heightened social unrest leading to both mixed and broadened expectations for schools, and at the same time greater scrutiny of how well schools are doing? One can project at least four major responses to this set of conditions:

1. There will be greater emphasis on delineating those functions which the school can reasonably and appropriately assume. A likely outcome, especially in our larger cities, will be more formalized linkages between schools and other agencies, to provide instruction and services usually provided largely by schools. Both more functional endeavors such as driver and career education, opportunities for involvement in various arts, and, yes, even athletics, are likely to be coordinated with other public and private agents. Teachers will increasingly be involved in communicating and planning with persons outside the school context.

2. Schools at all levels increasingly will incorporate into their instruction the use of microwave and cable television and the development of software for microcomputers which can be used by students in the home and community center environments. Affordability of this technology and a heightened need to better delineate educational responsibility could well fuel such a move in this direction.

3. Schools, especially at the elementary level, will increasingly be organized in different ways. Not only will there be a more explicit division of labor among teachers, assuming different and more specialized responsibilities, but there will be more clearly delineated functions for schools to attend to at different times. Both *expanded day* and *expanded year* concepts will be more prevalent. Cost-effective accounting schemes will influence schools to meet different goals in specific ways at different times.

4. The increased concern for competent teachers could contribute to more protracted initial preparation especially in terms of formalized support for teachers during their first years of teaching. The increased realization by the teachers' organizations that salary increases and job benefits are in many respects tied to (perceived) level of professional competence would provide additional impetus for a more expanded initial preparation for teachers and a further move away from inservice efforts which may in any way be viewed as remediative in nature. This could result in more differentiation in teacher roles and responsibilities at *different stages* of their careers than occurs at present, with selected experienced teachers assuming more monitoring responsibilities and beginning teachers more specialized functions initially.

Thus, extended and more effective use of current technology by teachers (to say nothing of the technology that will emerge within the next 10 to 20 years), closer cooperation and shared responsibility among colleagues and with other agencies, and more specialized and intensive forms of instruction provided by individual teachers would all imply changes in the preparation and continuing renewal of teachers. The suggestion is that increasingly there will be even more variation in teacher roles in a greater variety of instructional contexts. Some of these teaching roles will depart dramatically from the normative role model where an individual teacher works largely in a single classroom with approximately 25 to 30 students at a time, in an environment that is characterized by verbal interaction and engagement with written materials. More teachers will work primarily through the media of television and computers, others in focused, optional contexts for students such as interpersonal laboratories, and still others in coordinating and managing roles.

This is not to say that most teachers won't teach in familiar classroom contexts or that a much fuller understanding of the various interactions between teachers, students, and materials in more conventional instructional formats is not needed. Indeed it is. It is rather to emphasize that our conception of teaching and, in turn, teacher education must consider the variety of educational contexts which teachers are already in and will increasingly be involved with in the future. The relatively long-term nature of salient chains of research and development mandates a careful examination of likely future conditions.

It is important then that adequate resources and the best of our forecasting methods be employed to anticipate changes likely to alter the teaching role. Research and development into teacher education which has as its ultimate goal improved practice cannot ignore changes in the larger society which have obvious implications for the mission of schools and the roles of teachers. The brief speculation above concerning future events and conditions is just that. It is intended to illustrate potential ways that the context in which teaching occurs and the manner in which it is conducted may vary in the future.

What directions seem reasonable given the present reality? While we have gained some insights into the art and science of teaching and the means whereby teachers are prepared for and sustained in their roles, our knowledge base in terms of present teacher education practices and conditions is indeed limited (as the authors of succeeding chapters point out). Future research and development into teacher education must consider both what currently is and is not understood about the critical endeavor of teacher education. This writer has recently been involved in a series of investigations intended to provide more clarity about present policy and practice. This survey research into all phases of teacher education (initial, transitional, and continuing) has resulted in data which describe normative teacher education practices in the United States.

It also should be noted that these studies provide some insight into the very interesting question of who pursues teaching as a career. Again, while the data from these studies provide only a partial description, there are nonetheless some rather alarming implications which suggest we need to know more about those who pursue teaching careers just as we do need to know more about the programs which prepare them for those careers.

Thus, attention is turned at this time from possible future events to an overview of present practices and conditions in terms of their implications for further research and development. Just as more attention must be given to anticipating how events of the future might shape teacher education, more attention must be given as well to a better synthesis and critical analysis of extant data.

CURRENT PROBLEMS AND PRACTICE IN PRESERVICE TEACHER EDUCATION

Perceptions of the effectiveness of initial teacher education vary depending on what one uses as a benchmark. This writer in commenting on the Preservice Teacher Education Study (Joyce, Yarger, & Howey, 1977) was able to develop two seemingly conflicting scenarios from the same data base:

> *Scenario One*: Education professors generally are familiar with the daily activity, the curriculum issues, and the problems of schools. Education students generally are able to practice in classroom situations throughout their initial preparation. These same students at the completion of their programs generally are satisfied. They perceive themselves as competent to begin teaching. In spite of common retrenchments in personnel and resources, individual faculty are continuing to refine and even expand curricular offerings to accommodate changes in the schools.

> *Scenario Two*: For all their prior experience and current familiarity in schools, professors generally appear to influence but minimally those changes they often call for. For all their experiences in schools, student teachers receive but periodic and general feedback about their development. For all their confidence, a high attrition rate of beginning teachers suggests many may well have a false sense of confidence. The beginning teacher may be ready to teach in the suburban school; his or her readiness to assume responsibility in many schools in the core of our major cities is more questionable. Beginning teachers generally appear neither well prepared nor especially interested in confronting those problems attendant to the economically disadvantaged or culturally different. While teacher education professors spend more time in counseling, advising, and teaching undergraduates than they are generally given credit for, there is little individual or collective effort to study current practice. The empirical data to support what is done in preservice training is minimal. Coherent and comprehensive program reform, such as that initiated by many institutions under the "competency-based" umbrella, has rarely been achieved, and it appears that momentum for such effort has been lost. (Howey, 1977)

Thus, while teacher education programs, at least from the perspective of those who complete them, have provided reasonable requisite training to begin teaching, one can at the same time enumerate a number of problems associated with this endeavor. There is no doubt further research and development is needed, first, to better describe what is occurring (and why) and second, to better assess the effects of these efforts.

Initial training or teacher preparation programs across the country tend to appear quite similar at least in terms of the number and general types of experiences they afford students and the structure and framework in which these are organized. These programs are also characterized by their brevity. While there has been a proliferation of concerns which schools are asked to attend to and an expanded information base related to the craft of teaching, the number of hours future teachers spend in professional studies and related foundational work has *not* significantly increased. Neither has the basic format for study. Courses are still designed in three- or five-credit configurations, where faculty and students meet largely in college classrooms for brief but regular intervals throughout a quarter or semester.

In terms of the amount of professional preparation slightly less than 40 percent of a prospective elementary teacher's total undergraduate studies are devoted to what could be construed as professional training. While opportunities for preservice teachers to teach in schools are becoming increasingly frequent, it appears that less than 15 percent of a student's preservice career (at least as it is translated into credit hours) takes on the form of some supervised practice with students.

Secondary students engage in even less professional studies. Less than one-fourth of the secondary teacher education student's undergraduate academic career is devoted to professional training and only about 10 percent to some form of supervised practice teaching. Translated into quarter credit hours, elementary students receive on the average 47 credit hours in education, with 31 credits devoted to professional studies, and 16 credits devoted to supervised practice teaching. (About 120 such quarter credit hours would generally be needed to graduate.) Secondary students, on the other hand, average 29 hours of academic credit in a major, with 17 credits related to professional studies and 12 quarter credit hours given over to student teaching.

Yarger in summarizing the above data gathered from the Preservice Study (Howey et al. 1978) relative to the amount of time a student spends in different teacher preparation programs wrote:

> we were still puzzled by the nagging question of precisely how much training do students receive? Consequently, some extrapolations were performed in order to cast the data in a different context. Assuming the standard of 15 hours of instruction per semester hour of credit, a very interesting picture emerges. Elementary students receive slightly over 100 hours of instruction in

introductory and foundations courses and slightly under 200 hours in specific methods (i.e., teaching of reading, mathematics, social studies, etc.). One hundred hours of instruction is also received in supportive courses such as speech for teachers, handwriting, physical education, test and measurements, and others. Secondary students receive less direct instruction in all areas.

In terms of concrete amounts of training, imagine for a moment an unreal world where students receive training continually in 40-hour "work weeks." The following picture emerges: Between two and three weeks of training would occur in the foundations and introductory areas and in the supportive course areas, at least for elementary students. In curriculum and general methods courses, elementary teacher education students would receive nearly five weeks of training in specific methods while secondary students would receive somewhat less than two weeks of training. The most important impression conveyed by this analysis is that on a continuous training, 40-hour week basis, elementary teacher education students could be trained in less than 12 weeks and secondary teacher education students in slightly over six. Admittedly, clinical experiences are not included in this analysis. Even more important, time for study, time for reflection, time for informal exchange with colleagues and professors, and other such serendipitous yet extremely important aspects of teacher education programs are excluded. The point of this analysis is that although the academic credit in a training program may range from a year to a year-and-a-half, and this may be spread over a two or three year calendar period, the fact remains that teacher education students receive precious little direct formal instruction in their quest to master the complex skills of teaching.

THE APPARENT LACK OF VARIATION
AND ACCOMMODATION TO CHANGE

As stated earlier there appears to be limited variation among teacher education programs across the nation, at least structurally and organizationally. Very few programs have gone beyond state certification and program approval requirements. Seldom are district program alternatives found either in terms of content or form. The professional studies curriculum of the "typical" teacher preparation program offers methodology in content consonant with the modal curriculum found in the public schools. While graduating students in the Preservice Study generally believe they have been adequately prepared to begin teaching in their area of specialization and believe they are capable of managing a classroom in most school situations, they also acknowledge they have real limitations in:

1. diagnosing students' needs;
2. understanding the legal, political, and organizational dimensions of schooling;
3. working with both economically disadvantaged and multi-ethnic students.

Obviously the prospective teacher is limited in identifying what might be limitations in his or her preparation. After teachers have taught for a year, perceptions tend to change somewhat (Howey & Bents, 1979). One common additional concern of first-year teachers is the need for more assistance in classroom discipline and organization. This concern is quite understandable since nearly 20 percent of the prospective teachers in the Preservice Study stated that they had received no specific training in classroom organization and management and even greater numbers of students cited lack of training in the diagnosis and remediation of learning disabilities (35 percent).

It should also be noted that student-teaching and other school-based experiences in the great majority of instances are most commonly pursued in single-graded, separate subject, largely self-contained classroom settings. Preservice students report limited, if any, experiences in alternative instructional approaches such as an "open" school or classroom, specific diagnostic-prescriptive curriculum models, forms of team teaching, or multi-age instructional settings. In some programs preservice teachers have the option to student teach in a school or classroom reflecting a specific orientation to schooling but have only minimal preparation to engage in that type of instructional approach.

Questions can also be raised about the matter of how the future teacher is instructed or engaged with the content of teacher education as well as about the scope or adequacy of the content itself. One could logically expect that teachers of teachers would employ a wide variety of teaching technologies or methodologies. However, in general, instructional diversity is limited. The Preservice Study reports that the lecture-discussion format is still far and away the dominant teaching modality employed. There appears, in fact, to be a diminishment in the use of other instructional approaches which have been widely applauded. Human relations training in teacher education programs is still not common even though our knowledge (information) base has considerably expanded relative to various facets of social-psychological behavior (Johnson, 1975) and the potential utility of such training in a highly interpersonal endeavor such as teaching has been amply documented. Johnson (1968) reported that 14 percent of the teacher education institutions incorporated human relations training as part of their preservice programs and the 1977 study would suggest that this figure has risen by only about 1 percent per year in 10 years. The Preservice Study also suggests that such relatively adaptable and easy-to-use approaches as micro-teaching and simulation are not commonly used to help novice teachers acquire specific teaching skills in a systematic way. For example, the extensive use of videotape was reported by only 2.1 percent of the faculty surveyed, the extensive use of microteaching, by 6.4 percent, and the use of simulation by 3.4 percent. It would certainly appear that training efforts in other sectors incorporate such instructional aids and approaches more commonly than teacher educators in their instruction.

LIMITED RESEARCH AND DEVELOPMENT

To what extent do institutions which prepare teachers engage in the study of their teacher education programs? It would also appear that research and development *into teacher education practice* is rare in most of the institutions that prepare teachers. The research and development that is conducted within the higher education/teacher education institutions responsible for knowledge production is not largely directed toward studying teacher preparation per se. It is rather a situation of individual faculty who have *some* teacher education responsibility conducting research into the various disciplines or instructional domains in which they are expert.

When the faculty respondents in the Preservice Study were asked if there was a formal relationship between their teacher education programs and some type of formalized research and development organization, only about 1 in 5 responded that there was such a link. Those teacher education programs which did report some type of formal research and development capability identified this resource as most frequently residing in their own program unit (11.6 percent). Rarely was a linkage reported with any external research and development agency, whether it be another institution of higher education (4.5 percent), a regional laboratory or research center (1.2 percent), or a private firm (0.8 percent). It should also be underscored that the preparation programs which prepare the largest number of teachers—elementary and secondary—are the least likely type of programs to have any type of formal R&D linkage (only 12 percent and 8 percent, respectively).

Development, of course, often occurs without corollary research. The recent efforts to implement competency-based teacher education (CBTE) programs are examples of larger-scale efforts to alter preparation programs. In the Preservice Study, it was found that most teacher education programs had, in fact, developed competency statements. These written competency statements, however, appear a long way from characterizing a program as competency-based. What other characteristics of CBTE have been implemented in these programs? Pretesting, for example, is central to the competency approach. Yet, only 28 percent of the respondents in the Preservice Study indicated *any* type of formal preassessment of students entering the program. Preassessment in courses is even rarer. Criterion-referenced evaluation approaches were reported in less than 4 percent of the programs. Courses in which student evaluation includes assessments of the student's performance as a teacher (the most commonly called for form of "competence" are equally remote, as less than 5 percent of the faculty report they are able to integrate such practice into the courses they teach.

Thus, while we witnessed considerable rhetoric about moving to competency approaches, it appears the essence of the approach is generally lacking in practice. Whatever competencies are emphasized, they appear to be concerned primarily with the acquisition of information and to be assessed with paper and pencil. Perhaps the most glaring limitation in this approach has been the sparse data or even articulate rationales to justify which teacher competencies are needed for which teaching roles and functions. Further, most faculty appear at this time to have little enthusiasm for the competency approach to teacher education. While 60 percent of the faculty surveyed indicated that it existed in some form in their institution, over two-thirds said it would not be used at all in their programs in three years and only 3 percent of those surveyed view it as a potentially dominant approach in the future.

Whatever the future holds, the perception here is that the limited progress attained to this point in efforts at achieving more competency-oriented programs is a reflection of what has invariably happened to plans for comprehensive and altered schemes of teacher education. They have fallen short because the wherewithal, not only in terms of personnel and financial resources but also in terms of *conceptual* power, appears lacking. What is badly needed are more coherent, and I might add, realistic conceptions of different teaching role models which have empirical and rational support. The competency movement appears to have accomplished little in this respect. This approach appears, or more accurately appeared, to have sound guidelines for how future teachers should be instructed. There is no quarrel here with advocates who called for more explicit goals and criteria for assessing student progress towards these goals, more flexible time frames, more instructional options through which these goals could be reached, and increased opportunity for actual teaching experiences with more focused and continuing feedback. However, we have still largely begged the ultimate question of what is a competent teacher in the competency effort.

Rather than contribute to increased insights into effective teaching or clearer conceptions of viable teacher roles, these efforts often culminated in extended lists of competencies (objectives) for what is frequently an already overextended role. Thus, the relatively major changes envisioned for teacher education generally fell far short. The questions of what schools can reasonably be expected to do and what different types of teachers are likely needed in the schools rarely reached the level of serious dialogue.

COLLEGE AND SCHOOL COOPERATION IN INITIAL TRAINING

The "in" word which appears to have replaced competency in many teacher education circles is collaboration. One could expect relatively extensive correspondence between those in higher education primarily responsible for preparing teachers and teachers themselves, for example, in deciding the content of initial teacher education. This is simply not the situation. At the very least one would expect a high degree of collaboration between those in institutions of higher education and those in local education agencies in the student-teaching phase of preservice. Given the rather major responsibility of the cooperating teacher, one would also assume these teachers would be selected with considerable care, provided training in supervision, and substantially reimbursed for their efforts. This also is simply not the case. Fewer than one-fifth of the department chairs surveyed in the Preservice Study cited level of experience as a teacher, advanced training, or previous supervisory experience as the most important factors in the selection of cooperating teachers. Instead, the general reputation of the teacher and a willingness to work with student teachers appear to be the primary criteria for selection.

One cannot be sure about the motives of practicing professionals in this "cooperative" venture. Many work with the beginner out of a sense of professional responsibility. However, the assistance which can be provided by the student teacher in the classroom and what this motivating factor portends in terms of the kind of experience the preservice teacher is provided should not be discounted either (Haberman speaks to the problem in Chapter 4). Certainly, the token honorarium provided by most institutions to the experienced teachers cannot be the reason for taking on this responsibility.

In-kind considerations and faculty assistance to cooperating teachers are provided in some situations but these are also limited. No one form of reciprocation is common and there are considerable differences from one institution to another in terms of what, if anything, is provided to teachers. For example, about one in seven programs provide considerations such as tuition remission, admission to college functions, or library privileges. Another one in five provide some assistance to teachers in the way of media or materials. However, only one in four provide some formal inservice training to these cooperating teachers and the common focus when this does occur is on the teacher's responsibilities as a supervising teacher. Even less common is the practice of teacher educators in post-secondary education involving themselves in any substantial way in planning and program development with teachers and school faculties.

Since both higher education and local education agencies are financially strapped at this time, it appears that rather traditional and, in several respects, inadequate practices in student teaching will likely continue. One cannot clearly identify any overall trend toward improved practice other than more extended experiences in schools for the preservice teacher in several states. Exactly what those experiences should entail is far less clear. This is not to deny instances of exemplary practice, where many basic improvements have been made, for example, in terms of the selection and training of cooperating teachers.

In summary, the data drawn from the Preservice Study suggests the following concerns with respect to initial teacher education:

1. Professional programs of teacher education are characterized by their brevity; the total time spent on actual face-to-face instruction for future teachers is commonly less than that for trainees in semiskilled trades.

2. Professional programs appear quite homogeneous. In a profession characterized historically by disparate philosophical, sociological, and psychological perspectives of the nature of teaching and learning, and in a society founded on the implicit strength of pluralistic thought and life styles, programs of teacher preparation which reflect coherently planned variation or test alternative training technologies are exceedingly rare.

3. Research and development capabilities and resources are sparse and those which do exist appear underutilized with respect to the study of teacher preparation itself.

4. Professional programs are almost always labor intensive, technologically impoverished endeavors; even relatively simple procedures such as microteaching and forms of simulation appear to have declined in recent years.

5. Recent efforts toward more comprehensive program development such as forms of competency-based teacher education have achieved but limited success. This lack of programmatic change can be attributed to a variety of factors, including those which are organizational, political, and economic in nature. Not the least of these problems, however, is a fundamental lack of clarity about relevant and realistic teaching roles and equal uncertainty of just what, at various stages of teacher development, constitutes competence.

6. There is little concept of collaboration—despite the considerable rhetoric—between different professional constituencies, institutions of higher education, and local education agencies in initial teacher preparation. The notion of school practitioners themselves assuming a more active role in curriculum development and instruction for preservice teachers—as sensible as this notion might be—appears to be remote at this juncture in time. The modal collaborative condition in preservice is to employ cooperating teachers. It must be said that there has been little vision exhibited toward the concept of *the professions working together* toward the improvement of teacher education specifically and education personnel development generally.

It is hardly a question, then, of whether there is a need for more research and development relative to beginning teacher education, but where—given considerable options—intervention might contribute to better understanding and alleviation of a series of interrelated problems which continue to be compounded.

The perception here is that preservice teacher education is confronted with a rather formidable agenda on the one hand and the very real possibility of further retrenchment of a meager resource base on the other. It is essential then that present and future research and development needs be thought through most carefully. Certainly, more systematic attention must be given to questions of how teachers can best be educated for their roles. However, the question of preparation for what needs to be more fully addressed as well. The most common "professional" pursuit—teaching, especially teaching in elementary schools—can be characterized as highly labor intensive, technologically naive, overextended, non-specialized, and noncollaborative. Increasingly there will be a need for more differentiation and sharing of responsibilities especially among elementary teachers. Related research and development must address the question of teaching effectiveness as it is shaped by the conditions and role expectations which direct teacher behavior.

TRANSITION FROM PRESERVICE TO INSERVICE

As noted earlier, current programs of preservice are typically not designed so that the novice can do extended practice teaching in different school sites or with different types of students. Yet the beginning teacher is expected to be able to adapt the general knowledge and skills acquired in a preservice program to meet specific needs and expectations in whatever context he or she first teaches. Given the complex nature of teaching and the considerable differences that can exist in teaching assignments and in students of different ages or from different cultures this is a big order. One would expect considerable orientation, support, and continuing education for the beginning teacher to be provided since it is likely the beginning teacher will have little familiarity with the school to which he or she is assigned and but limited experience with children of any specific age or background.

However, there is little evidence that in most situations systematically planned support and educative experiences are afforded the novice to ease the transition or induction into teaching. Teachers in the Inservice Education Study (Yarger, Howey, & Joyce, 1979) were asked what help they received in this critical transition period. Only about one in five teachers indicated that they received the inservice assistance they needed. In fact, a little more than 10 percent of the teachers indicated that they received no inservice help at all when they first began their teaching careers. When asked who provided them with assistance—given what little was provided—the overwhelming response what that it came from other teachers. About 7 in 10 teachers responded that this was how they got on-the-job instructional assistance. Most of this help apparently came in rather random and informal ways rather than through any planned program. It was not a case where an experienced teacher was given specific responsibility for assisting a new teacher in meeting the demands of their new role. Only rarely were building principals or persons charged with some supervisory responsibility in their local education agency reported by these teachers as providing assistance. As might be expected persons in higher education were identified as the least helpful during this critical period.

The prevailing practice for assisting with this difficult transition appears limited basically to adding a few extra days for orientation at the outset of the school year for the beginning teachers and adding a few more formal visits from the principal throughout the year. This orientation is devoted to concerns of school policy and organizational functioning. Follow-up activities focused specifically on the needs of the beginning teacher are uncommon.

One reason advanced for this lack of support is that apparently many schools expect the beginning teacher to assume the same responsibilities at basically the same level of competence as the experienced teacher. Leight (1975) underscores the problem associated with the lack of differential expectations for the beginner:

> Most of our competency statements blur or ignore the difference between what might be called "entry-level proficiency" (what we will accept for Level I certification) and "mastery-level proficiency" (what we expect of a tenured, Level II teacher). The failure to make this distinction and to assist the teacher to become a master teacher is the most important confusion and shortcoming of teacher education. Teacher educators have brought the candidate to the point where he can enter the classroom with some competence, but the profession pretends that he is an accomplished teacher. Thus he receives the same assignment and treatment as veteran teachers. The result is that the first year of teaching is the greatest scandal in American education. It has allowed teacher educators to be the scapegoats for virtually all of the shortcomings in basic education. It has driven literally thousands of promising and idealistic young people in disgust from the profession. Worse still, it has soured and embittered a large percentage of the incumbents in the profession. And these young men and women are the future—they will be our schools for the next 20, 30, even 40 years.

One response to this problem would be to have the schools plan a more formalized induction into teaching. Another, complementary response to this problem would be to extend what is now basically referred to as preservice education. The AACTE Bicentennial Commission (1976) recommended the latter action be taken. They stated:

> It is apparent that federal programs in support of the search for better ways to educate teachers and teacher educators have had a significant influence on teacher education practice. New approaches have been developed. Much less successful has been the effort to institutionalize the new programs. The professional culture of teacher education has been significantly advanced, but

there has been a counterproductive failure to assist teacher education to increase the length of programs so that teachers could learn that culture. This has been the major flaw in the. efforts of EPDA and other U.S. Office of Education (USOE) programs. In order to make effective use of the new conceptual insights and instructional techniques, teacher education requires a significantly longer preparation program.

The commission underscored that simply extending programs by including more student teaching is not what they had in mind. It would be a major step backward to move toward essentially an apprenticeship model. They called rather for more substantive academic and professional training combined with more extended and focused forms of teaching in the schools. Their suggestions imply some collaboration between teacher education institutions and local school districts until a mastery level proficiency is reached. Certainly *learning* to teach is a developmental process in which the classroom itself may often not be the most appropriate context for the student teacher to learn initially. Haberman elaborates on the kind of experience needed in Chapter 4.

Those with a vested interest in teacher education need to be brought together to confront this challenge of providing a better *transition* from learning to teach to teaching others. State departments of education may be in the best position to coordinate discussion of legal, political, and financial options. There are a number of basic models which could be piloted. One model could be basically an extension of the initial teacher education program and primarily the responsibility of institutions of higher education. A second variation could also be viewed as a highly specialized inservice program and largely the responsibility of the local education agency. Finally, of course, any number of schemes in which there were more of a partnership or a shared responsibility for this type of transitional teacher training could also be developed.

Whether initial preparation is extended/enlarged, or initial teaching is more substantively integrated with teacher education opportunities and whatever the role/responsibility of those in higher education and schools, better articulation between pre- and inservice education is needed. Just what teacher education experiences are most appropriate at what stage of professional development are questions that those primarily concerned with inservice should examine with those whose basic responsibilities are in preservice. As it stands now, certain needs which are first addressed in an in-depth manner by teachers during inservice offerings would appear to be more effectively engaged in during preservice training programs. For example, the development and refinement of essential interpersonal communication skills, collaborative planning, and problem-solving strategies, or skills in documentation, measurement, and evaluation of classroom activities do not require extended teaching experience as a prerequisite. They are probably better practiced in focused laboratory sessions during preservice. Yet these are common inservice goals. Likewise, one could ask whether certain objectives now prevalent in preservice programs might better be addressed for the most part after one has more experience as a teacher. There is a need to rethink how a teacher develops personally and professionally over time.

Ryan (1979), one of the few persons who has studied the problems of the beginning teacher, underscores this need for new thinking:

> The fundamental changes needed to solve this problem are conceptual changes. We have to begin, first by realizing that it is a solvable problem, not something that is a necessary rite of passage into teaching. Historical roots and the fact that "everyone else has gone through it" are no excuse for letting the problem continue.

> Second, we should conceive of entrance into teaching as a *social* stage in a person's personal and professional life and respond to it institutionally and humanly in an appropriate way. Recently, some of the educational community have begun to identify the early years as the induction phase. Even this labeling begins to focus our attention more clearly on the problem. People need to be inducted. Special things need to happen. It is not the same as other teaching experiences.

> Third, we need new interpretive tools. The late Frances Fuller and her colleagues at the University of Texas have provided us with a very interesting start (Fuller, 1975). They have identified three stages of teacher development. The first stage, and the one that corresponds to the first year of teaching, is called the survival stage.

Basic needs during this "survival" stage have been well documented and whatever arrangements evolve, induction programs should provide:

1. ample time for the beginning teacher to study and reflect upon his or her teaching;
2. assignment of the teacher to a mentor;
3. systematic and continuing feedback about development in the teaching role;
4. orientation to both the "system" and the community, especially assistance in understanding social and political dimensions;
5. a more well-delineated, developmental sequence of broadened responsibilities over time.

It is also imperative that we involve those who are affected most in this critical transitional period. For it is in responding to personal needs in personal ways that one gets to the heart of this delicate part-professional/ part-learner phase of development. We have to know how the problem is experienced by those most directly affected. In our interviews with selected beginning teachers (Howey & Bents, 1979), it became apparent that even those students who were well prepared (or at least perceived themselves to be so) experienced problems, as this first-year teacher shared:

> I was really satisfied with my student teaching, in fact, with my whole under-graduate educational career. Individualization and discipline really haven't been a problem for me. It has been more establishing relationships in work-ing with the rest of the staff. We have been trying to develop a team teaching situation and although I felt that I knew how to work in that situation, actual-ly doing it became very difficult for me. I felt, for a long time, that people didn't understand and appreciate my expertise and skills, and I suppose, in turn, that I haven't fully appreciated nor understood the wisdom that comes from experience in the classroom. And that became very frustrating for me.

In summary, it appears there are at least four major needs to which research and development can be directed relative to this phase of teacher education:

1. the need for a clearer delineation between the entry-level capabilities of teachers (post-baccalaureate training) and that level of ability re-quired for initial licensure (post-residency or induction training);
2. the need to conceptualize and test different legal/political/economic schemes involving several parties which might provide better assis-tance to beginning teachers;
3. the need for more knowledge about how the beginning teacher is socialized and effects of this;
4. the need for more knowledge about the perceptions and expectations of beginning teachers and how these interact with their teaching and learning (Johnson and Ryan address these concerns more fully in Chapter 6 and outline in more detail potential directions for further re-search).

INSERVICE TEACHER EDUCATION

The respondents in our Inservice Teacher Education Study (Yarger, Howey, & Joyce, 1979) were fairly divided when asked about the general effectiveness of inservice education they were familiar with. A little more than a quarter of the respondents indicated it was either good or excel-lent. However, between 40 percent and 45 percent of the respondents described inservice education as only fair. The remaining 30 percent per-ceived inservice to be in poor or bad condition. Thus, the great majority of teachers, administrators, professors, and parents viewed inservice as only fair or even bad. Certainly more persons saw it as in need of im-provement rather than as generally satisfactory.

This is not to say there isn't a desire for more inservice. The teachers surveyed were also asked how often they experienced each of the following kinds of inservice:

1. inservice *embedded* in the job, that is, the type of growth activity which could improve teaching skills largely while teachers are engaged with ongoing duties (e.g., self-observation techniques);
2. inservice that is definitely tied or *related to the job* but does not take place while teaching is going on;
3. those experiences designed to improve *general teaching competence* but not tailored to meet the specific needs of the job;
4. those experiences engaged in to help one obtain a new *credential* or prepare for a different teaching role; and
5. those experiences designed to facilitate *personal development* which might contribute indirectly to greater effectiveness on the job.

The responses to these questions underscore the relatively small amount of inservice engaged in by teachers. The considerable majority of teachers indicated that they typically engaged in each of these types of inservice but once a year—or less. However, when teachers were asked whether these various forms of inservice or continuing education had any appeal for them the overwhelming response was that indeed they did. The great majority of teachers indicated considerable support (i.e., either an excellent or good idea) for each of the five types of inservice which were identified in the survey. This is to say they desired growth activities ranging from the general professional to the personal, in and out of the school context. Yet they do not commonly engage in such activity.

It should also be noted that very few teachers reported any *follow-up* in their classrooms to inservice which occurred outside of the school context. Only about 6 percent of the teachers in one state, for example, reported that they experienced this type of assistance. However, when the teachers were asked if they would like some periodic observation and analysis of their teaching in the classroom setting, their responses were again by and large positive. About two-thirds of the teachers, for example, indicated that they would like to engage in this practice with their peers and, moreover, a surprisingly high 55 percent report they could benefit from such an activity involving students. These sentiments would suggest a strong endorsement of classroom-focused forms of inservice where colleagues and even students might contribute to individual teacher development.

It also appears that most inservice occurs "after school." In response to questions about desired conditions for inservice, teachers in the Inservice Study stated that their primary reason for engaging in inservice was the belief that it could help them to do their jobs better. Teachers, however, were also asked how desirable certain secondary benefits or enabling conditions were. For example, teachers were asked their opinion of the desirability of a time for inservice other than the typical after-school format. Among the options which the teachers were asked to respond to were: (1) released time during the school day, (2) closing school for an extended period of time on a regular basis, (3) paying teachers for a month or more of summer study, (4) and paying teachers for weekends or holiday inservice. The teacher responses to each of these options were overwhelmingly positive. That is, the great majority of teachers perceived these options to be either an excellent or a good idea. There was somewhat less support for the concept of reimbursed weekend or holiday inservice but still the majority of teachers supported this scheme.

When teachers were asked how often they actually had an opportunity to engage in the four schemes enumerated above, they consistently indicated that such opportunities were rare or didn't occur at all. This reinforces the perception that inservice in many situations is little more than an occasional after school activity or courses pursued during the summer. The question must be raised as to the potency of inservice limited to such approaches.

This perception of potency or efficacy is an important one. McLaughlin (1978), in her analysis of federally funded change efforts in schools, reports the following about teachers:

> The most powerful teacher attribute in the Rand analysis was teacher sense of efficacy—a belief that the teacher can help even the most difficult or unmotivated students. This teacher characteristic showed a strong, positive relationship to all of the project outcome measures. Furthermore, the effects of a sense of efficacy were among the strongest of all the relationships identified in the analysis. Teacher sense of efficacy was positively related to the percent of project goals achieved, the amount of teacher change, total improved student performance, and the continuation of both project methods and materials.

Another factor that appeared related to teachers' involvement was the *scope* of the change proposed by a project. The Rand study found that the more effort that was required of project teachers and the greater the overall change in teaching style that was attempted by the project, the more likely the project was able to attract and commit teachers to it. More complex and ambitious projects were more likely to elicit the enthusiasm of teachers than were routine and limited ones. These observations suggest that not only is it important for teachers to believe that they can make a difference but that they must believe the inservice they participate in will also help them to make that difference. Experienced teachers especially realize that it takes major, coordinated efforts to make any significant change in schools. Few teachers apparently have had prior inservice experience to convince them that inservice is really capable of much help.

There is widespread endorsement among all educational professionals, but especially among teachers, for the greater involvement of teachers in all facets of inservice. Teachers desire to be involved not only in deciding what the priorities will be for their continuing education but also in monitoring, implementating, and evaluating these activities. Yet, constructive teacher involvement in many situations appears limited at this time.

The respondents to the Inservice Study do report that the content of inservice generally addresses their primary concerns and interests, although more than half of the teachers indicated that the inservice they engaged in did not adequately address contemporary issues or innovations in instruction and school organization. Again, however, the primary concern of the teachers is not so much with the lack of relevant content but rather with the lack of attention to the conditions in which they participate in their continuing education activities.

Teachers were also queried as to whether they were interested in serving as an instructor to their colleagues in specific inservice activities in areas where they believed they had some expertise. About half of the teachers (51 percent) responded that they were not at all interested in such a role; on the other hand almost half of the teachers expressed some interest and about one in five indicated that they were *very much* interested in assuming such a role. If 20 percent of the teachers were, in fact, able to contribute more substantially to their colleagues, a very considerable reservoir of ideas and skills would be available for continuing teacher development.

While teachers respect what their colleagues can assist them with, they also acknowledge others' help in a variety of ways contrary to what some of the literature would suggest. When teachers were asked who the most appropriate instructor would be for various types of inservice, they assigned this responsibility to different persons depending on the purposes of the activity. For example, they believed teachers would be the most effective and appropriate instructors for various forms of job-embedded and job-related forms of inservice but indicated that professors would be the more effective instructors for more general professional and theoretical forms of continuing education. These data suggest that the problem of inservice is not so much one of instructor ineffectiveness per se in many situations but rather that the wrong content may well be offered by the wrong person, in the wrong place, and at the wrong time.

While teachers want an expanded role in determining the direction of their continuing education, they hardly perceive inservice decisions as the teacher's exclusive domain. In fact, the Inservice Study indicated that there was a readiness on the part of all who have some vested interest in continuing teacher education to work together. This expressed willingness to work together was tempered, however, by the common perception that cooperative working arrangements, especially among different role groups, is indeed difficult to achieve. As stated earlier the rhetoric by many about collaboration is considerably tempered by reality. Educators in the study were asked to assess a number of potential obstacles to more collaborative decision making. These obstacles included: lack of skill in cooperative governance, competition among role groups with different vested interests, inadequate frameworks for engaging in cooperative ventures, lack of financial support, and limited time because of other priorities. Each of the role groups inventoried in the study suggested that *all* of these obstacles presented *severe* or *very severe* problems in the development of functional and ongoing cooperative working relationships. Thus, while there appears to be some willingness to work cooperatively, a number of problems appear to severely constrain such activity in most situations.

Yarger discusses future directions in research and development in inservice teacher education in some detail in Chapter 17 and thus needed future research need not be discussed at any length here. Nonetheless, the data from the Inservice Study reviewed here does suggest that the following general concerns need attention:

1. Not only *more*, but *more effective*, inservice is needed for a great many teachers and other educational personnel.

2. Inservice is in many situations largely an undifferentiated concept. The modal form of inservice still appears to be either lecture-discussion or a workshop format. More research and development is needed relative to forms of advisory approaches, psychological consultation, clinical supervision, organizational development, cooperative problem solving, child study, modeling behavior, observation and feedback, and self-directed instruction.

3. There is a definite need for more *follow-up* activities to those inservice activities pursued outside the school or classroom context. These classroom activities could well incorporate forms of peer instruction and even student involvement in certain activities. These follow-up activities could also incorporate more demonstration and opportunities for practice with feedback which appear lacking in many other forms of inservice.

4. Inservice increasingly needs to be more comprehensive in scope and intensive in nature. It appears that much inservice is fragmented in nature and often distant from the professional lives of teachers and the settings in which they work. More conceptually coherent inservice schemes are needed which attend both to the school as an organization and a social system and the teacher as a person and a professional.

5. There need to be more powerful incentives for teachers to participate in more authentic ways in growth activities. While monetary reimbursement and occasional released time are obviously important factors, there are other important considerations. For example, inservice opportunities must be perceived as powerful enough to improve teacher competence and/or alter conditions in the school in significant ways.

6. Teachers should be more centrally involved in all facets of the process. This involvement must transcend current "needs assessments."

7. Inservice must be consonant with the value systems held by teachers and this speaks especially to the where, when, and how of these activities. More personalized and individualized forms of inservice are needed.

8. Inservice must also be able to enhance the status and credibility of teachers. It must increasingly present opportunities for varying one's role and the opportunity to assume leadership in different ways while still assuming, largely, a teacher role.

9. While teachers have the preeminent voice in many decisions, it is apparent that more coherent and powerful forms of inservice will demand the cooperative efforts of several parties. There is much to be learned about how to achieve different forms of cooperation especially between role groups. One of the most important forms of cooperation between teachers and scholars is to pursue joint *research and development* as one form of continuing education.

RECRUITMENT, ADMISSIONS, SELECTIONS, PLACEMENT

What do we know about those who choose teaching as a career? Who is encouraged to enter the teaching profession? How do prospective teachers get into teacher education programs and eventually teaching? Various data speak to these questions. First, who is encouraged to enter the profession? Drumheller (1961) conducted an experimental study with over 100 secondary school counselors. He systematically varied records representing elementary and junior high school teacher aspirants in terms of scholastic aptitude, financial resources, ethnicity, and social class. His study indicated that the counselors were 24 times more likely to recommend students characterized by average ability, limited finances, and lower social and economic status to enter a teacher's college rather than a liberal arts college.

Numerous surveys have raised the question of whether parents would encourage their sons or daughters to pursue a teaching career. For example, a study by Auster and Bolstad in the late 1950s was repeated again by Pounds and Hawkins in the late 1960s. Although there was a span of 12 years between the studies, the results were very similar. While approximately 4 of 5 parents polled at that time reported they would encourage a daughter to enter teaching, fewer than 50 percent of them would encourage a son to pursue a teaching career. These results were uniform across urban and rural sites.

The general perception that teaching conditions have further deteriorated since the Pounds and Hawkins study is reflected in low opinions of the general public in the annual Gallop Poll of the Public's Attitudes Towards the Public Schools. A question repeated in this survey is, "Would you like to have a child of yours take up teaching in the public schools as a career?" In 1969, only 15 percent of the parents answered "no" to this question. Three years later, in the early 1970s, a trend had begun—22 percent answered "no". By 1980 a resounding 40 percent—almost a 200 percent increase from 1969—stated "no," they would not want their child to become a public school teacher.

Certainly, an analysis of elementary teachers in this country confirms elementary teaching is a career primarily pursued by women. The National Education Association in their 1975–76 *Status of the American Public School Teacher* report the following statistics relative to men and women in the teaching force. In 1976 a little more than two-thirds of *all* teachers were female (67.1 percent). In fact, the proportion of females teaching in elementary schools increased from 1971 to 1976 from 84 percent to almost 88 percent. It should also be noted that in 1976 more than 7 of 10 of these teachers (71.3 percent) reported that they were married. The majority of women teachers who are married also have children and spouses who are employed as well. These statistics strongly support the view that few men view elementary teaching as a career choice and that many of the women who do seek elementary teaching careers have family and child-rearing responsibilities as well.

ADMISSIONS

Setting aside for a moment the question of who is encouraged to or who decides to enter teaching, one can ask how one gains access to a teacher preparation program if he or she does view this as a desirable vocation. Certainly, gaining entry into a program does not appear to be too difficult. The enrollment figures in the majority of teacher education programs are determined basically by the number of students who desire to enroll. The almost universal criteria employed in deciding admissions are prior high school and college accumulated grade-point averages, letters of evaluation (or, in most instances, recommendation), and a consideration of SAT or ACT test scores (Preservice Study).

The Preservice Study also indicated that personal interviews with students were conducted in only about one out of three institutions. Speech proficiency was tested only in about 25 percent of the institutions surveyed. Standardized examinations and measures of personality and psychological factors were rarely part of the admissions procedure. There was no evidence in the study of the use of simulated techniques or structured group interviews as means to ascertain more information about specific attributes and characteristics of teacher candidates.

The admissions process itself appears to be a rather mechanical procedure. The limited student data is usually reviewed by selected faculty within specific teacher education program units to which admission is desired. Occasionally, administrators such as department heads, deans, or placement officers are also involved in this process. However, the involvement of faculty from other program areas, students themselves, experienced practicing professionals such as teachers, or measurement specialists, is exceedingly rare.

It appears then that little systematic attention has been given to the question of selection criteria (especially those that might have predictive validity), how these criteria are established, and which types of persons might be involved in more rigorous selection processes. The problem is long standing. In 1974, for example, the National Institute of Education brought in scholars from various disciplines throughout the country to help establish an agenda for research on teaching. One of the first panels of experts which they assembled focused on questions of recruitment, selection, and placement. This panel stated in their report:

> Selecting entrants into teacher education or into teaching jobs is only occasionally a rational process; more often it is nonsystematic or haphazard. A considerable body of theory and technology could make selection a more valid, objective, and efficient process (1974).

A similar sentiment was shared by the American Association of Colleges for Teacher Education's (Howsam et al. 1976) Bicentennial Commission. They conclude:

> The profession must find and support more effective guides for recruitment and selection. Current trends towards life long learning, recognition of the varieties of ways that people learn, value of human relationships, and respect for persons suggest the kind of teachers society needs. The profession needs new methods for finding these qualities in prospective candidates. Scholastic aptitude, test scores, rank in class, and grade-point averages are necessary but are not sufficient for quality selection of candidates.

This commission went on to suggest that evidence of voluntary social efforts, avocations that promote effective human relationships, attention to experiences that demonstrate a sense of responsibility for others, and indications of one's tolerance for uncertainty and ambiguity *could be* obtained and assessed if efforts were focused in this direction. Does what we know about those who pursue a teaching career suggest the characteristics called for by the AACTE Commission are common?

In the Preservice Study the "typical" future teacher was female, Caucasian, single, and in her early 20s. She tended to come from a smaller city, town, or rural area. She was likely to be monolingual (fewer than 3 percent of the future teachers reported they would be able to instruct in a language other than English). This "typical" teacher is likely to have attended a college or university relatively near to home. In fact, two-thirds of the students in the survey reported that they attended a college within 100 miles of their parents' residence. Given current and projected economic conditions this prevailing pattern of attending school in close proximity to one's home is likely to be reinforced. When these students were queried as to why they entered the programs that they did, the most typical responses were for economic reasons, convenience to home, and the perception of reasonable job prospects upon graduation.

That the great majority of these future teachers are largely unfamiliar with cultures other than the one in which they grew up is reflected in their responses about the types of students they would prefer to teach. Only about 25 percent of these future teachers indicated they would prefer to teach in an instructional setting where the student population would be multi-ethnic. On the other hand, over 40 percent of these teachers indicated a preference to teach a class which was predominantly Caucasian.

Lortie (1975), in his insightful portrait of teachers based upon questionnaires and interviews and buttressed with other survey data, identifies three common qualities or characteristics of classroom teachers. He concludes that first they are *conservative*. They are largely supportive of the current structure, organization, and purposes of school and prefer to do things the way they have done them in the past. He further suggests that teaching is seen by many as but a *partial profession* into which entry is relatively easy and the methods of teaching largely similar. He also defines teachers as "presentist." Many teachers, he suggests, view their role as but a *temporary occupation* and appear to obtain much of their psychological reinforcement from the day-to-day interactions with students in their classroom.

If his characterizations of teachers are accurate, one must ask what the implications are when (1) those with an inclination for stability are confronted continually with pressures to change, (2) those with a limited repertoire of relatively similar methods of teaching are confronted daily with considerable human diversity in terms of 30 or more students, and (3) those who treat teaching as a temporary job are in fact in a craft where it often takes several years to achieve excellence or even competence.

More recent data about those entering the teaching profession is shared by Weaver (1978) in his study of the effects of supply and demand on the quality of persons entering the teaching profession. Since cognitive ability is obviously a core attribute of effective teaching, his study is particularly pertinent. Weaver surveyed 19 post-secondary institutions in what is reported as a case study methodology. The basic premise which undergirds his inquiry can be stated as follows: as the market demand for new graduates in any given field diminished, the *quality* (in terms of academic credentials) of the pool of applicants desiring to enter that field of study will also decrease.

This premise assumes that institutions of higher education adapt to decline in market demands by selecting the best from a shrinking pool of talent. This strategy sacrifices absolute for relative standards since a percentage of the potential students who would enter any given field—in this instance teaching—choose not to do so when the job opportunities in that field are somewhat diminished and their academic credentials suggest they may have better career opportunities elsewhere. For example, a student whose combined SAT scores exceed 1100 will obviously have more options than a student whose combined scores fall below the 800 range. Thus, the reasoning is that when there are falling applications, it is likely there will be more applicants with lower test scores and an increase in the ratio of acceptances to applications will then result in a decrease in mean test scores.

His study of SAT scores of persons entering various professional schools supports this contention. He reports, for example, that the ACT English scores of college-bound students who plan to pursue elementary education as a major have declined substantially since 1970. While declines have been reported in other majors, the scores of the elementary education majors have declined at a more rapid rate than the total college-bound population. Likewise the ACT mathematic scores of college-bound students who plan either elementary or secondary education majors have also declined at a more rapid rate than the total college-bound population. Weaver reports that in the institutions he studied, elementary education majors had within a 5-year period declined from above the national mean of other college-bound seniors on SAT verbal and mathematics scores to means which were considerably lower than a national sample. He further reports that teacher education majors have on the average declined 23 points on the GRE verbal. Scores of the teacher education majors are significantly lower than scores of students in eight other professional fields including: nursing, biological sciences, chemistry, aeronautical engineering, physical sciences, sociology, political science, and public administration. (The verbal scores of education majors were higher than those of entering students in mechanical and chemical engineering among the 11 major fields which Weaver chose to examine.)

In summary then, Weaver's analysis of these standardized test scores indicates that students entering teacher education programs in 1975–76 scored considerably lower than those students who had opted for a similar academic preparation (teacher education) five years earlier. It should be noted that his sample is nonrandomized and limited. Yet he makes a persuasive argument.

There have been other studies which shed light on the cognitive ability of prospective teachers. Harvey, Hunt, and Schroder (1961) formulated a developmental model concerned with the conceptual potential of adults. Their *conceptual systems* model presents cognitive stages which are hierarchical in nature. Patterns of thinking are identified on a continuum from those characterized by considerable concreteness, minimal differentiation, and little or no integration, to those characterized by high levels of abstraction, high degrees of differentiation, and the ability to integrate information across a wide range of domains.

Each of the three theorists has subsequently defined stages of adult development in terms of somewhat different functional aspects. Harvey, for example, has focused on what he refers to as belief systems. Schroder has emphasized information processing. Hunt has focused more on the match between one's conceptual orientation and the type of instructional environment in which one is likely to function best. Harvey defines his beliefs systems as "deeply held attitudes or values." He examines belief systems in terms of a number of dimensions such as openness-closeness, complexity-simplicity, and consistency-inconsistency. He describes individuals in terms of the following four belief systems:

> *System 1*: high concreteness of beliefs, high absolutism toward rules and roles, a tendency to view the world in an overly simplistic, either-or, black-white way; a positive attitude toward tradition, authority; an inability to change set, role play, or to think creatively under conditions of high involvement and stress.

> *System 2*: a tendency to have strong negative attitudes toward institutions and traditions; low in self-esteem and high in alienation and cynicism; denounces power figures when of low status but appears to use power and authority rigidly once he/she acquire them.

> *System 3*: strong outward emphasis on friendship; efforts to manipulate through establishing dependency of oneself on others and of others on oneself; need to control others through dependency disguised under the desire and need to help others.

> *System 4*: most abstract and open-minded; manifests itself in information seeking pragmatism, a problem-solving orientation and a higher ability to change set, withstand stress and behave creatively; rules and structures used when utilitarian and instrumental to problem solving (1961).

In 1970 Harvey attempted to assess how college students, including education majors, were distributed along his four levels. He reports the following distribution: 45 percent of undergraduate education majors were measured as being at system 1, characterized by a high concreteness of beliefs. Another 5 percent were measured at system 2, and 25 percent more were measured at system 3. Only 5 percent of the undergraduate teacher education majors were characterized as system 4, or as abstract and open-minded in nature with a pragmatic information-seeking and a problem-solving orientation. These particular data correspond very closely to other studies of practicing teachers. In fact, the data reported on practicing teachers is even less complimentary. Fifty-five percent of the practicing teachers studied were reported at system 1 and only 4 percent at system 4 (see Table 1.1).

Studies have been conducted which report associations betwen these measures of conceptual abilities and various teaching behaviors. Murphy and Brown (1970), for example, report that the amount of teacher information which could be characterized as helping students to think divergently, theorize, and engage in self-expression increased with each higher system at which teachers were measured. Similarly, with increasing teaching abstractness, the sanctioning of more search behavior on the part of students was also observed. Likewise, Hunt and Joyce (1967) found significant positive correlations between indices of reflective teaching (which was defined by the use of the learner's frame of reference by the teacher in planning and evaluating their performance) and stage of teacher conceptual system. Harvey (1968) also reported that the students of teachers measured at his System 4 were observed as more cooperative, active, involved in their work, and higher in achievement than were students in classrooms with teachers who were assessed at systems 1, 2, and 3. (The Sprinthalls comment further about this line of inquiry in Chapter 3.)

There are, of course, indices of other characteristics or traits which appear essential to be effective in various teaching roles. Earlier it was stated that the Rand Corporation's study of federally funded attempts at change in schools suggests that a teacher's sense of efficacy is an important factor in efforts to initiate and sustain school renewal efforts. The many recent reports of teachers under stress suggest that tolerance for ambiguity and openness to change are important qualities for teachers to possess. The increasing demands placed upon schools suggest that in the future teachers may need to establish more cooperative working relationships. Hence, predispositions for working with others as well as the skills to do this increasingly may be important considerations in the selection and training of teachers.

TABLE 1.1   Distributions of Conceptual Systems Types among Liberal Arts Students, Education Majors, and Practicing Teachers

Educational Position	**1**	**2**	**3**	**4**
Liberal arts students	35%	15%	20%	7%
Undergraduate education majors	45%	5%	25%	5%
Practicing teachers	55%	0%	15%	4%

There appear to be numerous ways in which further study of specific teacher traits and characteristics could proceed. The work of Turner (1975) is helpful in this regard. He has identified a number of basic relationships which need to be studied in teacher education. Teacher selec-

tion variables were included in three of the seven relationships he identified. He suggested that one might first look at *selection* variables as these
interact with various teacher *training* variables.

This type of research about how students with different characteristics
perform in different instructional settings would be a common type of
study. Turner identifies related research which could be pursued as well.
He elaborates:

> The most frequent kinds of studies are those seeking "aptitude by treatment
> of interactions" (ATI), but a slightly different kind of study, one showing the
> influence of student characteristics on the type and intensity of training given
> by instructors is also possible. For example, does the admission of less able
> students lead to lower standards rather than to more intense weeding out?

A second basic relationship which Turner suggests needs further study is
that between *selection* and *placement*. Research here would look at how
individual teacher characteristics are associated or interact with various
types of teacher roles and role expectations or planned instructional
variations. The Sprinthalls (see Chapter 3) suggest that there are psychological factors which would predispose the degree of structure different
teachers would employ in their teaching, and thus the type of context in
which a teacher is placed could be critical.

Finally, a third type of inquiry he calls for would look at the relationship between *selection* variables and performance as a teacher, or the
relationship between teacher characteristics and various measures of desired student behavior. From this perspective, judicious selection of
teacher traits and characteristics can be incorporated into both prevalent
paradigms employed in research on teaching.

One common type of research on teaching has been to examine specific teacher behaviors in relation to specific student outcomes. This is
often referred to as process-product research. This research has progress-
ed to the point where data acquired in many small-scale correlational
studies over the last 25 years can now be used to design experimental studies. Selected teacher characteristics could be considered as well in pro-
cess-product/presage-process chains of inquiry. As clusters of teacher behavior are shown to be related to certain pupil outcomes, investigations
should proceed to examine whether those teacher behaviors are in turn
associated with certain personal or psychological traits. If certain desired
teacher behaviors are in fact associated with measurable psychological
attributes of teachers, the question of whether selection for these traits
may be as viable a process as training for them needs to be considered
more fully.

Any second major line of inquiry advocates examining teacher effects
from a molar, interactive perspective and calls for more conceptually
coherent and comprehensive ecological paradigms. Research is called for

which can attend to a variety of interrelationships among salient classroom variables and, in turn, the relationship between these and desired student outcomes. The concern is that we go beyond specific process-product relationships and develop more powerful explanatory models of what actually transpires within classrooms. Certainly, it would appear that more insight into how teachers are differentiated along selected characteristics would be helpful in studying how they both structure the classroom and interact in a variety of ways within that environment.

Doyle (1977) suggests that students learn how to locate and interpret what he calls "cue resources" for navigating various classroom tasks. He maintains that students acquire the responses needed to succeed in what he views as a "performance-grade" exchange between student and teacher. He contends that *interpretive* as well as academic skills are needed for students to succeed in the classroom. The relationship of teachers' perceptions or interpretive frameworks to certain teacher characteristics could be studied as well in examining a number of salient role relationships between teachers and students. The work of Combs (1974), for example, would be especially appropriate as one type of conceptual lens for ecological investigations in a classroom where selected teacher characteristics are also a focus.

There is no intent here to ignore the valid and long-standing concerns about our ability to measure adequately certain traits or characteristics nor the limited success achieved in studies of teacher characteristics in the past. Also the writer is cognizant of the importance of differentiating traits from more situation-specific responses. There are obvious limitations to the forms of inquiry suggested above. Nonetheless, the position taken is that there is enough data to suggest that certain teacher traits should be further examined in well-conceived *chains of inquiry* which would examine the interaction between selected teacher characteristics and (1) success in different types of teacher-training contexts, (2) accommodation to basically different teaching roles and functions, and (3) interaction with specific teacher behaviors which are, in turn, associated with students' success.

In summary, this overview chapter has attempted to address three basic objectives. First, it examined present and evolving conditions within the larger society which must be taken into consideration when planning future research and development for teacher education. Next, it examined (normative) practices and policies in all three phases of the teacher education continuum: initial teacher education, induction into the profession, and inservice or continuing teacher education. What these present practices and policies might imply for future research and development was also discussed briefly. Finally, the question of what we know about those who choose to become teachers was examined from several perspectives. Since the ultimate goal of developing a quality teaching force is related to matters of recruitment and selection, as well as to preparation and renewal, a plea for more research into selected teacher characteristics as well as into selected teacher preparation practices was made.

BIBLIOGRAPHY

Auster, D., & Molstad, J. A survey of parents' reactions and opinions concerning certain aspects of education. *Journal of Educational Sociology*, 1957, *31*.

Combs, A. W., et al. *The professional education of teachers.* (Rev. Ed.). Boston: Allyn & Bacon, 1974.

Doyle, W. Learning the classroom environment: An ecological analysis. *Journal of Teacher Education*, 1977, *28*(6), 51–55.

Drumheller, S. J. *The image of Teachers College as seen by high school counselors.* Doctoral dissertation, Columbia University, 1961.

Harvey, O. J. Beliefs and behavior: Some implications for education. *The Science Teacher*, 1979, *37*.

Harvey, O. J., Hunt, D. E., & Schroder, H. M. *Conceptual systems and personality organization.* New York: Wiley, 1961.

Harvey, O. J., White, B. J., Prather, J. J., & Hoffmeister, J. K. Teachers' beliefs, classroom atmosphere, and student behavior. *American Educational Research Journal*, 1968, *5*.

Howey, K. R. Preservice teacher education: Lost in the shuffle? *Journal of Teacher Education*, 1977, *28*, 26–28.

Howey, K. R., & Bents, R. H. (Eds.). *Toward meeting the needs of the beginning teacher.* USOE/HEW Grant No. G00700055, 1979.

Howey, K. R., Yarger S. J., & Joyce, B. R. *Improving teacher education.* Washington, D.C.: Association of Teacher Educators, 1978.

Howsam, R. B., Corrigan, D. C., Denemark, G. W., & Nash, R. J. *Educating a profession.* Washington, D.C.: American Association of Colleges for Teacher Education, 1976.

Hunt, D. E., & Joyce, B. R. Teacher trainee personality and initial teaching style. *American Educational Research Journal*, 1967, *4*(3).

Johnson, D. W., & Johnson, F. *Joining together: Group theory and group skills.* Englewood Cliffs, New Jersey: Prentice-Hall, 1975.

Johnson, J. A. *A national survey of student teaching programs.* USOE Project No. 6–8182, July, 1968.

Joyce, B. R., Yarger, S. J., & Howey, K. R. *Preservice Teacher Education.* Palo Alto: Booksend Laboratory, 1977.

Leight, R. L. The Teaching Internship as Delivery System for CBTE. *Performance Based Teacher Education* 3(9): 7; March 1975.

Lortie, D. C. *Schoolteacher: A sociological study.* Chicago: University of Chicago Press, 1975.

McLaughlin, M. W., & Marsh, D. Staff development and school change. *Teachers College Record*, 1978, *80*(1), 69–94.

Murphy, P., & Brown, M. Conceptual systems and teaching styles. *American Educational Research Journal*, 1970, *7*.

———. *National Conference on Studies in Teaching: Panel Summaries.* National Institute of Education, Washington, D.C., 1974.

National Education Association Research, *Status of the American public school teacher, 1980–1981*. National Education Association, Washington, D.C., 1982.

Pounds, H. R., & Hawkins, M. L. Adult attitudes on teaching as a career. Journal of Teacher Education, 1969, *20*.

Ream, M. A. *Status of the American public school teacher, 1975–1976*. NEA Research, 1977.

Ryan, K. Toward understanding the problem: At the threshhold of the profession. In K. R. Howey & R. Bents (Eds.), *Toward meeting the needs of the beginning teacher*. USOE/HEW Grant No. G007700055, 1979, 35–52.

Turner, Richard L. *An Overview of Research in Teacher Education*. The 74th yearbook of the National Society for the Study of Education, part 2. Ryan, K. (Ed.) Chicago: University of Chicago Press, 1975.

Weaver, W. T. Educators in supply and demand: Effects on quality. *School Review*, Fall 1978, 552–569.

Yarger, S. J., Howey, K. R., & Joyce, B. R. *In-service teacher education*. Palo Alto: Booksend Laboratory, 1979.

2

Methodological Considerations in Future Research and Development in Teacher Education

Del Schalock

Oregon College of Education

Within the context of educational research and development, methodology typically refers to how something is done. Methods employed in educational development include design teams, review panels, prototype preparation, pilot tests, field tests, third-party evaluations, cost-benefit studies, and validation studies. Methods employed in educational research most often refer to measurement alternatives—for example, observation, interview, surveys, standardized achievement/aptitude measures, applied performance measures—but the concept often is extended to cover design and analysis alternatives as well. As such the concept is extremely broad in meaning, and soft in definition. In spite of these weaknesses the concept seems to have utility, for it is commonplace in the language of all scientific and professional groups.

With its breadth of meaning, the methodology of educational R and D can be dealt with only cursorily in this chapter. Milestones with respect to method will be traced for both educational development and research,

The author would like to thank Jean Ferguson, Jessee Garrison, and Gerry Girod, Oregon College of Education; Meredith Gall and Dick Hersh, University of Oregon; Glen Fielding, Teacher Research Division; and Vern Rempel, the Chancellor's Office, for critiquing the chapter and suggesting improvements.

but the primary focus of the chapter is on the *future*. In keeping with the intent of the volume, the central theme of the chapter is on what is needed to improve the effectiveness or efficiency of our teacher preparation programs in the years ahead.

DEVELOPMENT IN TEACHER EDUCATION*

In general terms, educational development is seen as "a systematic process of creating new alternatives that contribute to the improvement of educational practice" (Hemphill, 1969, p. 23). The emphasis upon system design principles in nearly all current writing on the subject has led to the methodology of educational development being described variously as knowledge based, systematic, rigorous, empirical, data dependent. It is this dependency on the use of data to determine the effectiveness of what is developed that sets systematic educational development apart from developmental efforts of teachers, publishers, and national curriculum groups.

From this frame of reference, development in teacher education has been minimal. What is more, with the possible exception of Teacher Centers, no major development efforts currently are underway. It is my belief that this lack of attention to systematic development, more than any other single factor, accounts for why teaching and teacher education are commonly perceived as a semiprofession (Howsam et al. 1976).

The role of systematic development in the evolution of teacher education is described briefly in the paragraphs that follow. Some examples of the kind of development efforts that I perceive to be needed in teacher education are provided after this review.

Notes on the Past

When schools were first established in America, teachers had no special training. Persons who could read and write, and were acceptable to members of a community, were hired as teachers. This condition prevailed until early in the 19th century.

During the 1830s and 1840s teacher education was introduced to the United States from Europe, in the form of normal schools. In tracing the history of the growth of teaching as a profession, Howsam et al. (1976) point out that:

* This section of the chapter draws heavily on the work of the Bicentennial Commission on Education for the Profession of Teaching (Howsam et al., 1976) and a monograph prepared by the author on competency-based teacher education programs as a focus of and context for research and development in teacher education (Schalock, 1975).

At first, normal school students had less than a high school education; later, high school became a common requirement. Normal schools offered some subject matter and a smattering of pedagogy. . . . In the late nineteenth century and into the twentieth, normal schools lengthened their periods of preparation to two years. Then, impelled by the growing need for secondary teachers, and by the desire of the society to expand higher education opportunities close to home, they became teachers' colleges and state universities (p. 32).

This process was essentially complete by the end of World War II (Haberman provides a more detailed description of the evolution of teacher education up to this time in Chapter 4).

In 100 years teacher education in the United States has become a major industry. It has become a significant element in most colleges and universities; it consumes a sizable portion of a family's income during the preparation years; and it consumes a sizable portion of the funds a state provides in support of higher education institutions. Yet, for all practical purposes, teacher education has evolved in the United States without benefit of systematic development. No evidence has been collected along the way that teacher preparation programs in fact achieve the outcomes desired of them, or that one program achieves an intended outcome more efficiently than another.

Enter the Federal Government. Following the shift to a four- or five-year program of study, the next major development in teacher education was triggered by the launching of Sputnik. This event, in 1957, caused the nation to presume major deficiencies in its schools, and brought the federal government into education and teacher education in a way previously unknown. Howsam and his colleagues describe the growth of teacher education as a profession during the post-Sputnik era:

Because the government assumed that the problem was teachers' subject matter deficiency, it poured resources into curriculum development and academic inservice education, mainly in the sciences and mathematics. Obviously, there was significant upgrading in these subject matter areas, but pedagogy, the professional *act* of teaching, received little attention (p. 33).

The civil rights movement of the late 1950s and 1960s served to bring the federal government further into the business of teacher education:

In 1954, the courts began their succession of rulings on rights and education. During the 1960's, the nation's festering social problems erupted into civil rights movements. There was rioting in the streets and parts of cities were burned. . . .

From that time, the response of the federal government has been to concentrate on alleviating inequities. The government gave serious attention to teacher education for the first time by developing and funding such efforts as Trainers of Teacher Trainers (Triple T), Teacher Corps, The Comprehensive Elementary Teacher Education (CETEM) Project, Teacher Centers, the Education Renewal Project, multicultural education, and bilingual education (Howsam et al., pp. 33–34).

Of all the efforts funded by the federal government during these years only the elementary models (CETEM) and the "protocol" programs reflected a commitment to the process of systematic development, and both of these programs were aborted before implementation and testing could be undertaken.

The Development of Alternative Models of Teacher Preparation. The first serious and systematic effort to explore alternative designs for the preparation of teachers came in the late 1960s with the federally funded elementary models program. Ten competing models were developed by faculty from teacher preparation programs across the country, and though different in focus and content, all shared the design requirement of being clear about outcomes to be achieved and systematic in their achievement. Both pivoted on assessment, first, as a means of giving operational definition to the outcomes desired and, second, as a means of determining when and to what extent desired outcomes have been attained. A number of analyses have been made of the similarities and differences between models (see, for example, Burdin & Lanzillotti, 1969, and the 1970 spring issue of the *Journal of Research and Development in Teacher Education*), but the list of commonly shared assumptions provided by the authors of *Educating a Profession* (Howsam et al., 1976) is as good as any other:

1. Teaching is a profession; the teacher is a clinician and decision maker.
2. At work, the teacher shares with others the clinical and decision-making tasks; teaching demands team work and collegial relationships.
3. The competencies needed by teachers can be identified, specified as behaviors, and developed through training.
4. Management systems adequate for complex teacher education programs can be developed.
5. Teaching demands a long period of training extending throughout the employment period; effective training programs require collaboration between the several involved parties.
6. Development of the complex competencies of teaching will demand the effective use of both laboratory and field-centered approaches.
7. As an applied scientist, the teacher needs to be well versed in the behavioral sciences which are relevant to the profession.
8. The models—as with all preparation programs—are just early approximations of what is needed (pp. 34–35).

Even though funds for the implementation phase of the models program were never provided, and thus the full impact of the program blunted, a number of institutions implemented programs that reflected the models they had developed. These institutions, in turn, have been responsible for a disproportionately large share of the development work in teacher education during the latter half of the 1970s. The three institutions carrying model implementation farthest have been Oregon College of Education (Schalock, Kersh, & Garrison, 1976); the University of Houston (Houstin, Cooper, & Warner, 1977) and the University of Toledo (Dickson & Saxe, 1973).

Many other institutions, of course, have implemented pieces and parts from one or more of the models developed through the CETEM program, so even though not funded for implementation the program has had impact on teacher education in the United States far beyond the "think tank" effort that received federal funding. An additional outgrowth of the models program has been the controversial, but productive, competency-based teacher education movement.

The Application of New Technologies to Instruction. During the mid-1950s and early 1960s, two forces came to bear on instruction in higher education that have had a major and continuing impact. These were the application of technology through television and other media, and the application of learning principles—espoused most forcefully by B. F. Skinner—to what is now known as programmed instruction. Both led to instructional improvement efforts in higher education that were systematic in design and operation (Schalock, 1976). Multi-media instruction is now commonplace in teacher preparation programs, as are "media centers," to help professors prepare instruction, and "instructional modules," to facilitate both knowledge and skill mastery. Simulation materials, protocol materials, micro-teaching, and other approaches to laboratory instruction also are in wide use. While it is now clear that the application of the new technologies to instruction is not sufficient in and of itself to make teacher preparation programs appreciably more effective, and much of the initial enthusiasm for these approaches to instructional improvement has waned, they still enjoy relatively wide support in the teacher education community.

Projections for the Future

While progress has been made over the past two decades in applying systematic development procedures to teacher education, the efforts have been too few and too small. The instructional improvement efforts just reviewed have been piecemeal, and the full range of benefits that could have come from the elementary models program had it been continued have been lost. Large-scale, long-term, well-funded development efforts in teacher education simply are without precedent.

It is my belief that until such efforts are undertaken, and accompanied by research on the benefits and costs that accrue, teacher education will never progress in either its form or effectiveness far beyond what it is today. Improvement efforts, in the form of natural or planned variation studies—with sufficient replications for confidence to be established in observed effects—are necessary for significant improvement to occur. More importantly, the variations studied must be of sufficient magnitude and importance for noticeable effects to be observed. There is sufficient evidence that possession of a particular body of knowledge or a particular set of skills is not sufficiently strong as a variable in the preparation of teachers to be related to effective performance as a teacher (Schalock, 1979). To make a difference in teacher education development efforts must be sufficiently comprehensive, and deal with variables of sufficient power, that when modified they are likely to lead to an observed effect on the ability of prospective teachers to perform the functions of teaching in ongoing school settings.

In the next several pages examples are provided of the kind of program improvement studies that I believe to be needed if teacher education in the future is to be appreciably more effective than it is at present.

Example One: The Study of Benefits and Costs Accompanying Model Variations

Persons responsible for the allocation of resources in support of teacher education need to know whether the educational returns from one approach to preparation outweigh another, whether the costs associated with one approach are greater than those associated with the comparative approach, and the relation of costs to benefits in both cases. Information of this kind is needed by persons responsible for establishing state and national standards for teacher preparation, by institutional executives who must allocate resources in support of programs, and by employees of government who must recommend funding for such programs. Without comparative information, policy decisions of necessity must be made on some basis other than fact.

Three conditions are essential to implementing model variation studies. These are (1) criteria that define and differentiate model variations must be clearly specified; (2) ongoing preparation programs must exist that meet these specifications; and (3) persons responsible for such programs must be willing to take part in research that compares program costs and effects.

Put on other terms, benefit/cost studies of teacher preparation programs of any kind require:

- clarity as to program differences to be compared;
- essential *pure cases* of mature, fully functioning programs that reflect these differences; and

● teacher educators willing to submit themselves and their institutions to a comparative research effort.

Given these conditions, policy-oriented studies that focus on the comparison of model variations take the form of natural field experiments; that is, systematic comparisons of desired variations that can be identified in already established programs.*

The example that follows is taken from the monograph prepared by the author on CBTE programs as a focus of and context for research in teacher education (Schalock, 1975). One of the studies called for in the monograph was a comparison of CBTE/non-CBTE preparation programs.

When comparing CBTE and non-CBTE programs, care must be taken to include in the sample model variations that are dominant. These variations may be as significant in terms of benefit/cost relationships as the generic model variation being studied. With respect to CBTE and non-CBTE programs, model variations probably would involve, on the CBTE side, the selection of programs that focus instruction primarily at the level of (1) knowledge mastery, (2) skill mastery, or (3) the ability to perform the job of a teacher in a school setting. On the non-CBTE side, meaningful variations could include (1) traditional, discipline-centered four-year undergraduate programs; (2) programs that reflect a "phenomenological" approach to preparation; and (3) either a Master of Arts in Teaching (MAT) program or a traditional four-year program supplemented by a year of internship. These variations in CBTE and non-CBTE designs are shown schematically in Table 2.1.

While comparative studies of model-based programs are critically needed, their implementation is likely to be fraught with problems. The matter of defining and then finding pure cases of either CBTE or non-CBTE program variations of the kind outlined is likely to be a major stumbling block. So, too, is obtaining comparable outcome measures for all teachers or prospective teachers taking part in such studies, or being able to isolate and control factors that will act as sources of unwanted variation, for example, major personality, background or ability differences in teachers. Finally, there are the related problems of collecting data for and carrying out analyses on benefit/cost relationships. Methodology in this arena is primitive, and experience in applying the methodology that does exist is hard to come by.

---

* This discussion illustrates the lack of clear-cut distinction between systematic development and research. Development is needed before research of this kind is possible, and findings from the research are used to guide further development. A recognition of the functional interdependence of educational research, development, evaluation, and diffusion is slowly developing (see, for example, Schalock & Sell, 1972; Hood & Blackwell, 1975).

TABLE 2.1 Model Variations That Need to Be Taken into Account When Comparing CBTE and Non-CBTE Programs

Dominant Variations in CBTE Programs		Dominant Variations in Non-CBTE Programs	
Knowledge-centered definition of competence	Skill-centered definition of competence	Traditional, discipline-centered four-year undergraduate programs	Phenomenological four-year undergraduate programs
	Job performance-centered definition of competence		MAT Programs, or a traditional four-year program plus an internship

Given the problems embedded in model variation studies, their design is likely to assume some special characteristics. One of these is a small number of cases in each cell, probably three to five. Another is the limitations of such studies to model-based programs that exist in large enough numbers to meet a design requirement of even three programs per cell. Still another is the high cost of doing this kind of research. Field-based follow-up research is an expensive enterprise, particularly so where the collection of high-quality job performance data for a large number of subjects is involved (an initial sample of 100 teachers from each model-based program studied probably would be needed to complete three or five years of follow-up with an N of any size).

In combination, these considerations lead to the conclusion that model variation studies probably will have to be carried out on a nationwide basis. Resource and program access requirements leave little alternative. Preliminary thinking about the design of such studies is summarized in Table 2.2.

Example Two: A Study of Benefits and Costs Accompanying Within-Model Variations

Studies of this kind represent an elaboration of the model variation study described above. In the design proposed for the comparison of CBTE and non-CBTE programs, it was recommended that CBTE programs vary by level of competency definition. The example provided here calls for this differentiation to be carried one step further, and explore *within-level differences* as well.

The benefits and costs of at least two kinds of within-level differences in a model-based program need to be explored. One of these differences has to do with the content or substance of a program. It is possible, for example, for two programs to define teaching competence in terms of skills or behaviors to be performed, but in so doing, stress essentially different sets of skills. The consequences of such differences should be known.

The other has to do with the structure and operation of a program. It is possible for two programs to stress essentially the same content, but provide quite different learning experiences on the way to mastering that content. A case in point is the use of individualized learning modules, as opposed to lecture, reading, or class discussion, as a means to knowledge acquisition. Another is the use of micro-teaching or some other form of simulated practice experience, as opposed to field placement and supervision, as a means to skill acquisition. Since such differences have major consequences for program cost, they need to be studied for their benefit/cost relationships.

Operationally, within-model studies require that the same conditions be met as model variation studies. Mature programs having varying foci

TABLE 2.2 Illustrative Treatment Conditions, Control Variables, and Outcome Measures Appropriate to Model Variation Studies in Teacher Education

Treatment Conditions	Control Variables (through blocking designs and/or statistical manipulation)	Evidence of the Effectiveness of Program Graduated
Model Variations in Preparation Programs	*Program Characteristics*	*Program-related Benefits (Long term)*
Competency-based knowledge focus skill focus teaching focus	Match between program operation and definitional criteria Number of students graduated through the program Level of preparation, e.g., elementary teaching Kind of institution within which the program rests, e.g., private small college, large public university	Performance as a member of a school faculty (perceptions of principal/supervisor and colleagues)
Non-Competency-based discipline-based 4-year program discipline-based 4-year program plus internship	*Characteristics of Graduates* Academic ability	Performance as a facilitator of Learning I (perceptions of the graduate's students)
MAT programs	Predicted success as a teacher at the end of student teaching Attitudes toward self-as-teacher, job held and one's school as a context in which to teach	Performance as a facilitator of Learning II (perceptions of principal/supervisor)
Program-related Costs Dollar costs Human and political "costs"	*Characteristics of the Setting in Which the Graduate Is Teaching* The complexity of the instructional task, as determined by the nature of curricula, students being taught, availability of support services, etc.	Performance as a facilitator of Learning III (perceptions of an outside observer/interviewer)
Program-related Benefits (short term) To students To college faculty To school supervisors	Expectations for students and teachers in the school where the graduate is teaching, and in the neighborhood or community as a whole Amount of help/supervision received from district personnel, especially as a first-year student Number and kind of advanced study/inservice activities pursued after being hired as a teacher.	Performance as a facilitator of Learning IV (obtained through teacher summaries of student attainment with respect to designated learning objectives)

and emphases must be available; people in these programs must be willing to engage in a comparative study; the same unwanted sources of variation must be controlled; the same kind of dependent measures must be taken; and the same kinds of program benefit and cost analyses must be made. The fundamental distinction between the two designs is in the kind of program differences tested. In one, the difference is philosophical, as well as organizational and substantive. In the other, the difference tends to be limited to either organization or substance.

Another important difference between the two designs is that many individual institutions have the resources and capabilities needed to carry out within-model variation studies, while few are able to manage—for both political and financial reasons—model variation studies.

The example that follows is a within-model variation study that is being carried out currently by teacher education institutions in Oregon. The research addresses two problems that are faced by every institution that prepares teachers. One is the problem of meaningful follow-up evaluation of graduates of teacher preparation programs. The other is the kind and extent of field experiences to be included in a preparation program, and the purposes assigned to them. A third problem addressed by the study, though indirectly, is the problem of teacher selection.

The research addresses these problems through a longitudinal study of the costs and benefits associated with alternative patterns of field experience. All of the publicly supported institutions of higher education in Oregon, and two private institutions, are taking part in the study. Graduates from each preparation program offered by these institutions are represented in the sample studied. The design of the study is summarized in Table 2.3.

Example Three: A Study of the Effectiveness and Cost of Planned Variations within Programs

While policy makers need the kind of information coming from the studies just outlined, persons responsible for the implementation of teacher preparation programs need a different kind of information. Obviously, they must also be concerned with cost and benefit questions, but the central focus of program managers is the effectiveness of alternative instructional programs and procedures in bringing about a specified set of learning outcomes. Without such information, decisions as to program design and operation must also be based on something other than fact.

As used in the present chapter, planned variation studies are designed to bring about such information. Generally speaking, the design of these studies is much like the design of model-variation studies. They differ, however, in several important ways. First, planned variation studies are designed to test the cost-effectiveness of two or more instructional programs in bringing about a particular learning outcome. Second, they

TABLE 2.3 Illustrative Treatment Conditions, Control Variables, and Outcome Measures Appropriate to Within-Model Studies in Teacher Education

Program Variation Being Studied	Control Variables (through blocking designs and/or statistical manipulation)	Evidence of the Effectiveness of Program Graduates
Undergraduate Field Experiences That Vary in Time spent in schools Clarity of tasks to be performed when in schools Clarity of performance expectations with respect to tasks Time spent in teaching Amount and kind of supervision Amount and kind of performance evaluation Amount and kind of evaluative feedback about performance *Program-related Costs* Dollar costs Human and political "costs" *Program-related Benefits (short term)* To students To college faculty To school supervisors	*Characteristics of the Graduate* History of work with children, social involvement and the assumption of leadership responsibilities General academic ability (GPA combinations) Ability to communicate orally and in writing Adaptability Creativity Scores on the National Teacher Examinations at the end of student teaching Predicted success as a teacher at the end of student teaching Attitudes toward self-as-teacher, job held and one's school as a context in which to teach *Characteristics of the Setting in Which the Graduate Is Teaching* The complexity of the instructional task, as determined by the nature of curricula, students being taught, availability of support services, etc. Expectations for students and teachers in the school where the graduate is teaching, and in the neighborhood or community as a whole Discrepancy between preferred grade level or subject areas in which to teach and position held Discrepancy between the neighborhood/community/school context in which the graduate grew up and position held Amount of help/supervision received from district personnel, especially as a first-year teacher Number and kind of advanced study/inservice activities pursued after being hired as a teacher	*Program-related Benefits (long term)* Performance as a member of a school faculty (perceptions of principal/supervisor and colleagues) Performance as a facilitator of Learning I (perceptions of the graduate's students) Performance as a facilitator of Learning II (perceptions of principal/supervisor) Performance as a facilitator of Learning III (perceptions of an outside observer/interviewer) Performance as a facilitator of Learning IV (obtained through teacher summaries of student attainment with respect to designated learning objectives)

49

require a greater degree of control over unwanted sources of variation than naturally occurring program designs because the effects to be tested are more sharply targeted (the rifle vs. shotgun analogy). Third, they do not require for their conduct full-blown, fully operational programs that meet the requirements of a particular model.

Given these differences, planned variation studies typically assume the form of *systematically manipulated* field experiments, in contrast to the *natural* field experiments that characterize policy-oriented studies.

These differences, in turn, have two major consequences for the conduct of planned variation studies. One is positive; one negative. On the positive side, the resources required are such that individual instructors, or individual institutions, can carry them out. On the negative side, the constraints on program operation due to the demand for control over unwanted sources of variation are such that persons or institutions either back away from such studies, or they select aspects of programs to be studied that are so limited in scope that little of practical importance can come from them. These features of planned variation studies need to be fully appreciated before individuals or institutions go too far in committing themselves to engage in such developmental research efforts.

As in the case of model variation studies, two conditions must be met before planned variation studies can be implemented. First, programs must be in operation which reflect the variation of concern. Second, either programs must be found that are comparable in structure, organization, and student body that are willing to compare practices under experimental conditions, or an institution must be willing to establish and compare the variations of interest. Since program practices and procedures work their effects through interaction with learner characteristics, and kind of learning outcome desired, it probably is best to carry out practice-oriented studies within the context of a particular program or institution.

There are advantages and disadvantages to this strategy, however. On the positive side, it permits developers/researchers to more easily control unwanted sources of variation; for example, major differences in learner characteristics and the conditions under which an instructional practice is administered. On the negative side, it reduces the generalizability of findings. By following the general rule, however, that practice-oriented studies should be replicated in at least three contexts before treating the data on effects as trustworthy, the advantages gained from intrainstitutional studies far outweight the disadvantages.

This should not lure developer/researchers, or institutions, into thinking that planned variation studies are therefore easy to manage, or without consequence to program operation. Just the opposite is true. They require a willingness on the part of students, faculty, and administrators to engage in agreed-to program variations while keeping constant the learning outcomes desired from the program; they require that bona fide experimental and control groups be established, and managed in such a way that true treatment variations are in fact implemented; and they require that a reasonably large number of students be enrolled in a program in order to establish the experimental and control groups needed. Finally, they require that measures of learning outcomes of the highest quality be obtained, and that both cost and effectiveness data be collected and submitted to analysis. These are not easy conditions to achieve, but unless they are, planned variation studies would be better left undone.

Planned variation studies have few bounds as to the kind of practice that is appropriate to be tested. They may deal with the relative cost and effectiveness of competing curricular content in bringing about desired performance as a prospective teacher; they may deal with the relative cost and effectiveness of supervised micro-teaching as opposed to supervised in-classroom teaching in bringing about a particular teaching function; or they may deal with alternative sets of procedures designed to bring about understanding of self as teacher. The only limits to be placed on practices to be tested would seem to be those of size and significance: if a practice is so circumscribed as to have little effect in the overall effects of a teacher preparation program, even if it is found to be more cost-effective than some other practice, it probably should not be treated as planned variation research. Extremely circumscribed practices would probably be treated better within the context of basic research, and extremely global practices would probably be better treated within the context of policy research.

Another characteristic of practice-oriented studies is their variability in design. While they must always involve at least two competing instructional conditions, and one or more commonly agreed-to measure(s) of desired learning outcomes, they can involve all possible combinations of experimental and control groupings and before-after treatment patterns of measurement. They can also vary as to the number and kind of moderator variables to be controlled. Data can be taken, for example, only on such standard variables as age, sex, socioeconomic status and teaching experience, or extended to include measures of personality characteristics and the characteristics of the setting in which instruction occurs. It is in the province of the developer/researcher, of course, to move a so-called moderator variable to the status of an experimental variable, and block his experimental and control groups accordingly.

The example that follows is a planned variation study that is currently underway in the elementary preparation program at Oregon College of Education. Students entering the OCE elementary program during the 1980–81 school year as juniors will serve as subjects for the study. Planned variations to be investigated are (1) a version of the present award-winning program that carries special emphasis on understanding self as teacher, preferred learning and teaching styles, etc., and matching learning experiences to these understandings; and (2) a version of the present program that carries special emphasis on teaching as a decision-making process, with practice in linking instructional decisions to intended outcomes on the part of pupils and the characteristics of the context in which learning is taking place. Students will be assigned randomly to the two planned variations and a parallel section of the present program that will serve as a control. The design of the study is summarized in Table 2.4.

Example Four: The Development of Quality Control Procedures Within Teacher Preparation Programs

Undergraduate teacher preparation programs have two major purposes, the initial preparation of teachers and the initial selection of persons who are to enter the field as practicing teachers. From the point of view of impact on children, the selection of persons who are to be recommended for a certificate to teach probably is the most important of the two.

After entering a preparation program, selection out can occur at any number of points and for any of a number of reasons, but two screening points tend to be viewed as most critical. These are recommendation for student teaching, and recommendation for initial certification. Other steps are involved in the selection process; for example, the initial hiring of a teacher by a district, the decision of a district to extend a contract to a teacher for a second year, and the recommendation for tenure or continuing certification, but the initial decision to recommend for certification probably is the most crucial. Historically, institutions of higher education have been responsible for this decision through their teacher preparation programs. Arnold et al. (1977) have discussed the selection process in terms of the concept of quality control, a concept which appears to be both appropriate and timely.

When current teacher preparation programs are analyzed from the point of view of quality control, one is forced to conclude that the control of quality is lax. (Recall Howey's review in Chapter 1.) Screening for entry to teacher preparation programs tends to be minimal, if it exists at all; knowledge of subject matter to be taught is assumed on the basis of grades received in college courses; knowledge of subject matter pertaining to the history of education in the United States, the psychology of human development and learning, and to some extent the methods of teaching also are assumed on the basis of grades received in courses; clear-cut performance standards in practice teaching, as a condition for entry to student teaching, exist in only a few institutions; and performance standards as guides to recommendation for certification are only slightly more common. The plea by Howsam and his colleagues (1976) for more coursework and a longer period of time for the preparation of teachers is one approach to upgrading the quality of the profession. Another is to improve the quality control mechanisms within existing programs.

TABLE 2.4 Illustrative Treatment Conditions, Control Variables, and Outcome Measures Appropriate to Model Variation Studies in Teacher Education

Treatment Conditions	Control Variables (through blocking designs and/ or statistical manipulation)	Evidence of the Effectiveness of Program Graduates
Planned Variation A Emphasis on understanding self as a teacher, preferred learning and teaching styles, etc., and matching learning experiences accordingly	*Characteristics of a Prospective Teacher Likely to Influence the Effect of a Treatment Condition* Academic ability Learning styles Ability to relate interpersonally Adaptability/flexibility	*Performance as a Member of a School Faculty* Quality of relationships with colleagues Performance of professional responsibilities other than teaching Assumption of leadership responsibilities within the school setting
Planned Variation B Emphasis on teaching as a decision-making process, which practice in linking instructional decisions to (a) intended outcomes on the part of pupils, and (b) the characteristics of the context in which learning is taking place	*Characteristics of an Instructional Setting Likely to Influence Performance on Work Samples* The complexity of the instructional task, as determined by the nature of curricula, students being taught, availability of support services, etc. Expectations for students and teachers Discrepancy between preferred grade level or subject areas in which to teach and the grade level or subject areas in which work samples are taken	*Performance as a Facilitator of Learning* Quality of relationships with pupils Performance of teaching functions Ability to maintain a classroom that is task oriented and civil *Pupil Perceptions, Attitudes and Behavior* Perceptions of a classroom as a context in which to learn Attitudes toward school subjects Engagement in learning activities
Base Program The OCE elementary teacher education program as it operates	Discrepancy between the neighborhood/community/school context in which the subject grew up and the school where work samples are taken Discrepancy between the neighborhood/community/school context in which student teaching occurred and the school where a graduate is teaching Amount of help/supervision received as a practicing or 1st year teacher, including staff development activities pursued	*Pupil Attainment* Progress in basic skill attainment, provided a teacher is responsible for facilitating this aspect of school learning Knowledge of subject matter taught by a teacher
NOTE: All program variations will work from a common syllabus, and will carry common requirements for academic and field performance		

The example that follows is a framework for quality control in teacher education that is under development by representatives from teacher preparation programs in state-supported institutions of higher education in Oregon. Table 2.5 provides an overview of the framework as it presently stands. The framework is yet to be adopted, but it illustrates the application of the concept to practice. It is anticipated that a program of research will accompany whatever framework is adopted to determine the benefits and costs associated with alternative assessment procedures and performance standards at the various quality control points in the preparation process.

RESEARCH IN TEACHER EDUCATION*

Research on teacher education should be a diverse and many-faceted enterprise. It should chart the characteristics of those who enter teacher preparation programs, and those who survive to enter teaching; it should study the relationship between characteristics at point of entry to a program, or point of exit, and subsequent success in practice; it should focus on the interaction of program entry characteristics, the nature of preparation programs, and subsequent success in practice; it should be searching for much more than it has for the relationship between knowledge or skill mastery and subsequent success in practice; it should be searching for early indicators of competence as a teacher, and studying the extent to which these are effective as predictors of success in first-, third-, or fifth-year teaching; it should be investigating the relationship between the nature of field placements in preparation programs, subsequent job placements, and subsequent performance in those job placements. (Haberman elaborates on this in Chapter 4.) As indicated in the previous pages, it should also be investigating the matter of benefits and costs associated with alternative preparation programs. Basic to the views that follow is the assumption that if research in teacher education is to be this diverse and many faceted, the *methodology* needed for its support must be equally diverse and many faceted.

I will argue here the position that research on teacher education has not been this far-ranging, and that at present, we do not have the methodology that enables it to be so. After completing a review of the research literature pertaining to teacher selection (Schalock, 1979), I am of the

* This section of the chapter draws heavily on a recent paper by the author entitled "Eating Humble Pie: Notes on Methodology in Teacher Education Research" (Schalock, 1980) and a chapter appearing in the *7th Annual Review of Research in Education* entitled "Research on Teacher Education Selection" (Schalock, 1979). Appreciation is expressed to the publishers of these materials for permission to draw upon them as freely as I have.

opinion that we know very little about any of the items mentioned above, and what is more we do not even have good hypotheses about them. We clearly do not have "up and running" the research designs or measurement systems needed to get good information about them. A case in point is the essential absence of tested methodology that can be used by teacher education institutions in responding to the NCATE requirement for evaluative follow-up studies of graduates of teacher preparation programs. Cooper reviews the type of data that is being collected in the few institutions who have instituted some systematic follow-up at this point in time in his chapter in this volume.

I have come to the opinion that we have a very limited knowledge base about teacher education per se, and that we are essentially without tradition when it comes to teacher education research. It is my understanding that Peck and Tucker (1973), and those who have reviewed the literature before them (for example, Cyphert & Spaights, 1964; Denemark & MacDonald, 1967), hold a similar view.

This is not to say that teacher education is without a research base. In fact it draws upon a number of research bases, but these historically have come from the disciplines of biology, psychology, and anthropology. Within recent years educational researchers have begun to establish a knowledge base that pertains directly to teaching, but as yet little information that *informs decisions by teacher educators about teacher education* has come from research on teacher education.

One aim of this chapter is to suggest how the research base in teacher education can be expanded, and made more powerful. Another is to suggest how this might be done at relatively low cost.

A first step toward establishing a more powerful research base is to reach agreement on the substantive issues in teacher education that need to be addressed through research. This is the aim of other chapters in the volume. It also was the aim of the NIE-sponsored conference in January of 1979 on issues confronting teacher education (Hall, Hord, & Brown, 1980). Once a focus of inquiry has been established, questions of methodology come into play. (In practice, of course, the reverse is often true, that is, the availability of a methodology often shapes the research questions asked.) The intent in this section of the chapter is to sensitize readers to the methodological issues that need to be addressed in planning research in teacher education, and provide some conceptual handles for dealing with them.

My remarks are based on the assumption that issues of methodology that face researchers in teacher education are infinitely more complex than was once thought, and that at present we do not have either the concepts or the methods needed to implement a full-scale program of research on all issues that are critical to the preparation of teachers. If this assumption is true, research on substantive issues will need to be paralleled by research on methodology.

TABLE 2.5 Tests and Measures Being Considered by OSSHE Institutions to Assure Quality in Graduates from Teacher Preparation Programs

Assessment Points	Basic Skills	Subject Matter to be Taught	Knowledge That Pertains to Teaching and Learning	Skills of Teaching	Competence in Teaching	Manner in Teaching
1. Entry to college/university	Typically inferred from GPA or SAT scores					
2. General studies	Inferred if performance is satisfactory; formal assessment and remediation available if performance is unsatisfactory					
3. Field experiences prior to teacher education admission			Review of experience by college and school supervisors; performance evaluated when appropriate			Assessed by both college and school supervisors
4. Entry to the preparation program	Assessed through interview and formal examination					
5. Coursework in content		Examinations given by instructors				
6. Coursework in teaching and learning			Examinations given by instructors			

7. Practicum experiences prior to student teaching					
a. that accompany foundation courses	Application observed and evaluated by college and school supervisors		Applications of knowledge observed by college and school supervisors; performance evaluated when appropriate	Review of experience by college and school supervisors; performance evaluated when appropriate		Assessed by both college and school supervisors
b. that accompany methods courses	Application observed and evaluated by college and school supervisors	Application observed and evaluated by college and school supervisors	Application observed and evaluated by college and school supervisors	Skills demonstrated; evaluations usually made by both college and school supervisors	For short periods or with small groups; supervised and assessed by college and school supervisors	Assessed by both college and school supervisors
8. Student teaching	Application observed and evaluated by college and school supervisors	Application observed and evaluated by college and school supervisors	Application observed and evaluated by college and school supervisors	Skills demonstrated; evaluations made by both college and school supervisors	For extended periods of full responsibility teaching; performance assessed by both college and school supervisors	Assessed by both college and school supervisors
9. As a first-year teacher					Performance assessed by a college representative, principal, colleagues and students	Assessed by a college representative, principal, colleagues and students
10. As a third-year teacher					Same as above	Same as above

Notes on the Past

Any number of textbooks deal with methods of research in education. None, to my knowledge, deal with methods of research in teacher education. It can be argued that this is with good reason, for the methods described are sufficiently generic as to be applicable to any educational problem. It also can be argued, however, that while there are generic research methods, their application always requires adaptation to what is being investigated and the conditions under which a particular investigation takes place.

My intent here is to focus on some of the adaptations that have to be made in educational research methods when applied to teacher education. My comments will focus on conceptual clarification and use of methods, more than they will on methods per se.

Distinguishing between Research on Teacher Education and Research on Teacher Effectiveness. Just as research on learning is not research on teaching, research on teaching is not research on teacher education. Research on teaching contributes importantly to the substance or content of teacher education, but it does not deal with the *prediction* of teacher effectiveness (teacher selection); it does not deal with the effectiveness of teacher preparation programs; it does not deal with the interaction of program characteristics and the characteristics of students preparing to become teachers; and it does not deal with the pragmatic and increasingly political matter of costs and benefits associated with alternative preparation programs.

To some, research on teacher education may not be as glamorous or exciting as research on teaching and learning, but it is research that is no less important. Enormous sums of public and private funds are directed to the education of teachers each year, and reminiscent of the circumstances the teaching profession faced a decade or so ago (USOE, 1970) teacher educators at this point would be hard pressed to build a convincing case that teacher education programs "make a difference." More importantly, teacher education programs are the filters through which persons enter the schools as teachers, and the social obligation that accompanies recommendation for certification demands that those who are recommending be sure of their recommendation. I doubt that any teacher educators now believe they are able to accurately predict at point of exit from a teacher preparation program who is going to be effective as a teacher and who is not—let alone why that will be so.

Research on teaching is important to teacher education, but research on teacher education is important to the public trust. It also is important to children and youth, for what we know about the preparation and selection of teachers in the long-run affects the quality of education they receive.

Alternative Foci for Research on Teacher Education. In a recent volume of the National Society for the Study of Education, Richard Turner (1975) proposed a framework for organizing research on teacher education that appears to have considerable utility. The framework is organized around stages in the professional life of a teacher, and calls for research to be done on the transition between stages. The four stages he deals with are selection, training, placement, and job performance, with work success in job performance being the important criterion. Turner used the following schematic to depict the foci for research highlighted by the framework.

Selection   Training   Placement   Work Success

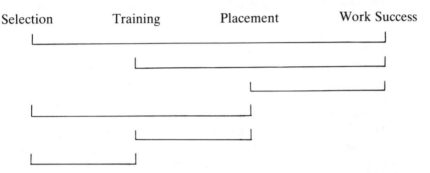

Turner's framework has to be viewed in light of his underlying assumption that "the aim of research in teacher education is to optimize that portion of teacher work success attributable to teacher preparation" (p. 87). In general I concur with this assumption, though I would add the political reality of having to pursue this aim within the framework of cost-benefit considerations.

Turner does not argue that all of the relationships identified in the schematic are equally important as foci for research, though all are possible and all are important. He also recognizes that one of the greatest handicaps to strong programs of research in teacher education is the problem of defensible criteria of work success, but this is an issue that has had to be faced in research on teacher effectiveness so it is not unique. Turner was able to find studies (done largely by doctoral students) that pertained to each of the research foci suggested by his framework, but in keeping with the view being advanced here he concluded his review by saying:

> In spite of recent improvements in research in the field, the amount of dependable information available compared to the amount needed to formulate more effective policies and practices of teacher education is miniscule (p. 107).

So far as I can determine nothing has changed in the five years since the publication of Turner's chapter to alter this conclusion, including the completion of the Beginning Teacher Evaluation Study (Fisher et al., 1978) designed to inform policies and practices in teacher education.

The Interaction of Focus and Method. It is stating the obvious to say that the focus of a research study determines to a large extent the nature of the design and methodology to be employed in carrying out the study, but when preparing a paper on methodology the strength of this connection needs to be fully understood. Using Turner's framework as a point of reference, research focusing on the relationship between characteristics of students entering a teacher preparation program and their subsequent effectiveness as teachers will take a very different form and will involve different sets of variables than will research focusing on the relationship between training and job placement. The strength of the connection between focus and method is even more notable when contrasting research on the costs and benefits associated with alternative preparation programs with the foci suggested in Turner's scheme.

The not-so-obvious point that needs to be made about the connectedness between focus and method is the point made in the introduction to this section of the chapter: we do not now have well-established methodology to support much of the research that needs to be done in teacher education. This is especially the case with respect to measurement systems and the conceptual framework on which they are based. Obviously, we are not altogether without method, so research of one form or another probably can take place around any of the foci that have been mentioned. The point that needs to be understood, however, is that from a methodological point of view much of this research will be relatively primitive, and as a consequence we should not expect too much by way of results from it too soon. For the immediate future research in teacher education probably should be as much concerned with the development of good constructs and methodology as it is with establishing empirically verified relationships (see Schalock, 1975, pp. 19–22).

The Effect of Context and Time. One of the most important contributions of research on teacher effectiveness to research on teacher education is the consistent finding that the effectiveness of a teacher is always time dependent and context specific. Learning on the part of students is clearly related to time allocated to learning (Block & Burns, 1976; Bloom, 1976; Fisher et al., 1978; Rosenshine & Berliner, 1978), and the behavior of teachers that facilitate learning clearly varies from grade level to grade level, and from subject to subject within grade level (Brophy & Evertson, 1974; Fisher et al., 1978; Medley, 1977). Having these data as a base on which to build teacher education research, especially teacher education research involving criteria of work success, doesn't make such research easier, but it does protect against assumptions about the nature of teaching effectiveness that are too simplistic and thus against the use of methods or designs that are inappropriate to such research.

Context and time enter research on teacher education in a number of other important ways. Both need to be considered, for example, in investigating the relationship between selection variables and training effects, or any research involving placement effects. Time also needs to enter the picture in research on program effectiveness, or in the study of costs and benefits associated with alternative program designs. It may well be, for example, that program effects are short lived, that is, they are reflected in the performance of first-year teachers but not third- or fifth-year teachers. On the other hand, it may be that program effects are cumulative, that is, they not only are reflected in the performance of first-year teachers but project a pattern of excellence or mediocrity that becomes more pronounced with time. Haberman speaks to this question in his chapter.

These are important considerations, and call for dimensions of context and time to be treated as critical variables in teacher education research. A recent paper by Doyle (1978) and work underway at the Far West Laboratory in the development of instructional theory from an "ecological" point of view (Tikunoff & Ward, 1978) point the way toward understanding why dimensions of context and time need to be incorporated into research on teacher education, and how this might be done.

The Dominance of Interaction Effects and the Likelihood of Curvilinear Relationships. In designing research studies in teacher education, and especially in analyzing data coming from these studies, allowance must be made for strong interaction effects and the likelihood of curvilinear relationships among the variables studied. Selection variables interact with training variables; both probably interact with placement variables; and all three interact with measures of work success. Moreover, different measures taken at each of these focal points are likely to have patterns of relationships that are inconsistent and anything but linear. For example, while a curvilinear relationship appears to exist between measures of academic ability and measures of teaching effectiveness; the curve looks somewhat different for elementary and secondary teachers. Interaction effects can also be expected between the socioeconomic background of teachers (or teacher preference as to grade level at which to teach), job placement characteristics, and success in teaching. Still another interaction that is likely to confound research on teacher education that involves measures of work success is the interaction that occurs between various measures of work success, for example, a supervisor's judgment of adequacy as to job performance, measures of student time on-task, and measures of learning gain. There is no assurance of any relationship between the first and the latter two measures, and when data are taken on individual students in classrooms, the relationship between the latter two measures tends to be weak (Fisher et al., 1978).

Again, while these realities do not prevent research in teacher education from progressing, they do not make it easier. As in the case of the effect of context and time they do protect teacher education researchers from progressing on assumptions that are too simple, and from using designs and methodology that do not accommodate the complexities with which teacher education research must deal. Turner (1975) recognized the impact of these realities when he spoke to the role of "moderator variables" in teacher education research generally.

> In all probability, teacher education is a field in which many variables are moderators. Because unidentified moderators twist, weaken, or obliterate linear relationships between variables, and since the dominant research methods anticipate linear relationships, research progress in the field might be anticipated to proceed slowly until the major moderating variables are identified (p. 89).

Confronting the Issue of External Validity in Research on Teacher Education. While research on teaching has influenced the content of teacher preparation programs, research on teacher education/selection appears to have had appreciably less influence on the manner in which teacher preparation programs are structured or operated. The Stanford research on the effects of micro-teaching, or the Far West Laboratory's research on "mini-courses," may be pointed to as an exception, but by and large, teacher education research has made little difference in the enterprise of teacher education.

In part, of course, this is due to the paucity of research that has been done in teacher education. There are two other reasons, however, that contribute to this lack of impact. First, experimental studies in teacher education have tended to be carried out in contexts that could tolerate the control and manipulation they require. The best example of such a context is an instructor's own class. Second, most research in teacher education has tended to involve practices that are narrowly conceived or limited in scope, for example, practices that cover a day or a week of instruction, a particular grading practice, or a particular set of role relationships between instructor and student that are to be tried for a term. Both strategies seem to stem from the fact that experimental studies make severe demands on the control of unwanted sources of variation, in both treatment conditions and outcome measures. The consequence of employing such strategies has been results of limited utility and generalizability, even within the context where the studies are carried out.

These are problems that have plagued educational researchers for decades, and only now are we coming to understand what must be done to overcome them. Bacically, they are problems that have to do with the *external validity* of educational experiments (Bracht & Glass, 1968; Snow, 1973). Shulman (1970) speaks pointedly to this problem when he says:

> Researchers are caught in a bind. To maximize the *internal validity* of experiments, they develop carefully monitored settings within which they can govern their research. This has long been recognized as a necessity, but it is likely that the experimental tradition in American education overemphasized the importance of reliability and precision at the expense of the characteristics affecting that other factor of equal importance (external validity). . . . It is not

sufficient that the individuals studied as a sample are truly representative of that human population to which the results of a particular experiment will be inferred. Researchers must also ascertain that the experimental conditions can serve external conditions of interest. That is, researchers must also attempt to *maximize the similarity* between the conditions in which they study behavior and those other conditions, whatever they may be, to which researchers may ultimately wish to make inferences. The similarity should hold them between psychologically meaningful features of the settings, not merely between the manifest aspects of the two situations (p. 377).

If Shulman's analysis is correct, three fundamental shifts in the nature and focus of teacher education research must take place if it is to be responsive to the criterion of external validity: (1) a shift in emphasis from the sampling of people to the sampling of educational environments; (2) a shift from the study of single, isolated variables to the study of the complex of variables that make up ongoing educational environments; and (3) a shift from piecemeal, unrelated, "one shot" research efforts to studies that are articulated through time, theory, and problem focus.

Projections for the Future

Recognizing that methodological considerations are tied always to the focus of a particular research study, it is hard to generalize about methodology, but the previous comments help put in perspective a growing uneasiness on the part of those who are doing research in education (and I presume teacher education) with the research paradigms that have been in use for the past several decades (Berliner, 1978; Fisher & Berliner, 1977; Shulman & Lanier, 1977). There is a growing awareness of the limitations inherent in large sample, cross-sectional studies that aggregate effects to class or school or program means. There also is a growing awareness of the limitations of looking for treatment effects of single variables within a class or school or program setting, even when these "variables" are conceived as broadly as teacher or curriculum effects. There also is growing awareness of the limitations inherent in looking at single outcome or dependent measures, especially when the focus of a research study is on something as complex as the consequences of selection decisions or program organization on the ability of prospective teachers to teach.

Finally, there is a growing awareness that looking only at teacher and student *behavior* in studies of teaching and teacher education is not enough. Attention also needs to be focused on the intentions of teachers and students (Fenstermacher, 1978), the decision making of teachers and students (Shavelson, 1976; Shulman & Elstein, 1975), and the context in which behavior, intentions and decisions occur (Dreeben, 1978). The chapter by the Sprinthalls clearly illustrates what may predispose specific behaviors in the classroom.

Signals of a Paradigm Shift. Collectively, these factors are pointing to research designs and methodologies in future studies of teaching and teacher education that are very different from those of the past. Projections of any kind are filled with risk, and stand to mislead as well as inform, but I foresee research in teacher education needing to reflect the following characteristics if it is to advance our understanding appreciably.

Design. Increasing use of longitudinal designs, coupled with a "case history" or "extreme case" or "clinical" or "ethnographic" orientation to data collection and analysis. Single subject designs (Kratochwill, 1978) may come into play, but if they do, I would expect them to be supplemented by design and analysis considerations that strive toward generalizability of findings. Since research in teacher education at this point in time needs to be as much concerned with construct development and delineation as it is the verification of empirical relationships, I would expect descriptive or hypothesis-generating designs to predominate over hypothesis-testing designs in the immediate future. Experimental designs will still be needed and employed, but only after constructs are reasonably well delineated and hypotheses reasonably well formulated. Whatever purpose a design is to serve, it will need to allow for the influence of context and time, and the interaction of variables that both imply.

Measurement. Multiple measures of any construct under investigation will be the order of the day, but particularly so with constructs serving as dependent variables. This is in keeping with the Campbell and Fiske plea more than twenty years ago (1959) for the "triangulation" of measures of constructs that are not yet well defined. Table 2.6 illustrates variables that are likely to figure most prominently in research on teacher education.

Analysis. Strategies of data analysis are more difficult to project, for they depend heavily on design decisions. To the extent that studies employ large sample, cross-sectional designs analyses are likely to take the form of those employed in the Beginning Teacher Evaluation Study or in the experimental study by Anderson, Evertson, and Brophy (1978) of effective teaching in first-grade reading groups. Generally speaking these researchers employed linear regression models, with entering differences in learners adjusted through covariance procedures, coupled with tests for the curvilinearity of relationships found. If longitudinal designs are employed, even more complex analyses apparently will have to be used (Borich, 1972).

Perhaps the greatest change that is likely to come in the analysis of data is in the form of exploratory data analysis. According to Berliner (1978), Tukey and others have shown that

> it is perfectly appropriate to work with sets of data throwing out some cases, keeping others, and doing things that the classical statistician never dreamed possible. Data analysis can be exploratory, not confirmatory, and the analyst

TABLE 2.6   Variables Being Considered by Oregon Teacher Preparation Institutions as Essential in Research on Teacher Selection and Preparation

Dimensions of Teacher Effectiveness to Be Assessed
- The ability to perform the functions required of the job held
- Leadership responsibilities assumed in the school and district
- Students' perception of a teacher's classroom as a context in which to learn
- Students' attitudes toward subject areas, and school generally
- The civility of a teacher's classroom as a context in which to learn
- The engagement of students in learning activities
- Student attainment of academic outcomes
- Student attainment of independence as a learner

Setting Characteristics Known or Assumed to Relate to the Effectiveness of a Teacher
- The content and organization of curriculum
- The instructional model used and instructional materials available
- The characteristics of students being taught
- The physical facilities within which instruction occurs
- Support services available to a teacher
- The characteristics of the neighbourhood/community served by the school
- The teachers' perception of the school and community as a context in which to teach

Personal Characteristics Known or Assumed to Relate to the Effectiveness of a Teacher
- The ability to communicate orally and in writing
- The ability to relate interpersonally
- Knowledge of content to be taught
- Knowledge of teaching principles, methods and skills
- Knowledge of human development and group dynamics
- General academic ability
- Adaptability
- Predicted success as a teacher at the end of student teaching
- Preference of grade level at which to teach

Background Characteristics Known or Assumed to Interact with Other Factors Influencing Teacher Effectiveness
- History of contact with children
- History of social involvement and the assumption of leadership responsibilities
- The nature of a teacher's own schooling experience, including the size of the school and the nature of the community it served

need not have preconceived notions about the data structures. In this kind of exploratory analysis you are urged to massage complex data such that new insights about the phenomena emerge (p. 21).

This approach to statistical manipulation would appear to be very much in keeping with the exploratory, descriptive, "hypothesis-generating" approach referred to above, and would appear to make eminently good sense in light of the size and complexity of the data bases that emerge as a consequence of such an approach to research in education. Case studies, clinical reports, single-subject research, and ethnographic research have reasonably well-established rules for reporting data, though these tend not to be as restrictive as the rules governing the reporting of data derived through inferential statistics.

The question of paradigm. It is still unclear whether developments of the kind described signal a genuine shift in the paradigm governing research in education (Kuhn, 1970), or whether they represent simply a maturing of awareness as to the complexity of the field with which we are dealing or a growing sense of independence from the designs and methodologies of the parent disciplines that have held sway for so long. They may also be simply a response to the frustration of not being able to establish powerful, conclusive, and generalizable findings on anything that has to do with teaching and the preparation of teachers. Doyle's recent paper on alternative paradigms for research on teaching effectiveness (1978), however, along with the "teaching as decision making" thrust of the new Institute for Research on Teaching (Shulman & Lanier, 1977) and Berliner's call for clinical studies of classroom teaching and learning (1978), would suggest that a genuine shift in paradigm may be forthcoming.

Whatever it is that is accounting for this shift in the way people are thinking about research in education and teacher education, it is likely that we will not continue for long the kind of studies that were the hallmark of the last decade. Just as "process-product" studies of teacher effectiveness emerged in response to a growing awareness of the limits of educational research carried out in the 1940s and 1950s, a new way of conducting educational research appears to be on the horizon. As we debate an agenda for research in teacher education we need to be aware of this fundamental shift in thinking about methodology, respond to the needs it creates, and take advantage of it to the extent possible.

Teacher Preparation Programs as Contexts for Research in Teacher Education. Much that has been written here rests on the proposition that ongoing teacher preparation programs are the most appropriate contexts for research on teacher education. The proposition rests on two broad assumptions. One is that teacher preparation programs represent "naturally occurring" contexts for such research. Persons wishing to become teachers always are screened against criteria that have been established for entry to a preparation program, entry to student teaching and recommendation for initial certification. Looked at from the view of research on teacher selection, these are points in preparation programs where predictors of success are regularly obtained and predictions of success regularly made. A second assumption is that teacher educators care more than anyone else about the ability to predict who is likely to succeed as a teacher. As the preparation and selection of teachers are now structured in the United States teacher education personnel carry the burden of this prediction, for they carry primary responsibility for determining who enters the profession. A great many lives are affected by each "prediction" that is made in this regard and teacher educators, as well as everyone else, want these predictions to be as accurate as possible.

Treating teacher preparation programs as contexts for research presumes that measures are taken routinely at these various stages of preparation to inform decisions that must be made relative to a student's continuing in a preparation program. Three additional conditions must be met for programs to be effective contexts for research: (1) measures taken for purposes of decision making within a teacher preparation program must be of sufficient quality to be used in research; (2) follow-up studies are carried out on graduates to determine how accurate predictions of effectiveness have been; and (3) all this can be done without being disruptive to the program, or making it inordinately expensive. At first blush these assumptions would appear to be beyond the bounds of reason. They are not. They do not require major changes in either the organization or the operation of most present day teacher education programs. What they do require are a lot of minor changes, and a sense of purpose that is now lacking. The nature of the changes needed, and how they have been implemented in the elementary teacher preparation program at Oregon College of Education has been described (Schalock & Girod, 1975; Schalock, Kersh, & Garrison, 1976).

In many respects what is being proposed is analogous to research laboratories that have been established in other disciplines. If the conditions that have been called for could be implemented, it would mean essentially that all of the requirements necessary for a teacher preparation program to become a functional "laboratory" for research on teacher preparation/selection would exist. This is especially the case if the content and operation of the preparation program itself could be varied systematically. Moreover, since data would be collected as part of ongoing preparation and follow-up programs, the laboratory could be operated at relatively low cost. The most expensive feature of most research is data collection, and this cost, for purposes of research, would essentially be eliminated.

Finally, the opportunity to replicate studies with each new group of prospective teachers entering the program would permit a line of inquiry to be pursued over a sufficiently long period of time, and with a sufficiently large number of replications, that trustworthy knowledge would actually have a chance of being produced. This is a condition that has never before existed in teacher education, and if established, represents for the first time the possibility that teaching and the preparation of teachers could move to the status of profession.

Teacher Preparation Programs as Contexts for Basic Research. The logic behind and the payoff from both policy- and practice-oriented research is apparent to most teacher educators. This is not the case for basic research. In fact, there often is open hostility on the part of educators, of all shades and descriptions, toward research activities labeled as basic. While understandable, this is an unfortunate circumstance, for like it or not, the kind of research activities that typically get classified as basic are at the center of how members of a particular profession think, work, and extend the knowledge base of their profession.

While the distinction between basic and applied research has never been particularly clear, the term is used here to describe research activities that cannot be classified either as policy- or practice-oriented studies. Typically such studies deal with matters that have little direct utility to the educational practitioner. Most commonly they deal with *variables affecting* instruction, rather than with full-blown features or aspects of an instructional program. Because of this, they tend to be linked more closely to the development and testing of instruction-related theory than they are to the development and testing of instructional programs and procedures. As a consequence, educational practitioners tend to find the results of basic research to be of little direct utility and, as a by-product, of little interest. Persons concerned with the development of instructional theory, however, or persons attempting to carry out practice-oriented research, find the results of basic studies to be essential to their work. The distinguishing features of policy-oriented studies, practice-oriented studies and basic research studies are summarized in Table 2.7.*

In some respects, basic research studies place fewer demands on an ongoing teacher preparation program than practice-oriented studies. They tend to involve fewer students; they need not involve a large segment of a program; and they need not extend over long periods of time. In other respects, however, their demands are greater. Quality in measurement must be assured, and experimental designs must be employed with sufficient rigor that causality can be attributed to the experimental or treatment variables being investigated. Both of these conditions are above and beyond the requirements of normal program operation, but there is reason to believe that both can be achieved if introduced with care and foresight. When these conditions are met much is to be gained, for basic research can be carried out as an adjunct to the normal operation of educational programs at little added cost.

While it is possible to combine basic research with program operation by meeting these two conditions, it needs to be pointed out that considerable risk is involved in attempting such a venture. High-quality measures,

* Survey research is another class of research activity frequently engaged in by teacher educators, but because of its relative simplicity it has not been dealt with in this chapter. Obviously, surveys can produce information that is of considerable use to educational practitioners, particularly if they supplement information gained through policy- and practice-oriented studies.

TABLE 2.7 Features That Distinguish Policy-oriented, Practice-oriented, and Basic Research Studies in Teacher Education

Type of Study	Experimental or Treatment Variables	Dependent or Outcome Variables	Control Over Unwanted Sources of Variation	Collection of Benefit and Cost Data
Policy-oriented studies	Teacher education programs or elements of such programs	Short- and long-term measures of success as a teacher	Loose	Yes
Practice-oriented studies	Aspects of a preparation program that are designed to bring about designated learning outcomes	Intended and unintended effects of the program dimension being tested	Moderate	Yes
Basic research studies	Practices, procedures or variables assumed to be related to learning and instruction	Performance on a conceptually relevant measure of learning effects	Tight	No

for example, are not easily nor inexpensively obtained. Also, requiring program operations to meet the constraints of experimental design almost always creates a cumbersomeness and rigidity that frustrates program managers and participants. Heretofore, efforts to design data collection systems that support both program operation and basic research *have tended to end in the design of research programs instead of operational programs that have good data.* When this has occurred, the reaction has been nearly universal on the part of program managers and participants: throw the researchers out! (Parlett & Hamilton, 1972).

Recognizing this pitfall, it still should be possible for teacher educators to design data generation systems that will support both applied and basic research, as well as program operation. When this is the case, the best possible context for research exists: it can be carried out at low cost, and it has a chance of meeting the requirements of external validity that are not met in most educational experiments.

CONCLUSION

Teacher education research has not had a strong history, and during the past decade it has been essentially overshadowed by research on teacher effectiveness. While much can and should be taken from the teacher effectiveness research when planning research on teacher education, both in substance and methodology, teacher education research has its own unique set of research questions and methodological dilemmas. I have argued that these questions are as important to the public good as questions revolving around teaching effectiveness and school learning, for they pertain directly to who enters the teaching profession and the likelihood of their effectiveness once there.

In planning an agenda for teacher education research close attention needs to be paid to what appears to be a fundamental shift in how people are beginning to think about educational research, and how it should be conducted. Some of these emerging views have been described in the previous pages. In addition to what has been said, however, I would argue that for teacher education research to make an appreciable difference in the manner in which teachers are selected and prepared in institutions across the nation, multiple sites must be engaged in both hypothesis-formulating and hypothesis-testing studies. I would also argue that in order to make a difference these studies will need to be longitudinal in nature, reflect a high degree of external validity (Shulman, 1975), and be subject to numerous replications. As Gage (1977) has pointed out, "Far more than the statistical significance of any single study, confirmation by independent studies is relied upon by behavioral scientists before they begin to take a finding seriously.... what we want in most fields of research, before we become truly impressed, is replication" (pp. 1–2). For this to be feasible, ways must be found to carry out research on teacher education at low cost.

Finally, I have argued that the only context that has a chance of meeting these requirements is that of ongoing teacher preparation programs. A number of conditions must be met for preparation programs to become viable, low-cost contexts for research, but these are not impossible conditions to meet. It is my belief that until these conditions are met, and at least a large number of our teacher preparation programs are functioning as counterparts to the laboratories that our colleagues in the parent disciplines so long have had at their disposal, and through which they have contributed so much, we will not be able to do much better in the preparation/selection of teachers than we have in the past.

BIBLIOGRAPHY

Anderson, L. N., Evertson, C. M., & Brophy, J. E. *An experimental study of effective teaching in first-grade reading groups.* Austin, Texas: Research and Development Center for Teacher Education, The University of Texas, 1978.

Arnold, D. S., Denemark, G., Nelly, E. R., Robinson, A., & Sagan, E. L. *Quality control in teacher education: Some policy issues.* Washington, D.C.: American Association of Colleges for Teacher Education, 1977.

Berliner, D. C. *Clinical studies of classrooms in teaching and learning.* Paper presented at the annual meeting of the American Educational Research Association, Toronto, March, 1978.

Block, J. H., & Burns, R. B. Mastery learning. In L. S. Shulman (Ed.), *Review of research in education,* Vol. 4. Itasca, Illinois: F. E. Peacock, 1976.

Bloom, B. S. *Human characteristics and school learning.* New York: McGraw-Hill, 1976.

Borich, G. D. *Linear and curvilinear models for aptitude-treatment interactions.* Paper presented at the meetings of the American Psychological Association, Honolulu, Hawaii, 1972.

Bracht, G. H., & Glass, G. V. The external validity of experiments. *American Educational Research Journal,* 1968, *5,* 437–474.

Brophy, J., & Evertson, C. M. *Learning from teaching: A developmental perspective.* Boston: Allyn and Bacon, 1974.

Burdin, J., & Lanzillotti, K. (Eds.). *A reader's guide to the comprehensive models for preparing elementary teachers.* Washington, D.C.: American Association of Colleges for Teacher Education and ERIC Clearinghouse on Teacher Education, 1969.

Campbell, D. T., & Fiske, W. Convergent and discriminant validations by the multitrait-multimethod matrix. *Psychological Bulletin,* 1959, *56,* 81–105.

Cyphert, F. R., & Spaights, E. *An analysis and projection of research in teacher education.* USOE Cooperative Research Project #F–015. Columbus, Ohio: The Ohio State University Research Foundation, 1964.

Denemark, G. W., & MacDonald, J. B. Preservice and inservice education of teachers. *Review of Educational Research,* 1967, *37,* 233–247.

Dickson, G. E., & Saxe, R. W., et al. *Partners for educational reform and renewal.* Berkeley, California: McCutchan, 1973.

Doyle, W. Paradigms for research on teacher effectiveness. In L. S. Shulman (Ed.), *Review of research in education*, Vol. 8. Itaska, Illinois: F. E. Peacock, 1978.

Dreeben, R. *The collective character of instruction.* Invited address presented at the annual meeting of the American Educational Research Association, Toronto, March, 1978.

Fenstermacher, G. A philosophical consideration of research on teacher effectiveness. In L. S. Shulman (Ed.), *Review of research in education*, Vol. 8. Itaska, Illinois: F. E. Peacock, 1978.

Fisher, D. W., & Berliner, D. C. *Quasi-clinical inquiry in research on classroom teaching and learning*, Technical Report VI–2, Beginning Teacher Evaluation Study. San Francisco: Far West Laboratory for Educational Research and Development, 1977.

Fisher, D. W., Filby, N. N., Marliave, R., Cahen, L. S., Dishaw, M., Moore, J. E., & Berliner, D. C. *Final report of the beginning teacher evaluation study*, Technical Report V–1. San Francisco: Far West Laboratory for Educational Research and Development, 1978.

Gage, N. L. *Four cheers for research on teaching.* Review draft, 1977.

Hall, G E., Hord, S. M., & Brown, G. (Eds.). *Exploring issues in teacher education: Questions for future research.* Report of NIE sponsored conference on research and development in teacher education, at the R and D Center for Teacher Education, Austin, Texas, 1980.

Hemphill, J. K. Educational development. *Urban Review*, 1969, *4*, 23–27.

Hood, P. D., & Blackwell, L. *The educational development, dissemination and evaluation training program.* San Francisco: Far West Laboratory for Educational Research and Development, 1975.

Houston, W. R., Cooper, J. M., & Warner, A. W. *School based teacher educator project: Report of second year activities.* Houston: University of Houston, 1977. SP 011 355.

Howsam, R. B., Corrigan, D. C., Denemark, G. W., & Nash, R. J. *Educating a profession.* Report of the Bicentennial Commission on Education for the Profession of Teaching. Washington, D.C.: American Association of Colleges for Teacher Education, 1976.

Kratochwill, T. *Single subject research.* New York: Academic Press, 1978.

Kuhn, T. S. *The structure of scientific revolutions.* (2nd Ed., enlarged). Chicago: University of Chicago Press, 1970.

Medley, D. M. *Teacher competence and teacher effectiveness: A review of process-product research.* Monograph. Washington, D.C.: The American Association of Colleges for Teacher Education, 1977.

Parlett, M., & Hamilton, D. *Evaluation as illumination: A new approach to the study of innovatory programs.* Occasional Paper, Centre for Research in the Educational Sciences, University of Edinburgh, Scotland, October, 1972.

Peck, R. F., & Tucker, J. A. Research on teacher education. In R. W. M. Travers (Ed.), *Second Handbook of research on teaching.* Chicago: Rand McNally, 1973.

Rosenshine, B., & Berliner, D. C. Academic engaged time. British *Journal of Teacher Education*, 1978, *4*, 3–16.

Schalock, H. D. *Closing the knowledge gap: CBTE programs as a focus of and context for research in education.* A position paper of The Consortium of CBE Centers. Albany, New York: The Multi-State Consortium for Performance-Based Teacher Education, Syracuse University, 1975.

——. Improving educational outcomes. In O. T. Lenning (Ed.), *New directions for higher education.* San Francisco: Jossey-Bass, 1976.

——. Research on teacher-selection. In D. C. Berliner (Ed.), *Review of research in education,* Vol. 7. Washington, D.C.: American Educational Research Association, 1979.

——. Eating humble pie: Notes on methodology in teacher education research. In G. E. Hall, S. M. Hord, & G. Brown (Eds.), *Exploring issues in teacher education: Questions for future research.* Report of NIE sponsored conference on research and development in teacher education at the R and D Center for Teacher Education, Austin, Texas, 1980.

Schalock, H. D., & Girod, G. R. The Oregon College of Education-Teaching Research Division paradigm for research on teacher preparation. In G. E. Dickson (Ed.), *Research and evaluation in operational competency-based teacher education programs,* College of Education Educational Comment, The University of Toledo, No. 1, 1975, 21–38.

Schalock, H. D., Kersh, B., & Garrison, J. *From commitment to practice: The OCE elementary teacher education program.* Washington, D.C.: The American Association for Colleges of Teacher Education, 1976.

Schalock, H. D., & Sell, G. R. A framework for the analysis and empirical investigation of educational RDD&E. In H. D. Schalock and G. R. Sell (Eds.), *The Oregon studies in educational RDD&E, Vol. III, Frameworks for viewing educational RDD&E.* Monmouth, Oregon: Teaching Research Division, 1972, pp. 193–261.

Shavelson, R. J. Teacher's decision making. In N. L. Gage (Ed.), *The psychology of teaching methods.* Chicago: National Society for the Study of Education, 1976.

Shulman, L. S. Reconstruction in educational research. *Review of Educational Research,* 1970, *40,* 371–396.

Shulman, L. S., & Elstein, A. S. Studies in problem solving, judgment, and decision making: Implications for educational research. In F. N. Kerlinger (Ed.), *Review of research in education,* Vol. 3. Itaska, Illinois: F. E. Peacock, 1975.

Shulman, L. S., & Lanier, J. E. The institute for research on teaching: An overview. *Journal of Teacher Education,* 1977, *28,* 44–49.

Snow, R. E. Theory construction for research on teaching. In R. M. W. Travers (Ed.), *Second handbook of research on teaching.* Chicago: Rand-McNally, 1973, pp. 77–112.

Tikunoff, W. J., & Ward, B. A. *Ecological theory of teaching: Proceedings of the seminar of scholars.* San Francisco: Far West Laboratory for Educational Research and Development, 1978.

Turner, R. L. An overview of research in teacher education. In K. Ryan (Eds.), *Teacher education.* Chicago: National Society for the Study of Education, 1975.

U. S. Office of Education. *Do teachers make a difference?* A report on recent research on pupil achievement. Washington, D.C.: Bureau of Educational Personnel Development, Office of Education, 1970.

3

The Need for Theoretical Frameworks in Educating Teachers: A Cognitive-Developmental Perspective

Norman A. Sprinthall

North Carolina State University
University of Minnesota

Lois Thies-Sprinthall

St. Cloud State University

INTRODUCTION

Teacher education in the eyes of some of its kindest critics is at best a reluctant giant. While there is an extensive body of research on the teaching-learning process itself, there is a major lacuna on the process of teacher education. Gage (1978) and Good (1979), among others, have pointed out through a version of meta-analysis that a growing number of major propositions vis-à-vis teaching are supported by both theory and research. As a result, this knowledge base can be formed into a framework as guidelines for the teaching process. It is certainly not complete. There is no need to close down the patent office section on research in teaching. Yet, on the other hand, there is direction, evidence, and cumulative information.

Compare, for a moment, the state of the "art" in teaching with teacher education. If we accept the proposition that the two are not synonymous, then what do we find? Are there theories, or even promising conceptual frameworks, for teacher education? And, on the other hand, is there research evidence? On the first point, both Ryan (1979) and Shutes (1975) provide extensive "explication du texte" to the conclusion that theory is notably absent. Ryan points out that teacher education program decisions, namely the content and process of undergraduate education, rarely if ever are derived from theory. He poignantly suggests that teacher education content is a camel, the product of a committee. Instead of a cohesive and coherent program, "these creatures of committees are dumpy and lumpy, made by so many people with different views of the human condition and of what are learning, teaching, and the characteristics of skillful teachers. In effect, a teacher-education program is a compromise of these many views and, sometimes, of many powerful factors" (Ryan, 1979, p. 1). Haberman in Chapter 4 also suggests that content and process are based on political rather than educational decisions. This does not mean, however, that such decision makers are necessarily venal or self-serving. The present arrangements, rather, are the natural consequence of the lack of theory and research. As Ryan notes, there are no blueprints to follow.[1]

Shutes essentially underscores the same theme in his recent and most provocative essay. He notes that all major advances in complex fields of study result from theory. In the absence of requisite theoretical principles, then, practice suffers, "guided at best by folk-wisdom and unevaluated experience, and is noncumulative in building a growing body of reliable, replaceable information" (Shutes, 1975, p. 85).

In other words, there is no critical mass. The result is a practice and a profession which wanders between the cosmic and the trivial, without necessarily knowing one from the other. Fads we adopted in one era, just as quickly disappear without a trace in the next. Our recent excursion, or incursion, into humanistic education is simply a case in point. Without theory and certainly without empirical evidence, many teacher education programs cavalierly solved the content-process distinction by announcing that process *was* content and that the experiential "here and now" is all that we had anyway. We cite this simply to remind ourselves that one of our early godparents, E. L. Thorndike, was, of all things, an optimist when he concluded years ago that education and psychology had reached the point where progress would be determined by theory and evidence rather than by statements ex cathedra.

While Ryan and Shutes have essentially emphasized the missing theoretical agenda for teacher education, Schalock focuses on the absent research (recall Chapter 2). His conclusions are hardly sanguine. He cites numerous omissions, a lack of "up and running" research designs, inadequate measurement systems, hardly any good hypotheses tested, and generally a methodology borrowed from other fields without a "goodness of fit."

Howey suggests the over-all problem is broader. What is the basis for admission, for the content and process of the program, and for the outcomes in teacher training/education? Admittedly this is a complex question, yet it is time for the profession to begin work on such an agenda. Certainly it is important to continue to improve the study of teaching effectiveness. At the same time we should initiate more research in teacher education as the authors of this volume so clearly indicate in their various chapters. It is time for the profession to take more systematic steps in the service of theory, research, and practice for teacher education. Toward that goal we will now suggest some emerging theorectical perspectives as well as research findings which may lead to a promising start for teacher education.

Cognitive-Developmental Goals

Certainly the most difficult and complex question facing any profession concerns the ultimate outcome of its educational efforts. Management by objectives can be a great idea once we know what the objectives are. Teacher education, like other fields, can benefit by a theory of instruction in the Bruner sense, since that provides a basis for prescription rather than simply description. Such a theory would enable us to elaborate our programs within teacher education. We could better articulate the relationships between the what of teacher education and the how. Still, without a clear view of over-all objectives even a prescriptive theory of instruction ends up as basically directionless. Sooner or later, then, we have. to face the statement of goals. Just what are the objectives that we aim for? Shades of J. Abner Peddiwell's famous *Saber Tooth Tiger.* Do we teach specific skills, with today's laundry list of behaviorally based teacher competencies, serving only as a latter-day version of paleolithic skills with firebrands, clubs, and hand fishing? Or do we teach for humane generalizations with today's call for educating the teacher as a whole person reminiscent of the tribal elder's desired goals of generalized agility, strength, and noble courage? Obviously, enlightened professionals aren't limited only to one or the other direction. A cognitive developmental perspective avoids an imbalance in one direction or the other. A framework built from this perspective can represent a synthesis of specific skills and generalizations. It is possible to have it both ways; a dual focus on highly specific behavioral teaching skills on one hand and general human development on the other.

In the tradition of John Dewey, and buttressed by recent work on a variety of developmental domains by contemporary theorists, we wish to call attention to a broadly based growing theoretical consensus as directing constructs for teacher education. The propositions are indeed direct. Cognitive developmental theory assumes:

1. All humans process experience through cognitive structures called stages—Piaget's concept of schemata.
2. Such cognitive structures are organized in a hierarchical sequence of stages from the less complex to the more.
3. Growth occurs first within a particular stage and then only to the next stage in the sequence. This latter change is a qualitiative shift—a major quantum leap to a significantly more complex system of processing experience.
4. Growth is not automatic nor unilateral but occurs only with appropriate interaction between the human and the environment.
5. Behavior can be determined and predicted by an individual's particular stage of development. Predictions are not, however, exact.

These propositions have been supported through a large body of empirical investigation scattered widely through the literature and will not be reviewed here.[2] We will present, however, a review of the work from a variety of developmental domains which are most appropriate for teacher education. There is no single cognitive-developmental theory which is superordinate. Rather, given the emergent nature of research efforts literally scattered over the globe, the current state of the art reveals small clusters of researchers working independently and in relative isolation. This gives a sense of partial overlap and at times a sense of relativistic frustration which inhibits the creation of an overall synthesis. Coordinated research efforts may lie in the future; at present we have a series of very loosely connected and mostly idiographic efforts. Figure 3.1 presents a description of some of the theorists, their domains, and their stages. Essentially, the domains represent that aspect of human functioning which that particular theorist found most challenging and rewarding.

Do Developmental Stages Make a Difference?

Another way to phrase this question is to ask the Dewey proposition—should education be designed to promote cognitive development? In other words, if humans move from less complex stages to more, does it mean anything in the real world of thought and action? A series of studies of adult functioning in general seems to provide a qualified yes to the question. Studies of adult accomplishments reported by numerous researchers employing slightly different but related indices of psychological maturity reached similar conclusions. Estimates based on psychological constructs of cognitive developmental competence levels yielded consistently positive predictions. In other words, persons identified during high school or college as functioning at higher, more complex stages than their colleagues were shown to function more successfully in their careers. It should also be noted that in each case, traditional measures of academic/

FIGURE 3.1 Domains of Developmental Stages

Theorist	Jean Piaget (1961)	Lawrence Kohlberg (1969)	Jane Loevinger (1966)	David Hunt (1971)	William Perry (1969)
Domain	Cognitive	Value/Moral	Ego/Self	Conceptual	Epistemological/Ethical
	Sensori-Motor	Obedience-Punishment	Pre-social Impulsive	Unsocialized Impulsive	—
	Pre-Operational	Naively Egoistic	Self-protective	Concrete Dogmatic	
	Concrete	Social Conformity	Conformist	Dependent Abstract	Dualist
	Formal Substage 1	Authority Maintaining	Conscientious	—	Relativist
	Formal Substage 2	Contractual Legalistic	Autonomous	Self-directed Abstract	Committed-Relativist

scholastic aptitude did not predict success, while estimates of cognitive development did.

Kohlberg, for example, reviewed literally thousands of studies on childhood predictors of adult performance. He noted that school academic achievement made no independent contribution to successful life adjustment. Instead, he found that indices of psychological development did predict success—success in this case measured by occupational achievement and absence of crime, mental illness, unemployment, and expert ratings of life adjustment (Kohlberg, 1977).

A sixteen-year longitudinal study sponsored by the Ford Foundation (Nicholson, 1970) yielded similar results. With an overlapping design and sample sizes of 400 to 500 students, the study reported that estimates during school of psychological-developmental maturity were effective predictors not only for college success but also in follow-up. Employing a combined index of success (*Who's Who*, peer judgment, advanced graduate work, economic success, etc.), the findings indicate that scholastic aptitude score (with a 150-point difference in some of the samples) was not related to 'life success" but that once again estimates of developmental maturity were.

Most recently, Heath's longitudinal studies with college-age samples reached similar conclusions. Carefully identified constructs such as ego maturity and competence were significantly related to a broad and multiple definition of life success, while academic achievement was not (Heath, 1977). The ability to symbolize one's experience, to act allocentrically with compassion, to act autonomously with self-control and a disciplined commitment to humane values—these formed part of the core of psychological maturity. Ironically, he found, especially for the American in his cross-cultural study, that, "Adolescent scholastic aptitude as well as other measures of academic intelligence, do not predict several *hundred* measures of the adaptation and competence of men in their early thirties. In fact, scholastic aptitude was inversely related in this group to many measures of their adult psychological maturity, as well as to their judged interpersonal competence" (Heath, 1977, pp. 177–178).

Finally, on this point, McClelland very clearly suggests that success in living apparently has a small relationship to academic content mastery. In noting the educational version of Catch 22, he underscores the point that scholastic tests only predict grades in school, yet grades do not predict success in life. He quotes from a series of studies of successful performance in jobs as varied as bank tellers, factory workers, air controllers, and scientific researchers as evidence of unpredictability. As a result, he suggests as the others already noted, that psychological competence is a far more significant educational outcome than content acquisition (McClelland, 1973).

If cognitive-developmental stage predicts differential functioning for adults in general, then what about adults in the helping professions, especially teachers? Are they a specific instance of the same generalization? Most recent studies of physicians by Candee (1977) quite clearly indicates that MD's at more complex stages of development (in this case, in the Kohlberg domain) function more democratically with patients than lower-stage colleagues even though both groups did not differ on traditional measures of academic achievement. The more developmentally complex doctors were more empathic, flexible, and responsive in enlisting the patient as a colleague in the service of their own treatment plan. The other doctors were more rigid, authoritarian, and perceived patients as fitting highly simplified cultural stereotypes. Similar findings were reported in studies of physicians (N = 348) by Sheehan (1979), who reported a positive correlation (+.57) between indices of psychological/moral development and humane physician competencies—similar to Candee's criteria.

Silver's (1975) study of school principals, in this case measuring development with David Hunt's system, indicated significant differences in perceived leadership style in accord with developmental level. She found that principals who scored at the more complex levels on Hunt's estimate of conceptual development were perceived by their teachers as more flexible in problem solving, more responsive, less rigid, and less authoritarian—in other words, a pattern of functioning highly congruent with Candee's and Sheehan's physicians.

Studies of teachers are both more numerous and equally supportive of the general thesis.[3] For example, studies by Hunt & Joyce (1967), Murphy & Brown (1970), and Rathbone (1970), reached highly confirmatory findings. Teacher's behaviors consistently associated with High Conceptual Level scores are described as flexible, responsive, adaptable, empathic. Such teachers employ different levels of structure according to pupil needs, use a wide variety of teaching "models" in their classrooms, are "indirect", and "read and flex" with pupils. In short, High Conceptual Level teachers perform in the classroom in a manner which fits closely with several behaviors associated with effective teaching.

This is particularly important to underscore. Gage (1978) has recently noted that there is a consistent scientific base for the art of teaching. His quite elegant meta-analysis indicates that the "know-nothing" view of teaching effectiveness is neither valid nor fashionable. He provides a systematic review of research suggesting very strongly that indirect (I/D) teaching as measured by Flander's instrument is positively associated with certain pupil gain. The ability to solicit student ideas and respond accurately to their feelings are critical abilities. He concluded that such teacher behaviors are highly significant as a causal factor in pupil achievement. He further indicated that particular elements of the Flanders categories were noteworthy. For example, the use of teacher praise and accepting pupil ideas were positively related to positive attitudes and achievement by pupils while criticism and disapproval were negatively correlated. In other words, such teaching is consistently associated with pupil gain and is a major characteristic of psychologically mature/high conceptual level teachers.

The same set of findings, although not as well documented, is emerging from recent research in counselor effectiveness. In fact, in their exhaustive review of the literature, Bergin & Garfield (1978) conclude that the only consistent factor associated with counselor/therapist effectiveness is positively associated with higher stages of cognitive complexity. Counselors rated at higher developmental stages were more positively interactive with clients (Lichtenberg & Heck, 1979), employed a greater variety of counselor models (Goldberg, 1974), and manifested more accurate levels of empathy than counselors at more modest levels of developmental maturity (Magnus, 1972).

A most recent study by Bielke (1979) found major differences in patterns of effective parenting according to developmental level, in this case Loevinger's index. Mothers at more advanced developmental levels were rated on a series of observational scales as more responsive, empahtic, and sensitive to the needs of their infants, on a longitudinal basis at 6, 12, and 18 months. Videos of actual mother-child interactions formed the basis for the observations. In other words, the higher-stage mothers were better able to exhibit complex and effective nurturing behaviors than their lower-stage cohorts.

All these studies point toward the same conclusion. The samples differ widely, the research methods varied, and the instruments themselves were dissimilar to a degree. However, in each situation, different aspects of cognitive development were the focus of different studies. Some used Hunt's theory and Conceptual Level tests, others used Kohlberg's theory and either the MJI (Moral Judgment Interview) or the Rest Defining Test, still others employed the Loevinger theory and her Sentence Completion Test. Regardless of these specific differences, however, the overall results were highly similar, namely that persons judged at higher stages of development function more complexly, possess a wider repertoire of behavioral skills, perceive problems more broadly, and can respond more accurately and empathically to the needs of others.

Hunt (1978b) has termed this the "New Three R's"—responsiveness, reciprocity, and reflexivity, or a person's ability to "read and flex" with pupils. Kohlberg refers to the process as the ability to role-take, to empathically place one's self in the shoes of another and to make decisions according to standards of democratic and justice principles. Loevinger denotes higher-stage functioning as the ability to tolerate stress, attend to the least compelling stimulus, process decisions according to democratic principles, and perceive questions from an objective "third-party" perspective. Other theorists such as Heath, and William Perry, employ somewhat differentiated concepts: Heath's psychological maturity comprehends both rationality and allocentrism; Perry's advanced stages are referred to as the process of "commitment in relativism." At an abstract level, however, there are basic similarities across all developmental domains. Loevinger has stated the truism that all developmental theories must positively correlate, while Sullivan et al. (1970) has proved the point empirically with moderate positive correlations in the +.4 to +.6 range between measures of difficult constructs (Hunt, Kohlberg, & Loevinger). Also, to a significant degree, the variations in theory and the degree of independence by the different theorists can serve as a means of cross-validation. The theorists themselves have worked very much independently, created and tested out their own instruments, and have only recently (in the past decade) become aware of each other's work. Such independence, of course, does have its limits if synthesis is the goal. However, during initial phases of theory building and heuristic activity, the independence and "inner-directedness" of the researchers does add credence to a cumulative body of promising theory as an explanatory base for complex human functioning. We still are a long way from closure, of course, yet some elements for an overall framework of directing constructs are emerging.[4]

Now the Switch: Cognitive-Developmental Stage from an Independent Variable to a Dependent Variable

If, as the previous studies have indicated, different cognitive-developmental domains predict different levels of functioning, then is it possible to consider stage as a dependent variable? If we can approximately assess a person's stage then we can make certain behaviorally based predictions, e.g., lower-stage teachers, will generally employ high-structured instruction (rule, example, rule, etc.) regardless of pupil needs and responses. Such teachers will also employ a limited number of teaching models, and tend to provide teacher-centered instruction. In other words, there will be very little interaction. The pupils will have almost no impact on the teacher. Regardless of circumstances, the classroom atmosphere will remain stable. Similarly, the reverse would hold in predicting the performance of higher-stage teachers. The teacher would employ significantly different strategies with groups of children according to their current functioning. Given this picture, then, is the conclusion that we (simply) pick the higher-stage candidates for teacher education programs and then move on to look for new problems to solve? Certainly, as Howey points out in this overview there should be more systematic consideration of indices of psychological maturity when prospective teachers are admitted to teacher education programs. It's hardly a question of a simple screening process, however. At present it would be most dangerous to assume that a young adult's present stage is a permanent classification. In fact, it would be a mistake of the greatest significance to assume that an individual's current stage is fixed. Such an assumption would be at least as great a theoretical error as Terman's original Americanization of IQ as a measure of native and immutable intellectual functioning. Instead, developmental theory must avoid such a reification. The theories all are based on the assumption of growth as a result of appropriate interaction in facilitating environments. This basic tenet must not be forgotten in any review of stage as an independent variable. Those studies have been cited here to establish the basic point that stage does make a difference in complex human performance. The major question now at hand concerns what is called "modifiability" (Cronbach & Snow, 1977), "malleability" (Hunt, 1978), or, more simply, "educability" (Dewey, 1916).[5] In other words, can we as educators do anything to stimulate developmental stage. What happens if cognitive-developmental stage becomes a dependent rather than independent variable, a criterion rather than a predicator, a target of educational programs rather than a fixed trait? This is a key question for all the obvious reasons, the most obvious being that such a switch transforms developmental theory from a later-day version of fixed-trait and factor personality theory to a theory of instruction. Rather than describing relationships in terms of a theory of learning, such a change would involve prescribing instructional (teacher training) activities to induce developmental growth. For teacher education, then, such a transfer would move toward the creation of different learning atmospheres, a teacher education curriculum differentiated by developmental concepts. In short, this would mean, in the Thomas Kuhn sense, a major paradigm shift from description to prescription.

The developmental assumption of interaction holds that effective teaching involves the process of "matching" and "mismatching" environments according to the developmental level of the learner. Thus, developmentally immature persons would interact best in a highly structured environment, with rule/example/rule teaching, short-term rewards, low ambiguity as to expectations, etc.* The opposite would hold for psychologically mature learners.

But are we sure that such a shift is justifiable? After all, the basic Attribute-Treatment-Interaction (ATI) concept has been judged wanting, almost constantly over the past decade. Is the idea of developmentally based intervention inviting a new round of criticism and failures, snatching defeat from the jaws of victory one more time so to speak?

On this point we think not. We agree with Hunt's cogent comments on the premature funeral of ATI, an idea abandoned before its time (Hunt, 1978a). Essentially, the research basis for ATI in the past has focused too minutely on a search for statistical interactions before the investigators had created carefully defined and developmentally differentiated teaching programs. Also, the studies did not employ assessments of deve-

* The term "high structure" itself is composed of multiple components. These are only a few as examples. A recent thesis by Bents (1978) contains a most impressive analysis of the complex meaning of the concept of structure.

lopmental level as dependent variables. Thus, it would be difficult if not impossible to find empirical evidence supporting the concepts of matching and mismatching without creating differentiated instruction on one hand and using measures of psychological development on the other. This does not mean that there is a huge body of evidence supporting the efficiency of developmental interventions, e.g., programs designed to differentially raise developmental stage. However, there is some and it may represent a most important harbinger.

With college students, programs developed by Widick, Knefelkamp, & Parker (1975) suggest that a differential curriculum can stimulate cognitive-development and that different instructional strategies are effective only for particular groups. They designed their curriculum using William Perry's theory and measures and instructed college students in English classes in significantly different modes. One group assessed at Perry's concrete-"dualistic" stage (highly analogous to Hunt's 1.5 stage and Loevinger's Stage Three) received substantially structured teaching, explicit homework assignments, positive short-term feedback, and encouragement. These are the usual recommended approaches for how to start instruction with lower-stage pupils. A second group, similar in background characterisitics, but at higher stages, i.e., Perry's "relativistic-abstract" (similar to Hunt's 2.5 stage and Loevinger's Stage Four), received more open-ended, self-directed, interactive teaching and negotiated assignments. The results indicated that the differentiated curriculum worked for the first group and not the second.

For the first group, the high-structured English teaching at the outset followed by more open-ended strategies seemed to promote growth on Perry's stages from Dualist to Relativist for pupils originally classed as Dualist. The student originally grouped as Relativist did not show movement to the next stage on the scheme (Widick & Simpson, 1978). The pupil's English essays were rated at the end of the term according to Perry's system as a measure of developmental stage.

As Table 3.1 indicates, within one college class of 31 pupils, 21 of 22 students who started at the Dualist levels on the Perry scheme, improved significantly on level of psychological maturity. The higher-stage pupils essentially broke even, with five improving and four remaining the same.

Similarly, a long series of "first generation" curriculum trials at the secondary level reached analogous, however, serendipitious conclusions. The high school classes were set up to deliberately raise the general developmental level of secondary school age pupils. The results indicated that such classes on the *average* were successful as a means of stimulating psychological maturity. Comparing experimental classes as a whole to "regular" classes favored the special programs. Table 3.2 presents the overall findings employing the Rosenthal technique (1978) to combine the results for independent studies. This quite clearly suggested that the educational classes which included significant student role taking as peer

TABLE 3.1 Summary of Within-Group Effects College of Liberal Arts English Classes (N = 31 pupils)

Initial Development Stage (Perry's Scheme)	Major Stage Gain (From 2/3 to 1 Stage)	Main Gain or No Change (1/3 to No Change)
Dualist/Multiple Concrete (N = 22)	21	1
Relativist Abstract (N = 9)	5	4
	26	5

$$X^2 = 4.85^*$$
$$P < .05$$
Yates Correction

SOURCE: Widick & Simpson, 1978 (table compiled by the authors from the data presented in the source material).

counselors, peer and cross-age teaching, and community internships, positively impacted the general level of psychological stage development estimated from the Loevinger and Kohlberg/Rest indices.

TABLE 3.2 Overall Effects of Programs Designed to Promote Psychological Development*

Study	Loevinger Estimate Ego Stage Change			Kohlberg-Rest Estimate Moral Judgement Stage Change		
	t	df	One Tail P	t	df	One Tail P
Hedin (1979)	+3.65	43	.001	+5.31	36	.001
Cognetta (1978)	+3.49	42	.001	+2.13	30	.05
Exum (1977)	+5.67	23	.001	—		
Rustad & Rogers (1975	+3.58	39	.001	+1.35	41	.10
Mosher & Sullivan (1975)	+1.96	27	.01	+1.98	27	.05
Dowell (1971)	+8.54	37	.001	+1.80	37	.08
Sum	26.89	211		12.57	171	

$t = \Sigma t$
$\Sigma(df/(df-2))$
  Square Root

$t = +10.67 < .001$ $t = +5.46 < .001$

* For summary of the specific studies, see Sprinthall, 1980. The authors compiled this table from data presented in the source material.

When a post hoc analysis of some of the within-class differences was conducted, that is, pupils who gained versus the pupils who showed no change, it was found that the curriculum had a differential impact. Students at the so-called modal or "regular" developmental stages for adolescents improved while their higher-stage colleagues remained the same. Of 34 students at the equivalent of Loevinger and Kohlberg Stage Three (initially), 25 demonstrated significant stage growth. However, of 17 high school students at Stage Four or higher, only 3 demonstrated significant growth (see Table 3.3). The semistructured, role-taking curriculum had a differentiated impact on the subgroups of teenagers, depending on their initial-stage characteristics. We may tentatively infer from this that developmental stage, as a dependent variable, can be impacted by particular instructional procedures. Analysis of within-group differences tends to support the view that specific learning environments may promote developmental growth. A role-taking curriculum for secondary school pupils (Sprinthall, 1980) and a high-structured English curriculum for liberal arts students (Widick, Kneflekamp, & Parker, 1975) had differential effects. When the curriculum and teaching strategies matched and then positively mismatched the pupils' level of development, we can tentatively infer that cognitive-development growth occurred.

TABLE 3.3 Summary of Within-Group Effects Secondary School Programs (N = 51 pupils)

Initial Development Stage

		Significant Developmental Gain	No Change
Loevinger Kohlberg/Rest	Stage 3 or Below	25	9
Loevinger Kohlberg/Rest	Stage 4 and above	3	14

$$X^2 = 14.29$$
$$< .001$$

Three Studies of Differential Effects

Post hoc analyses of three recent studies have been conducted which may shed more light on the possible positive and negative effects of developmental matching and mismatching. On the positive side, Hedin (1979) set out to deliberately differentiate instructional programs for secondary pupils according to cognitive-developmental level. She subdivided a high school class of 21 pupils according to assessed stage. This created three subgroups in a social studies class—a low-concrete-stage group (on Loevinger & Kohlberg-Rest), N = 6; a middle-stage group on the same instruments, N = 11; and a high-stage subgroup, N = 4. She identified a matched control with three similar subgroups according to initial stage. Next, she devised a "differentiated curriculum" and teaching strategy (see Table 3.4). After examining several first-generation studies, she varied structure, role-taking responsibilities, and cognitive examination of experience according to initial stage. The control class received a general "action-learning program.

TABLE 3.4   Learning Environments Matched to Stage

	Structure:
Stage of	Close supervision in field experience.
High School	Simple, clear tasks.
Pupils	Grade based on quantity of work and fulfilling contract.
Kohlberg	Gradual increment of responsibility and initiative from modest levels.
Stage 2	
Loevinger	Required journal writing—specific questions to respond to weekly.
1–2	
Delta	Work in team to develop loyalty and responsibility to others.
Delta Three	
	Types of Experiences:
	Empathy or caring experiences with persons likely to show appreciation, such as children, elderly, handicapped, or retarded children.
	Volunteer in nursing home or daycare center with specific, clearly defined duties.
	Discussion of moral dilemmas through role playing original dilemmas or those encountered in field experience.
	Peer counseling.
	Grade based on student's as well as instructor's judgment.
	Colleagial relationships with adults.
	Types of experiences:
	Research projects.
	Internships in government, corrections, law, regulatory agencies.
	Attempts to influence public policy.
	Peer counseling regarding sensitive, controversial issues, e.g., rape, birth control.
	Cross-age teaching—moral dilemmas, controversial issues—where students have freedom to design their own curriculum.
	Systematic experiences in rule making and democratic governance of schools.

SOURCE: Hedin, 1979

The results are summarized in Table 3.5. Generally, each of the experimental subgroups improved on developmental indices while in every instance the matched control subgroups essentially remained unchanged. This could indicate that matching the content and process of so-called action-learning programs is necessary if all students are to benefit psychologically from the experience. When compared to the first generation of studies at the high school level, there is a clear difference since each subgroup improved in the Hedin study. By systematically varying the classroom structure and field assignments, each group was able to manifest significant stage growth. Of course, this single study does not prove the point. The sample size is relatively small, an intact high school class, and replication is requisite. However, it may point the way to more studies with a *deliberately differentiated curriculum according to initial stage characteristics of the learners*. The overall effect of the Hedin study, of course, was highly congruent with the prior studies. The experimental groups as a whole always demonstrated positive gains on developmental indices while control and/or quasi-control groups always remained essentially unchanged. Thus, there is strong support for the general proposition as to the "modifiability" of developmental stage. What we now need to work out is more careful instructional prescriptions which can be tried out and evaluated with other populations to learn more about the limits and opportunities for matching learning environments according to stage characteristics.

TABLE 3.5   Subgroup Developmental Gains Scores

Experimental Subgroups: Developmental Gains Scores (Loevinger & Kohlberg-Rest)*	Control Subgroups: Developmental Gains Scores (Loevinger & Kohlberg-Rest)
Initial Stage Group Low N = 6 $\bar{X}$ gain = +4.3 (Loevinger = A, $\triangle$3 and Kohlberg-Rest $\bar{X}$ = 12.4P)	N = 8 $\bar{X}$ gain = −1.53
Middle N = 11 $\bar{X}$ gain = +5.53 (Loevinger = 3,3/4 and Kohlberg-Rest $\bar{X}$ = 22.7P)	N = 11 $\bar{X}$ gain = +.01
High N = 4 (Loevinger = 4,4/5 and $\bar{X}$ gain − +5.45 Kohlberg-Rest = 30.2P)	N = 4 $\bar{X}$ gain = −.50

* For purposes of illustration, we added the average gain scores on Loevinger with the Kohlberg-Rest for a combined index of developmental changes, e.g., for the middle group (E) this gain on Loevinger was +.73 and the Rest was +4.8—for the middle group (C), it was −.09 on Loevinger and 1.0 on the Rest.

A second study on effects of matching was conducted recently by the second author of this chapter. Hedin, of course, had not examined the possible effects of teachers at different stages interacting with pupils at different stages. Since she taught both the experimental and control classes herself, and was obviously at a relatively high-developmental stage, it was possible to examine the curriculum structure but not differences due to different stage characteristics of teachers. To examine this second question, namely the possible effects of developmental stage matching and mismatching between teachers and learners, a study was conducted with a sample of student teachers and their supervisors (Thies-Sprinthall, 1980). This permitted an examination of matching by dyad pairs according to developmental levels. In the earlier matching studies the attempt was made to match a single teacher to a classroom of pupils. The procedure as described by Hunt did not yield productive results largely because of so many natural setting and uncontrolled events. In the current study it was thought that by focusing on dyad matches and mismatches it might be more feasible to assess possible effects. As a result, the researcher identified two samples of student teachers who were significantly different on developmental characteristics using the Rest as an estimate of psychological-moral development and the Hunt as a estimate of conceptual maturity. There were 16 student teachers identified as high-principled thought and conceptual level—a combined index of Rest and Hunt, and 13 student teachers identified as low on the two measures (they were drawn from total population of 93 student teachers). The student teacher sample, by design, was almost equally divided by conceptual level, 16 high versus 13 low. The classroom teacher supervisors were measured on the same instruments. However, since they had already been assigned to the student teachers, the distribution of developmental and conceptual level of the classroom supervisors were not equally split. Only 9 of the supervisors were classed as high and 20 as low.

To assess possible interaction effects according to developmental stage dyads, the supervisor ratings were compared to classroom performance ratings by a 20-minute video near the conclusion of their student teaching. The supervisors' judgments, of course, were highly subjective even though a scale was used complete with behavioral descriptions of effective versus ineffective teaching modes. The videos were analyzed and blind scored by an independent judge trained in the Flanders system, (recall that Gage's summary had emphasized the validity of the ID ratio as an index of effective teaching). This was to provide a more objective analysis of the student-teaching behavior. Finally, four-year grade-point averages were computed for the two student groups. Table 3.5 presents the comparison across the two samples of student teachers grouped by developmental level. The results indicated that there was no difference in GPA but a difference in the predicted direction favoring the high-stage group on the ID ratio, as expected. This is quite consistent with prior studies by Hunt (1971). The student teachers at more advanced developmental levels were more indirect in their teaching and employed a greater variety of teaching modes. See Table 3.6.

Table 3.7 presents the results of student-teacher performance according to the four dyad groupings. The supervisors' subjective ratings are compared with the average Flanders ratio in each of the matched and mismatched groups.

TABLE 3.6   Academic Performance, Flanders Ratio, and Developmental Level of Student Teachers*

Student Teachers (only)	Academic Average	Flanders Indirect Ratio (1, 2, 3, 4, = 1 through 7)
High Group		
N = 16 mean score	3.15	45
s.d.	.41	
Low Group		
N = 13 mean score	3.01	31
s.d.	.35	
	t = n.s.	t = 1.9
		p <.03 (1 tail)

* The high and low groups were designated by a combined index of the Rest (DIT) and Hunt (CL) tests.

TABLE 3.7   Student-Teacher-Supervisor Groups

Supervisor Ratings and Flanders Ratios		
	Supervisor Ratings	Flanders Indirect Ratio for student teaching
Group One		
High CL/PT Student Teachers Matched with High Supervisors N = 5 pairs	Superior teaching flexible, innovative, responsive, etc.	45
Group Two		
Low CL/PT Student Teachers Mismatched with High Supervisors N = 4 pairs	Average ratings adequate but not outstanding, oscillates between rigid & flexible, etc.	38
Group Three		
High CL/PT Student Teachers Mismatched with Low Supervisors N = 11 pairs	Average to Mediocre ratings: limited teaching styles	45
Group Four		
Low CL/PT Student Teachers Matched with Low Supervisors N = 9 pairs	Same as Group Two	28

The results suggest that there may be a major difference in the observation and judgment between the matched high group of 5 pairs of student teachers and their supervisors and the 11 pairs of mismatched in

Group Three. In the latter group the 11 student teachers had high-developmental-stage scores and were supervised by cooperating teachers who had low-stage scores. The student teachers in that mismatched group received the lowest subjective ratings even though their more objective Flanders ratio was the same as for Group One. In Hunt's studies of teacher-pupil interaction in classrooms, he found that low-stage teachers were rigid, inflexible, demonstrated a more limited repertoire of teaching tactics—in other words could not "read and flex" with pupils. In the current study the pattern may be the same except in this case it occurs in a two-person dyad between supervisor and student teacher. Audio or video recordings of the actual supervision session in the four subgroups may have provided more information on the actual interaction between supervision and student teacher and should be included in further research of this type. Similarly, such recordings might have revealed more information on the other groups, particularly the possible differences between Group Two—high-stage supervisors and low-stage student teachers—and Group Four—the matched low-stage group. In any case, the over-all findings suggest that there may be very significant differences in the interactions according to matched and mismatched teacher-learner groups. This is not to suggest, however, that we should simply strive for compatible matching. Theoretically, at least, there is a strong argument that the higher-stage teacher, or supervisor, is always preferable since such a person can provide for differential learning environments depending upon the developmental needs of the learner.[6]

A study by Hanson (1975) attempted to further illuminate the possible impacts of developmental matching and mismatching. In her case, she studied the three-way complex of the developmental level of the pupils (junior college students), the curriculum materials, and the faculty. She tested the pupils directly on the Hunt. The materials (readings, course objectives, etc.) were assessed through a method she created based on Bloom's Cognitive Taxonomy. The faculty were assessed through ratings of their tape-recorded tutorials and complexity level of their quizzes. Her findings for four sections of a freshmen introductory course (N = 35 pupils) were quite provocative. The curriculum itself required readings and course objectives which were quite high on the Bloom—66 percent of the course objectives were classified from Level Three through Six and only 33 percent in One and Two.

The students presented average CL scores of 1.78 (.35 s.d.) and could be considered as moderate to moderately high CL for pupils in that range. The tests and the teacher questions, however, were quite low. Ninety-one percent of the quiz items were rated as Bloom One or Two. Eighty-one percent of the instructor statements in the tutorials were rated at I or II, and 93 percent of the questions which the instructor asked called for an answer at the One or Two level. One cannot really conclude from these data that the course instructors were themselves at a lower developmental level than the pupils, as was the case with the Thies-Sprinthall study. On the other hand, the instructors were certainly engaging in critical dialogue and asking exam questions at very low developmental levels. This three-way interaction is depicted in Table 3.8.

TABLE 3.8   Developmental Levels: Junior College Curriculum, Pupils and Teachers

Curriculum	
Materials & Objectives* (N = 138 Units)	High 66% Bloom 3–6
Pupils (N = 35)	Moderate X̄ = 1.78 Hunt sd = .35 CL
Teachers (N = 4) Written Quiz* (N = 168) Tutorial Statements (N = 306) Tutorials Questions (N = 266)	Low 91% Bloom 1–2 80% Bloom 1–2 93% Bloom 1–2

* The interjudge reliability for the rating schemes were +.91 for course objectives, +.89 for quizzes, +.82 for statements and +.79 for questions.
SOURCE: The table was created by the authors from the data presented in the source material.

The Hanson findings suggest, at minimum, that there can be a substantial mismatch between the *curriculum objectives* and *teaching strategies*. Also, it appears in this situation as if the pupils are somewhere in the middle between more abstract goals and more concrete exams and questions. It is not surprising then that there was little change at all in the CL of the pupils between their freshmen and sophmore years; in fact, the score was exactly the same, 1.78, for both years.

Obviously, none of these studies, either singly or cumulatively, can be considered definitive. They are *exploratory* investigations which may help us better understand the complex interactions which occur in teacher education and better plan for them.

SUMMARY AND IMPLICATIONS FOR THE FUTURE

We began this chapter with the suggestion that there is a great need in teacher education for theoretical frameworks to generate a cumulative research and practice basis which could guide programs in teacher training. We noted the current dearth of effective directing constructs for such efforts. We attempted to make a strong case for a cognitive-developmental approach as one potentially productive framework. Based upon a selective review, we indicated the possible effectiveness to the profession in adopting developmental goals as program objectives. Studies of successful adult functioning in complex careers, such as the educational and medical professions as well as studies of adults in general, supported the validity of developmental stage as a predictor. We also suggested that developmental stage could well become a dependent variable—that programs or program components could be created to test out procedures to deliberately impact or modify one's current stage. We reviewed some recent studies at the high school and college level which supported the idea that different learning environments may have differential psychological impacts upon various stage characteristics of these students.

The implications are multiple. Further research studies are clearly needed. We would certainly urge our colleagues to adopt the cognitive-developmental model. For example, in preservice programs, we could foresee the possibility of applying a series of differentiated learning environments and different supervision techniques to groups of student teachers according to their entry developmental level. The initial stage represents that individual's current preferred style and matching the general instruction (both content and process) to this initial level is really nothing more than Dewey's original dictum of starting where the learner is. The difference now is that we do have a more precise means of assessing psychological maturity of the teacher education student. Bents (1978) has shown that student teachers initially classed as low to moderate on the Hunt CL system tended to learn more adequately under the so-called rule/example/rule method than prospective teachers at higher stages.

In a sense we are suggesting that a preservice program could be constructed in a manner paralleling Hedin's work with teenagers. In other words, one could carefully articulate two or three distinctly different learning environments for preservice teachers. The content and process throughout the various phases of training could be designed in accord with our "best shot" as to developmental matching principles. With careful assessment through formative evaluation, such a program could continually be refined. In any case we need such a field-based try-out in order to add to our current knowledge base. We certainly take the position that there is enough logic to the theory and supportive empirical evidence to merit more systematic trials. As Howey noted at the outset, there is very little logic and apparently no research evidence to support the current highly general approaches now common to teacher education.

A second and related implication comes from the Thies-Sprinthall study. The supervision of student teaching has long been a significant but understudied endeavor as Haberman points out in Chapter 4. Mosher and Purple (1972) in their seminal work referred to supervision as a "reluctant profession", while Blumberg (1974) more recently was even less kind. At least part of the difficulty seems to derive from an inability to specify the supervisor's role. Often the role is either so global that it is most difficult either theoretically or empirically to create a systematic approach. The study pointing out possible positive and negative effects in the student-teacher/cooperating teacher dyad suggests a need for careful work with inservice cooperating teachers as Howey has called for.

In the third area, the Hanson study suggests that we need to attend to the so-called formal curriculum in developmental terms. Thus, the readings, homework assignments, and even examinations can represent different developmental levels and thus could conceivably be incongruent with the developmental level of the student. Systematic assessment and initial matching on formal content could represent a more adequate theory and practice of developmental growth.

It can be said that good teachers have probably known all these ideas at least intuitively for over 2,000 years. To start where the learner is and gradually challenge and support is after all at the heart of effective instruction. Recent theory and research studies present us with a somewhat more articulated version of this ancient truism. Higher stages of psychological development benefit both the teacher and the learner. Higher is better in the sense that it is more complex both intellectually and empathically. Thus, the higher-stage teacher is more adequate as an instructor and can meet the needs of a broader group of pupils. Also, the higher-stage supervisor may be capable of providing different levels of supervision according to the needs of the student teacher. Finally, higher-stage curriculum content would connote differentiated levels of materials in order to accomodate different learner needs.

The challenge is to begin to put these principles into practice. Naturally, this is only a beginning, but it is our contention that pilot studies of differentiated teacher education programs are now needed as a first step. A cycle of trial and formative evaluation can provide feedback for further research and development. Such a process would begin to accumulate wisdom for teacher education theory and practice.

NOTES

1. As a recent example, after an unnamed university committee examined its own teacher education curriculum the conclusions were almost exactly as Ryan would have predicted. The content was arrayed across 22 knowledge domains representing the current interests of the on-site faculty. Somewhat realistically, the report noted that domains listed should not be viewed as exhaustive, but rather as representative of "all types for which we could find persuasive advocacy."

2. There is major empirical support for all of these propositions scattered widely throughout the research literature. Piaget's studies are easily the most numerous in support of his stages of growth. Flavell has summarized the validity of his contributions as "nothing short of stupendous, both quantitatively and qualitatively" (Flavell 1971). Kohlberg, Hunt, Loevinger, and Perry validated their own work in a series of original studies, many of which have been subsequently cross-validated by other researchers.

3. Ryan's studies in the 1950s may be distant precursors. Although he did

not employ direct measures of cognitive-developmental stage, his descriptions of characteristics of effective versus ineffective teachers seem theoretically consistent with the most recent Hunt, Kohlberg et al. studies (Ryan, 1960). Similarly Knoell's (1953) denotation of educational fluency as a significant teacher characteristic seems highly analogous to the high-stage attributes on the Hunt, Perry, Kohlberg, and Loevinger domains.

4. William Perry has remarked that the current state of the art in cognitive-developmental theories is biblical. We have various accounts of the Gospel according to Saint Jane, Saint Larry, Saint David (and Saint Bill?) usually in chart form. There are concordances and then where there are disagreements—blank spaces.

5. From extensive discussion of the value implications of cognitive-developmental goals for educational practice in the generic Dewey sense see *Value Development . . . As the Aim of Education*, N. A. Sprinthall and R. L. Mosher, Character Research Press, Schenectady; 1982 (2nd Edition).

6. The second author is currently conducting a pilot study with a small group of ten classroom teacher-supervisors. The objective of the instruction is to explore possible modes of impacting the developmental level of the supervisors.

BIBLIOGRAPHY

Bergin, A., & Garfield, S. *Handbook of psychotherapy and behavior change.* (2nd Ed). Wiley, 1978.

Bielke, P. *The relationship of maternal ego development to parenting behavior and attitudes.* Unpublished doctoral dissertation, University of Minnesota, 1979.

Candee, D. Role taking, role conception, and moral reasoning as factors on good physicians' performance. *Moral Education Forum*, 1977, *2*, 14–15.

Cronbach, L. J., & Snow, R. E. *Aptitudes and instructional methods.* New York: Irvington Press, 1977.

Dewey, J. *Democracy and education.* New York: Macmillan, 1916.

Flavell, J. Stage related properties of cognitive development. *Cognitive Psychology*, 1971, *2*, 421–453.

Gage, N. *The scientific basis of the art of teaching.* New York: Teachers College Press, 1978.

Goldberg, A. Conceptual system as a predisposition toward therapeutic communication. *Journal of Counseling Psychology*, 1974, *21*, 364–368.

Good, T. Research on teaching. Paper presented at Exploring Issues in Teacher Education conference, Austin, Texas, 1979.

Hanson, M. Student conceptual level and instructor-student interaction: A cognitive developmental analysis. Unpublished doctoral thesis, University of Minnesota, 1975.

Heath, D. *Maturity and competence.* New York: Gardner, 1977.

Hedin, D. Teenage health educators: An action learning program to promote psychological development. Unpublished doctoral thesis, University of Minnesota, 1979.

Hunt, D. *Matching models in education.* Toronto: Ontario Institute for Studies in Education, 1971.

———. Theorists are persons, too: On preaching what you practice. In C. A. Parker (Ed.), *Encouraging development in college students*. Minneapolis: University of Minnesota Press, 1978a, 250–266.

———. In-service training as persons-in-relation. *Theory into Practice*, 1978b, *17*.

Hunt, D., & Joyce, B. Teacher trainee personality and initial teaching style. *American Educational Research Journal*, 1967, *4*, 253–259.

Knoell, D. Prediction of teaching success from word fluency data. *Journal of Educational Research*, 1953, *46*, 673–683.

Kohlberg, L. Stage and sequence: The cognitive-developmental approach to socialization. In D. Goslin (Ed.), *Handbook of socialization*. Chicago: Rand McNally, 1969, 347–480.

Kohlberg, L. Moral development, ego development, and psychoeducational practices. In D. Miller (Ed.), *Developmental theory*. St. Paul, Minnesota: Minnesota Department of Education, 1977.

Lichtenberg, J., & Heck, E. Interactional structure of interviews conducted by counselors, of different levels of cognitive complexity. *Journal of Counseling Psychology*, 1979, *26* (1), 15–22.

Loevinger, J. The meaning and measurement of ego development. *American Psychologist*, 1966, *21*, 195–206.

Magnus, R. Development of an individualized autoinstructional program to improve the ability to understand and communicate empathically. Unpublished doctoral thesis, Mississippi State University, 1972.

McClelland, D. Testing for competence rather than for intelligence. *American Psychologist*, 1973, 1–14.

McNergney, R. F. Review of N. L. Gages, The scientific basis of the art of teaching. *Educational Researcher*, 1979, *8*(8), 19–20.

Murphy, P., & Brown, M. Conceptual systems and teaching styles. *American Educational Research Journal*, 1970, *7*, 529–540.

Nicholson, E. Success and admission criteria for potentially successful risks (project report). Providence, R.I.: The Ford Foundation and Brown University, March, 1970.

Perry, W. G. *Forms of intellectual and ethical development during the college years*. New York: Holt, Rinehart & Winston, 1969.

Piaget, J. The genetic approach to the psychology of thought. *Journal of Educational Psychology*, 1961, *52*, 275–281.

Rathbone, C. Teachers' information-handling behavior when grouped with students by conceptual level. Unpublished doctoral disseration, Syracuse University, 1970.

Rosenthal, R. Combining results of independent studies. *Psychological Bulletin*, 1978, *85*,(1), 185–193.

Ryans, D. *Characteristics of teachers*. Washington, D.C.: American Council on Education, 1960.

Ryan, K. Mainstreaming and teacher education: The last straw. In M. C. Reynolds (Ed.), *A common body of practice for teachers*. Minneapolis: University of Minnesota National Support Systems Project—Draft Report, 1979.

Sheeha, J. T. Moral judgment as a predictor of clinical performance, Paper presented at Conference on Research in Medical Education, Oct., 1978.

Shutes, R. Needed: A theory of teacher education. *Texas Tech Journal of Education*, 1975, *2*, 94–101.

Silver, P. Principals' conceptual ability in relation to situation and behavior. *Educational Administration Quarterly*, 1975, *11*(3), 49–6.

Sprinthall, N. A. Psychology for secondary schools: The saber tooth curriculum revisited? *American Psychologist*, 1980, *35*, 4, 336–347.

Sullivan, E., McCullough, G., & Stager, M. A developmental study of the relationship between conceptual, ego, and moral development. *Child Development*, 1970, *41*, 399–411.

Widick, C., Knefelkamp, L., & Parker, C. The counselors as developmental instructor. *Counselor Education and Supervision*, 1975, *14*(4), 286–296.

Widick, C., & Simpson, D. Developmental concepts in college instruction. In C. A. Parker (Ed.), *Encouraging development in college students*. Minneapolis: University of Minnesota Press, 1978, 27–59.

Addendum:

Bents, R. *A study of the effects of environment structure on students of differing conceptual levels*. Unpublished doctoral dissertation, University of Minnesota, 1978.

Blumberg, A. *Supervisors and teachers: A private cold war*. Berkeley, California: McCutchan, 1974.

Mosher, R., & Purple, D. *Supervision: A reluctant profession*. Boston: Houghton-Mifflin, 1972.

4

Research on Preservice Laboratory and Clinical Experiences: Implications for Teacher Education

Martin Haberman

University of Wisconsin, Milwaukee

OVERVIEW

Study and research related to student teaching can be characterized as meager, diverse, and trivial. Its meagerness is a function of the fact that the knowledgeable people who work with student teachers are essentially practitioners, not researchers. Its diversity is a function of the fact that there are few monies for research available in this area and thus the most common inquiry into student teaching has been one-time-only doctoral dissertations. These studies all conclude with a chapter advising others on ways to follow up on research but rarely if ever is this done. The often trivial nature of this research is a function of the fact that those who do an occasional study are unfamiliar with the basic nature of student teaching and regard it as *teaching* behavior rather than *learning* behavior. They also make the mistake of viewing it as largely individual behavior driven by knowledge and personality rather than as *organizational* behavior driven by the press of various conditions, norms, and events in the school setting.

In order to understand the development of student teaching it is necessary to have a general grasp of how teacher education has developed. Essentially, teacher preparation has evolved out of the lower levels of schooling into postsecondary and finally into university forms.

As this transformation occurred there was an inevitable shift from the practicalities of apprenticeship to a broader form of training and, ultimately, to a higher education rooted in theoretic-like concerns. My basic argument is that this development, while an improvement in quality, has shifted the locus of preparation from the school to the university, and that there is a current set of pressures which seek to return teacher preparation to the schools. Related to this argument are issues which deal with the inevitably disfunctional nature of lower schools and universities as "cooperating" organizations.

HISTORICAL DEVELOPMENT

During the colonial period the teacher training available was a form of apprenticeship. Its nature was usually of the "sit-by-Nellie" variety. For example, the following agreement was made in 1722:

> This indenture (apprenticeship) witnesseth that John Campbell . . . hath put himself . . . apprentice to George Brownell Schoolmaster to learn the Art, Trade or Mystery of teaching . . . And the said George Brownell doth hereby covenant to teach or instruct . . . the said apprentice in art, trade or calling of a schoolmaster by the best measure he or his wife may or can (Cubberly, 1920, p. 386).

Gradually, a primary school education became the accepted requirement for future teachers and mere apprenticeship was replaced by some form of practice teaching in conjunction with the study of school subjects. In 1823 Reverend Samuel Hall's School was established in Concord, Vermont as the first private normal school in America. It was a three-year program. In addition to his *Lectures on Schoolkeeping* the third-year students in Hall's school were offered the opportunity of practicing on a few children who were admitted for the specific purpose of demonstration lessons. Hall's school, along with the second private normal school founded in Lancaster, Massachusetts, in 1827 by James G. Carter, soon closed because of financial difficulties. Carter, however, was successful as a lawmaker, and the 1837 law which created the State Board of Education and the first public normal school in Lexington, Massachusetts, earned Carter the title "Father of the Normal School." The school began with a faculty of one and a student body of three. It is interesting to note that the term "normal," which was borrowed from the French, derives from the Latin term *norma* meaning "a carpenter's square, a rule, a pattern, a model" (Elsbree, 1939, p. 145).

In 1839 Cyrus Pierce was appointed as the first principal of this first state normal school in Lexington, Massachusetts. He also conducted a model school for 30 boys and girls aged 6 to 10. The students in the normal school were the teachers in the model school. Mr. Pierce visited the school twice daily and thereby became the first supervisor of student teachers. In one of his letters to Henry Barnard, then secretary to the Massachusetts Board of Education, Mr. Pierce outlined his pedagogical goals as:

> To Teach the pupils (i.e., the future teachers) by my own example, as well as by precepts, the best way of teaching the same things effectually to others. I have four methods of recitation. First, by question and answer; second, by conversation; third, by calling one, two, three, or more or less, to give an analysis of the whole subject contained in the lesson; and fourth, by requiring written analysis, in which the ideas of the author are stated in the language of the pupil (Norton, 1926, p. 1).

It is interesting to note that unlike our modern admonition that teacher educators use the same *methods* with student teachers that they prescribe for students' use with children, Pierce was attempting to teach the very same *content goals* to his student teachers in the hope that they would then achieve these goals with their children. Also, unlike many of today's teacher educators, Mr. Pierce recognized and accepted individual differences among his student teachers.

> I see more the distinctive character of my pupils. I am glad to see them show plainly their individual and peculiar characteristics. A little observation would show the visitor that we have no block or mold by which we are all cast, so that there may be uniformity of character in the Prepared Teachers. I would have a way, a mode, a system; but still I would not have it so unyielding and restrictive as to preclude rather than aid individual developments (Norton, 1926, p. 33).

It is noteworthy that Cyrus Pierce's work as the first supervisor of student teachers led him to a most remarkable insight: that the teacher-to-be needed not only specific instruction in the "normalities" but the encouragement to experiment and identify new methods of teaching and self-evaluation. In a remarkable statement of self-analysis he wrote:

> What can I do? What am I doing? I am stating to my Pupils in a Series of Conversations and Lectures the duties and qualifications—The Principles of Governing and Teaching a School—I am showing them daily by my own Method of Teaching them, and teaching the Scholars of the Model School, how they should teach their pupils. I am giving them an opportunity of experimenting themselves in the way of teaching—while I, as much as I am able, observe their manner, and at proper times, remark upon it. What more can be done or rather what different; I know not. (Norton, 1926, p. 18–19).

Pierce was prophetic since his simple process of criticizing has lasted almost 150 years and will persist further. Unfortunately, his willingness to let his student teachers experiment and to have them observe his own teaching of children are no longer common supervisory practices.

Prior to the Civil War there were only 11 state-supported normal schools in this country (New York, Massachusetts, Connecticut (4), Rhode Island, New Jersey, Illinois, Michigan, and Minnesota) and the number of graduates made no appreciable impact on the quality of public education. By 1898 there were 167 public normal schools and even more private ones. The public normal schools had graduated 8,188 teachers and the more numerous private ones another 3,067. This was still a modest influence on the schools since there were 403,333 practicing teachers at that time plus an annual need for 50,000 new ones. It is obvious that the vast majority of teachers were not receiving even the meager training of the state normal schools. "Meager" since in 1900 the entrance requirements to normal school training was usually the modest prerequisite of an elementary school education.

With a few exceptions the normal schools prepared only elementary school teachers. By 1890, 114 colleges and universities (there were only 400 in total) were preempting the secondary field and preparing these teachers. The number of secondary education students numbered about 3,414 at this time.

In 1900 most of the normal schools preparing teachers were really offering high school level education with an infusion of pedagogy. For all its inadequacies, however, there was greater relevance in the teacher education of 1900 than there is now since almost all the subject matter content which teachers learned was the same or a slightly advanced version of what they were supposed to teach children. In terms of connections, linkage, and relevance, we have deteriorated in the last 80 years.

In addition to the state normal schools and the private ones, there were cities involved in teacher training. By World War I (1914) every city in the United States with a population of 100,000 or more, had a normal school or a department in its high school for teacher training. (This amounted to almost 100 cities.) The growth of those city training schools resulted from the demands of a growing population. State normal schools simply could not provide enough graduates. By the 1930s only about 20 of these city-run training schools remained, and the budgetary problems of cities in the Depression pushed these institutions into state subsidies or into oblivion. The common criticism of the city normal schools was that they fostered inbreeding and provincialism. The local girls from the local districts were trained and became teachers in the same neighborhoods, frequently in the very same buildings, where they had grown up.

At the same time urban areas were training teachers, rural areas in 24 states were using specially designated high schools for training teachers from their areas to serve in these more remote locales. The pattern was to extend high school one year and to provide a certificate. The better programs (e.g., in Minnesota) included practice teaching, the poorer ones (e.g., in Kansas) did not.

As we consider the teacher training offered by city schools or by schools in rural areas, it is clear that it was highly relevant to practice. It was of the schools, by the schools, and for the schools. The content learned by teachers to be taught to pupils was essentially the same, with some minimal study in pedagogy tacked on. There was in this relationship the opportunity to safely assume that teachers would be appropriately trained. One could also assert, with some justification, that this situation of great relevance of training to practice *should* be so since it was frequently the very same bureaucracy (i.e., the public schools) that trained both teacher and pupil.

Having licked the problems of relevance and appropriateness leads one to wonder why these training institutions disappeared. In addition to lack of money, which was the primary explanation, there were a few other reasons. The fields of human development, learning, educational philosophy, and pedagogy were growing. Similarly, the fields of general knowledge were also expanding rapidly. It became painfully and increasingly clear that most teachers were semiliterate, poorly educated people, in truth, a short step (usually one chapter in a textbook) above the masses they were supposedly extricating from the pools of ignorance. The response to this state of affairs was to insist upon more university education for teachers. From 1900 until the present that is precisely what has occurred, and as a result teacher education is now inextricably ensconced in the bosom of higher education. In exchange for a highly relevant but almost ignorant corps of teachers we now have a better educated but less appropriately trained teaching profession.

Under the influence of Dewey the concept of practice teaching was dropped and the notion of a student teacher engaged in professional laboratory experiences was introduced. The cadet or practice teacher concept emphasized an apprentice practicing the techniques of school teaching. The notion of a student experimenting in a professional laboratory is intended to convey the continuous search of the student of teaching. The student teacher is expected to make mistakes and to learn principles as a result. The practice teacher is expected to practice correct responses. The practice teacher can be evaluated on the same basis as the regular inservice teacher; that is, the performance of effective behaviors. The student teacher is evaluated as a learner; that is, what he or she learned from today's lesson is of paramount importance. As stated at the outset, this confusion between the role of practice and student teacher is a major cause for the low quality and quantity of research on student teaching. If the neophyte is essentially an apprentice who must practice, why bother with special study? Simply apply the research literature on effective teaching to the neophyte.

Lest this distinction seem new to you, permit me to point out that it was made in 1904. In drawing the distinction between preparing a student of teaching—one who would act on developing principles and who would continue to grow—and a technician who acts with no undergirding rationale, the following description is offered:

> For immediate skill may be got at the cost of power to go on growing. The teacher who leaves the professional school with power in managing a class of children may appear to superior advantage the first day, the first week, the first month, or even the first year, as compared with some other teacher who has a much more vital command of the psychology, logic, and ethics of development. But later "progress" may with such consist only in perfecting and refining skill already possessed. Such persons seem to know how to teach but are not students of teaching. Even though they go on studying books of pedagogy, reading teachers' journals, attending teachers' institutes, etc., yet the root of the matter is not in them, unless they continue to be students of subject matter and students of mind activity. Unless a teacher is such a student, he may continue to improve the mechanics of school management, but he cannot grow as a teacher, an inspirer and director of soul-life. How often do candid instructors in training schools acknowledge disappointment in the later careers of even their more promising candidates. They seem to strike twelve at the start. There is an unexpected and seemingly unaccountable failure to maintain steady growth (Dewey, 1904, p. 8).

The difference between the teacher who has one year's experience thirty times and the teacher who grows each year is attributed to the teacher education program. This debate is the genesis of the gulf that has come to separate those who talk about teacher *training* and *practice* teaching on the one hand and those who use the terms teacher *education* and *student* teaching on the other.

It is similarly noteworthy that the admonition to help student teachers analyze their own teaching rather than to receive constant criticism is also not new and refers back to the concept undergirding direct experiences. Is the experience intended to perfect correct behavior or is the experience to prepare a professional who can monitor his or her own behavior? This debate on the goal of student teaching is manifested most clearly in how the student teacher would be supervised (i.e., taught).

> It ought to go without saying... that criticism should be directed toward making the student thoughtful about his work in the light of principles rather than induce in him a recognition that certain special methods are good, and certain other special methods bad. At all events, no greater travesty of real intellectual criticism can be given than to set a student to teaching a brief number of lessons, having him under inspection in practically all the time of every lesson, and then criticize him almost, if not quite, at the end of each lesson, upon the particular way in which that particular lesson has been taught, pointing out elements of failure and of success. Such methods of cri-

ticism may be adapted to giving a training-teacher command of some of the knacks and tools of the trade, but are not calculated to develop a thoughtful and independent teacher (Dewey, 1904, p. 22).

In terms of research, there has been and remains no greater need than to systematically gather data to support or refute this contention that certain kinds of practice teaching lead to technicians and other forms of student teaching lead to students of teaching.

The reason for this very brief overview is to simply initiate a pause for thinking. There will, in the future, be an inevitable price for making teachers more relevant to school practice. It may not be the same price we paid when we felt any good high school should be able to train teachers, but there will nevertheless be a price!

There is a finite amount of time and energy for training. In the push-pull of competing subject matters demanding the neophyte's attention there are limits on the liberal education, the specialization and the professional education which can be crammed into any period—whether the period is four years, five years, or six years. We must simply accept the fact that if greater connections are to be made between preparation and practice something will be squeezed out of present programs. In today's world of electronic media, films, libraries, and other resources, today's teachers will not lapse all the way back to the low quality of nineteenth century teachers. We need to be realistic, however. There will be some academic price to pay for gaining increased relevance.

Finally, this review permits me to underscore the initial point that student teaching is a process learned in disfunctional bureaucracies. Since teacher training is not under the aegis of the schools and is in fact under the administration of higher education institutions which are, in part, mindful and proud of their freedom from social pressure, there should be realistic horizons set for the degree of relevance which can be *re*infused into preservice teacher education. And let us also be aware as we seek to *re*infuse this relevance that we do not go to the extreme of advocating ignorance as the trade-off for practical knowhow. I am certain that if we had training programs in school settings involving four years of student teaching with little or no college work whatever, that we could train more teachers to keep better order and to help children reach higher reading levels than they presently achieve. The question is, dare we implement such "improvements' and risk not having teachers who are first well educated and only second, professionally prepared.

An immediate implication of the foregoing is that I believe I know how to prepare more effective teachers (defining "effective" as having pupils score higher on achievement tests). This is true. I believe that if we placed high school graduates in a four-year career ladder as paraprofessionals, aides, assistant teachers, student teachers and interns into schools—the very same schools where they would eventually teach—that they could be trained to be more proficient and competent (in behavioral terms) than any graduates of present university teacher education programs. It might be possible to then have the state require the subsequent completion of a bachelors degree in general-liberal studies within a ten-year period. This is precisely what some states did in former times with normal school graduates. The question of purpose remains: Is it better to prepare a technically competent teacher who will subsequently pursue a bachelors degree, or is it better to require a bachelors (or masters) degree and thereby limit the professional know-how of beginning teachers? Stated another way, is it better for the practicing teacher to be *primarily* concerned with professional or academic development. "Wise persons" will, of course, answer "both"; however, the reality of the situation is that most practicing teachers study, and are required to study, little beyond education courses once they are certified. At present, our system clearly prepares beginning teachers with minimal professional skills who spend almost all of their subsequent study in areas of professional development. It is, theoretically, possible to reverse this entire process. But the organizational linkage between state departments of education and institutions of higher education is too fixed to be changed. Teacher education is largely owned by the universities. The most that we can do is to use the state to pressure teacher education institutions (within limits) to make *their* preparation more relevant and, on occasion, to use the universities to pressure the state departments (within limits) to loosen up "restrictive" requirements.

This brings us into the well-circumscribed arena where we play by gentlemen's rules. If you in the state will not permit school districts to train teachers, we in the university will continue to support your authority to certify and if you in the university show at least some small effort to make your teacher training more relevant to school practice, we in the state will continue to accredit you—and you alone.

What has happened in the century-and-one-half since we first adapted and created student teaching in America? Has its evolvement been a regression from a noble beginning, or, has it been refined and improved from crude fits and starts? What critical trends can be identified in this history? The analysis is worth the effort since the development of student teaching is, in effect, parallel to the evolution of teacher education in general. Student teaching has always been the heart and mind of teacher preparation: to understand its development is to grasp the essence of the professional development of educators.

THE NATURE OF STUDENT TEACHING RESEARCH

As Howey has pointed out in his overview, there is no instance of any widespread practice in student-teaching programs which is the result of research. Conversely, there are no common practices which have been dropped from student-teaching programs on the basis of research evidence. Essentially, student-teaching programs, like all college curricula, are political agreements among faculty and differ only in response to power variations in the organizational setting of the particular college or university. Nevertheless, it would be useful to review some of the types of studies that have been done in relation to student teaching.

First, are the studies which derive from the study of teaching and which are simply extrapolated to include what should be taught to student teachers. The most popular examples of this practice are various forms of interaction analysis, micro-teaching, and competency-based teaching. These trends grew out of efforts to systematically improve the practices of inservice teachers. It soon became clear that systems for describing and analyzing teaching could also be used for judging and finally for improving the work of teachers. Once this point was reached it became a short step to studying student teaching using these same modalities. Except for micro-teaching, the roots of all these studies derive from the effort to improve inservice teaching, not from attempts to prepare students more effectively. And the research literature of micro teaching, although impressive in its ability to specify important pedagogic acts, essentially proves that students who are taught specific behaviors remember and use them more than students who are not taught these behaviors.

The closest thing we have to a continuous pattern of study grew out of the widespread use of the Minnesota Teacher Attitude Inventory by numerous institutions over a period of years. Once the concern of teacher educators shifted from an interest in predispositions, values, and attitudes to actual behavior, the descriptive studies of students' attitudinal changes dropped into the background.

Finally, the lack of systematic study of student teaching cannot be highlighted more dramatically than to cite the profession's response to the accreditation requirement of Standard VI of the National Council for the Accreditation of Teachers of Education. Even though it is required that student teachers be evaluated upon completion of their preparation programs, there are few if any institutions which can mount such an effort. Jim Cooper speaks to the few institutions which have done this in the following chapter. We tend to regard this as the failure of an individual institution when the common nature of this inability to follow up graduates demonstrates with ringing clarity that our programs are not conceptualized or offered in ways which permit evaluation. My contention is that this situation is, in part, a function of having a political/organizational base rather than a research/knowledge base for student-teaching programs and for teacher education programs in general.

Without doubt, there is infinitely more calling for research and agreements among experts about what needs to be studied than there is actual production of research. For example, experts generally agree that student teaching is the most important part of the preparation program because students rate it as the most useful part of their preservice (Davies, 1969; Amershek, 1969, pp. 1376–1387). Different advocates have also stated that student teaching at various times could be the significant educational experience in preparing students to fight the war on poverty, increase school integration, mainstream the handicapped, disseminate new methods into the schools, implement the improvement of reading instruction, and indoctrinate a new breed of militant teachers who will serve as change agents in the schools. It is noteworthy that at the same time many call on learning to teach as the process for accomplishing this brave new world, they generally agree that student teaching does not adequately prepare students for success in their first year of teaching normal children in traditional schools.

In addition to literature "calling for" student teaching to help implement educational and social movements there is also much advice on what student teaching "should be." It "should" include an internship, involve theory as well as practice, sequence experiences from easy to hard, encompass various school situations and grades, affect the student affectively as well as cognitively, and lead to specific behavioral teaching competencies.

In addition to what some "call for" and assume "should be" in student teaching, what we actually know about this process in practice can be summarized in one Word—varied. How is student teaching organized? Varied. How is it administered? Varied. What admission criteria are used? Varied. How are assignments made? Varied. How is it evaluated? Varied. Is it required for certification in every state. Yes (Ebel, 1969). The final paragraph of a 1969 research review would have been equally accurate in 1979 and will probably be as true in 1989.

> given its ascribed importance in teacher education, it is alarming to find so little systematic research directly related to it. Discussion and descriptive reports are plentiful, but comprehensive basic study of the process involved is lacking (Ebel, 1969, p. 1384).

Most of what happens around student teaching is not research but a continuous flurry of developmental effort. And most of the developmental effort relates to administrative arrangements (i.e., how many hours, placements, and observations should be made) and does not deal with the *content* of what is taught. Research studies generally agree that when "new" content is developed students who are offered the new content learn it better than students not offered the new content.

In the last decade, a summary of the available research on teacher education reached the conclusion that this situation would change.

> Teacher education seems likely to become a far more systematic process in the years ahead. Its objectives seem likely to be stated in terms of concrete, observable, and trainable teaching behaviors (Peck & Tucker, 1973, p. 970).

Peck and Tucker obviously saw this as an advance over the recent past and in truth it was. In the sweep of things, however, simply making teacher education more specific and concrete is a throwback to Reverend Hall's normal school of 1823. The 1973 summary is superior to the 1969 summary only because it adds all the feedback studies. In sum, these studies tell us that when students are given specific criticism they have a better likelihood of improving and that students taught specific behaviors will demonstrate them more frequently than students not taught those behaviors. To what extent do such studies contribute to knowledge? What research on student teaching has *not* helped us to do is answer the ultimate question. What are the behaviors and knowledge which student teachers must learn in order to become effective teachers subsequently? On this question (i.e., the content of student teaching) the variance among the more than 1,000 institutions that offer student teaching remains extremely great. Our present knowledge base simply does not derive from research.

In two areas we do have the beginnings of some solid evidence, and it is interesting to note that the content of these studies relate to aspects of student teaching which we seek to counteract rather than to implement. The first generalization which we can make with a fair degree of certainty is that cooperating teachers influence students more than college supervisors (Yee, 1969; Seperson & Joyce, 1973; Chie, 1975; Friebus, 1977; Karmos & Jacko, 1977). Nevertheless, I would argue we should continue to use and even expand college supervision since the university personnel emphasize concepts and principles as well as behaviors. If the cooperating teacher's power over the student teacher is permitted to become the total value of the student-teaching program we will regress to preparing technicians, not educators.

While cooperating teachers may be the most important people influencing students, we also know that student personality is a more powerful determinant of ultimate teaching style. (Veldman, 1970, p. 165–167). We also know that when what is to be learned relates to more general aspects of teaching rather than to techniques, cooperating teachers are not the most influential mentors of student teachers (Boschee, Prescott, & Hein, 1978, p. 57–61).

In a study which contradicts the simplistic notion that cooperating teachers' influence on student teachers is always greater than college supervisors', Zimpher, deVoss, and Nott (1980) indicate several specific functions and forms of influence which are directly tied to the role of the college supervisor. The first function not performed by others which is left to be accomplished by the college supervisor relates to goal setting. This involves setting both the purposes for the student-teaching experience and establishing the expectations for the particular student teacher. A second function performed by the college supervisor relates to setting a sequence of activities of increasing complexity. This graduated induction process which includes observation, planning, tutoring, and small-group instruction is contrary to the tendencies of cooperating teachers to "throw students in" from the first day and thereby make the student-teaching experience an undifferentiated one with no real qualitative difference between the activities performed by a student teacher on his or her first and last day. A third function of the college supervisor is to offer criticism. There is a tendency for cooperating teachers who have established rapport with students and college personnel, to leave any difficult or negative feedback to the college supervisor. The outsider role of the college supervisor is in this sense an advantage since the professional social distance which is maintained by the college supervisor vis-à-vis the cooperating and student teachers permits the college supervisor to be more objective, analytical, and critical. Additional findings indicate that the college supervisor serves to increase communication and to introduce ideas which would ordinarily be ignored by cooperating teachers and students as of little practical application (Zimpher, deVoss, & Nott, 1980).

There is no question that the preponderance of evidence supports the notion that cooperating teachers have greater influence than college supervisors over techniques that students adopt. One reason which might account for less research to support the influence of college supervisors is that the influence issue is usually couched in terms of specific techniques rather than principles, goals, or personal growth (as the Sprinthalls advocate in Chapter 3), and most college supervisors would agree on their secondary role in the area of technical training. It is also possible that the issues raised in the Zimpher, deVoss, Nott study might be so generally accepted by those directly involved in student teaching that there is a low-(no-) felt need for systematic study to support this contention.

The second area in which we have sufficient data to feel we know something definite to act upon again relates to an aspect of student teaching which we seek to correct rather than continue. We know that often as students move closer to graduation they become more dogmatic (Johnson, 1969, p. 224–226). In an effort to counteract this long-standing phenomenon Roy (1972) developed a special student-teaching program (Project Together) as a treatment designed to overcome the "natural" inclination of students to become less idealistic, less theoretic, and more practical and control oriented as they approached graduation and their first teaching experience. This is a landmark study in that the literature of student teaching includes no more carefully planned, systematic effort to countervene the decrease in college influence and the increase in school influence. The content of the treatment involved an elaborate theoretic concept of creating a professional and emotional support group for students. This support group was developed to help student teachers fight against the socializing influences of their cooperating schools. The dependent variables were group centeredness, dogmatism, pupil control ideology, and perception of problems. The hypotheses advanced were that Project Together students would be (1) more cohesive, (2) less dogmatic, (3) more humanistic in their outlook toward pupil control, and (4) likely to perceive fewer school-related problems. In comparing these students with student teachers not given any special treatment, only the hypothesis that the students could be made more supportive of each other was supported. The nonsignificant results of this study are indeed significant! Even elaborate methods (ones that go well beyond what colleges and universities can typically afford to provide their student teachers in the way of class size, personalized placement, special instruction, etc.) cannot stop the process whereby students become socialized by classroom teachers. The conclusion reached was that student teachers could be treated in ways which gave them emotional support but could not be made less dogmatic and less custodial without changing the institutions in which the students teach.

Taken together, the two generalizations we can be most secure about deriving from research related to student teaching are the following:

1. Students and cooperating teachers tend to agree that student teaching is primarily an opportunity to practice methods and, therefore, people or opportunities for furthering such practice will be defined as relevant and useful, while activities which distract from the pursuits of technique will tend to be regarded as less necessary or impractical.

2. The definition of the beginning teacher's role usually defines classroom management as not only a major priority but a concern of overriding magnitude. (See Johnston and Ryan's review of the literature in Chapter 6.) Student teachers often focus on learning skills which they perceive will help them to control and thereby survive. As a result, individual differences in ability, personality, or professional ideology among student teachers becomes increasingly less important in understanding or predicting their future teaching behavior. This is in contrast to opportunities to clarify an educational philosophy; increase self-evaluation skills; test out personal strengths and weakness; try out concepts learned in development or learning courses; or seek ways of breaking down and connecting subject matter concepts with individual pupils' interest.

WHAT SHOULD BE STUDIED IN RELATION TO STUDENT TEACHING

The first major area of fruitful research relates to occupational socialization. At this point, we should apply ideas from the studies of organizations and from socialization studies in related service professions. Occupational socialization may be defined as the process by which the neophyte learns the culture, norms, and role behavior of the group he or she seeks to be accepted by and to join. Given this definition it is possible to view many problems of teacher education as essentially related to occupational socialization. Major content to be studied in this realm are the interactions between neophyte and others in particular settings. It may be, for example, that not only are cooperating teachers more influential than college supervisors (regarding technique) but that others in the workplace (e.g., other teachers, principals, janitors, secretaries, school nurse, etc.) are also more influential in shaping the student's total role concept. Medical trainees, for example, who were isolated from the medical faculty often shaped their definition of a doctor on the basis of the nurses' and patients' perceptions (Becker et al., 1961; Mumford, 1970). The principle that might be accepted (on a tentative basis) as a starting point for future study is that the more frequently trainees observe their trainers actually performing and the more frequently the trainee is observed trying to perform the practitioner's role by the trainer, the more influential the interaction becomes.

The most important question for future study is the degree to which the particular situational press controls the performance of both trainer and trainee and the degree to which the particular situation is merely incidental to the fact that trainer and trainee are interacting by observing each other's performances. My hunch is that both factors are critical; however, we need more precise information to act upon. If the interaction proves most powerful, then college supervisors face the long-standing problem of making more and better supervisory visits. If the school setting is shown to be of greater influence than the university supervisors (and other university personnel), we have the responsibility of seeking to influence other school practitioners and the setting itself as well. As an extreme example, should the setting prove the most potent force, then we might need university personnel who can help change school curriculum materials, rather than supervisors who engage in the traditional practice of criticizing student teachers' lessons.

A second major area of needed research should be directed at the comparison of learning styles of cooperating teachers and student teachers. (Again, recall the Sprinthall chapter.) How does the match-up of cognitive style and level between cooperating teacher and student teacher affect the student's learning? Even more important again may be the question of how this match-up is affected by the particular school setting in which trainer and trainee interact.

A third area I would propose as a fruitful area for research on student teaching relates to the sequence of activities which lead students from the beginning to the final stage of preservice preparation. Figure 4.1 is my paradigm of the levels through which a student teacher will naturally move (i.e., from I through VI). My hypothesis for future study is that student teachers move in the reverse order, from Stage VI through Stage I.

FIGURE 4.1 Stages of Student Development in Professional
Laboratory Experiences

Stage I.   **Ritualistic-Imitative**
Student teacher seeks to replicate as much of the behavior of other teachers as possible. (Can I do what these teachers do?)

Stage II.   **Reality-centered**
Student teacher selects the teaching behaviors to be imitated and focuses on controlling behaviors as the highest priority.
(Can I control the class as well as Teacher X?)

Stage III.   **Learning Skills Director**
Student teacher seeks to perfect skills aimed at teaching skills to children and youth.
(What specifically did I teach anyone today?)

Stage IV.   **Self-evaluator**
Student teacher develops skills for self-evaluating his/her own instruction. (What specifically did I learn about teaching today?)

Stage V.   **Insightful Analyst**
Student teacher develops feel for, hunches, intuitions regarding the pupils' behavior, their own reactions and the nature of their interaction with pupils in the particular setting.
(What is really happening to me and to these pupils in this setting?)

Stage VI.   **Professional Decision Maker**
Student teacher seeks to connect daily activities with school's more general curriculum goals. (What might I do to expedite the process of moving children and youth toward the achievement of program goals?)

My perception is that student teachers begin with prestudent-teaching courses which give them the broadest possible overview and frequently end up at the lowest levels of learning. This contention is an elaboration of our present knowledge that students become more dogmatic and custodial as they approach their first day of teaching. Future study should help teacher educators more fully describe students' *stages* of professional development.

A fourth area of research should focus on the costs of individuals who seek to become professional (socialized) teachers. It has been found that stress is not caused so much by interaction among individuals but rather by the organizational climate of the school, and that 70 percent stress at the start of an experience can decrease to 20 percent by the end of the experience. (Sorenson & Halpert, 1968, p. 28–33).

Graen (1976, p. 1235) has described the induction process of beginners in work situations as including three phases: initial confrontation, working through, and integrating. The initial confrontation stage is most interesting since it described a "disillusionment phenomenon" whereby high expectations before experience are followed by much lower expectations after experience. Vroom and Deci (1971, pp. 36–49) found these less favorable expectations beginning just prior to experience, then deepening during the first year, and lasting approximately 2½ years. This phenomenon has been so reliably documented that it is now expected that newcomers will be "turned off"—that they must inevitably go through such a stage—before they can be integrated into the work group. Some commentators on the research literature conclude that the most a training program or an induction process can do is to delay the full impact of disillusionment until the newcomer is prepared to cope with it.

We also need to know more about how teachers learn different needed skills, both academic and social. Although it is clear that individuals in organizations are substantially dependent upon members of their work groups for gaining the knowledge and skills they need to perform their jobs adequately, little controlled research has been done to explain how this takes place *in* organizational settings. These are psychological theories of stimulus and response and sociological explanations of inherent needs for group approval and belonging, but little to explain the apparently universal drive of inductees to be part of a work group, or at the very least, to not incur its displeasure.

Studies on deviation which seek to identify how much tolerance can be given newcomers would have important implication for laboratory experiences in teacher education. Current findings suggest that the freedom to deviate is fairly fragile even for members who have paid their dues with long years of obedience. Pressures to conform to group norms are greatest when group members are motivated to achieve uniformity, when the norm is of importance to the group and when a member's deviant behavior is especially noticeable (Hackman, 1976, p. 1504–1505).

It seems to me that the present public emphasis on basic skills triggers each of these three conditions in teacher groups. It explains why a student teacher, for example, educated in principles of child development will be steamrolled into the role of reading tutor by the operating norms of the particular teacher group. Pressures to conform are strongest when the norm is of high intensity and highly crystallized (Jackson, 1965). But this doesn't mean that there are not sufficient controls at all times. As long as a member needs or desires resources over which the group has control, as long as he or she seeks their approval, and most importantly for teacher groups—so long as he or she seeks to not be criticized by the group, the member is likely to conform.

The issue is not one of placing students in schools where the teachers get along well together. Research by Janis (1972), for example, suggests that high cohesiveness can in some cases be actively dysfunctional for the group as a whole. Janis suggests that as a group becomes excessively close knit and develops a clubby feeling of "we-ness" it becomes susceptible to a pattern he calls "groupthink." The major symptom of groupthink is a marked decrease in the openness of the group members to discrepant or unsettling information. These interpersonal strategies, Janis argues, result in an increased likelihood that the group, in a spirit of goodwill and shared confidence, will develop and implement a course of action which is grossly inappropriate and ineffective. When we reflect about it, this dynamic of groupthink could explain much of the behavior among university groups as well.

Should cohesiveness be avoided? Obviously not. Group norms provide many desirable supports which teachers use to counterbalance the bureaucracy. The question becomes the content of the norms; and the issue for teacher educators becomes the influence of these norms on student teachers and beginners.

A NEXT STEP TOWARD SOLVING THE PROBLEM OF IMPROVED RESEARCH IN STUDENT TEACHING

In order to increase the production of usable research regarding student teaching, individuals who are not now involved in college supervision will have to be attracted to the study of educating and inducting beginners. Those involved in student-teaching programs (and in teacher education generally) understand the problems but usually lack the proclivity for research or skills of systematic study regarding proposed solutions. Skilled researchers, on the other hand, who are untroubled by history, a full knowledge of practices, or direct experience with the problems, tend to study what is researchable rather than what is important. What is needed in the future is a *preresearch step* which involves future researchers with practicing college supervisors in the process of clarifying and specifying the problems to be studied. Since such cooperative problem definition is not always possible, the questions with which I conclude this chapter are intended to serve as a capsule briefing for those who would study student teaching. On the basis of the preceding analysis it should be clear that I regard items 19, 20, and 21 of greatest importance.

The fact that these questions are stated as "shoulds" does not make them only policy questions. These questions must now be translated from problems solved by political processes into hypotheses or questions to be studied. If such translations do not occur, the next 150 years of teacher education will simply perpetuate the same forms of student teaching as the past. The cycle of too few researchers picking off neat but relatively unimportant topics while the main body of college supervisors ask, "What more can I do?" will be broken only by *cooperatively* attacking and specifying most critical questions. The challenge is both great and interesting. The question is whether sufficient numbers of skilled researchers can be attracted to this very complex area of study and whether they will begin with sufficient intellectual humility to work cooperatively in problem definition.

QUESTIONS MOST COMMONLY RAISED REGARDING PROFESSIONAL LABORATORY EXPERIENCES

1. Which courses in teacher education should include direct experiences?
2. How should these experiences be organized and integrated?
3. Is there an arrangement of direct experience (e.g., from observation to full teaching).
4. What criteria should be used for selecting students to begin professional laboratory experiences?
5. At what point in their college programs should students be admitted to major student-teaching experiences?
6. In how many different situations should student teachers work?
7. With what age(s), in addition to those they have designated as their primary concern, should students work?
8. In which and how many nonschool settings should students work?
9. What should be the bases for determining the length and nature of students' various direct experiences?
10. What courses and other experiences should precede, concur, and follow direct experiences?
11. To what extent should direct experiences be individualized?
12. What are the roles of college faculty, other school personnel, and students in developing, shaping, and changing direct experiences?
13. How should responsibilities for evaluating students be divided among college faculty, school personnel, and students?
14. What criteria should be used in evaluating student teachers' achievements?
15. Who should make written evaluations of student teachers' direct experiences?
16. What controls should public school personnel (and teachers' associations) exert over professional laboratory experiences?
17. What should be the special training of college faculty who supervise direct experiences?
18. What should be the special training of other personnel who supervise students?
19. How should settings in which students are placed be evaluated, selected, and controlled? By whom?
20. What should be the content goals of direct experiences? Who should be involved in developing these?
21. What are the impacts of various settings on student teachers?

BIBLIOGRAPHY

Becker, H. S., Greer, B., Hughes, E. C., & Strauss, A. L. *Boys in white.* Chicago: University of Chicago Press, 1961.

Boschee, F., Prescott, D. R., & Hein, D. D. Do cooperating teachers influence the educational philosophy of student teachers? *Journal of Teacher Education*, 1978, *29*(2), 57–61.

Chie, L. H. Influence of student teaching on perceived teaching competence. *Perceptual and Motor Skills*, 1975, *40*, 872–874.

Cuberly, E. *Reading in history of education*. New York: Houghton Mifflin, 1920.

Davies, D., Amershek, K. Student Teaching. *Encyclopedia of Educational Research 4th Edition*, Ebel, R. L. (Ed.) MacMillan Co., Collier-MaMillan Ltd. London, 1969.

Dewey, J. The relation of theory to practice in education. In Charles A. McMurry (Ed.), *Third yearbook of the national society for the study of education*. Chicago: University of Chicago Press, 1904.

Ebel, R. L. (Ed.). *Encyclopedia of educational research*. (4th Ed). London: Mac-Millan, 1969, 1376–1387.

Elsbree, W. S. *The American teacher*. New York: American Book Company, 1939.

Friebus, R.J. Agents of socialization involved in student teaching. *Journal of Educational Research*, 1977, *70*, 263–268.

Graen, G. Role waking process within complex organizations. *Handbook of industrial and organizational psychology*. Chicago: Rand McNally, 1976, 1235, 1504–1505.

Hackman, J. R. Group influences on individuals. *Handbook of industrial and organizational psychology*. Chicago: Rand McNally, 1976, 1504–1505.

Jackson, J. Structural characteristics of norms. In I. D. Steiner & M. Fishbein (Eds.), *Current studies in social psychology*. New York: Holt, Rinehart, and Winston, 1965.

Janis, I. L. *Victims of groupthink: A psychological study of foreign policy decisions and fiascos*. New York: Houghton Mifflin, 1972.

Johnson, J. S. Change in student teacher dogmatism. *Journal of Educational Research*, 1969, *62*, 224–226.

Karmos, A. H., & Jacko, C. M. The role of significant others during the student teaching experience. *Journal of Teacher Education*, 1977, *28*, 51–55.

Mumford, E. *Interns: From students to physicians*. Cambridge, Massachusetts: Harvard University Press, 1970.

Norton, A. O. *The first state normal school in America*. Cambridge, Massachusetts: Harvard University Press, 1926.

Peck, R. F., & Tucker, J. A. Research on teacher education. In R. M. W. Travers (Ed.), *Second handbook on research in teaching*. Chicago: Rand McNally, 1973.

Roy, W. E. *Project together, a group centered student teaching program*. Unpublished doctoral dissertation, University of Wisconsin-Milwaukee, 1972.

Seperson, M. A., & Joyce, B. R. Teaching styles and student teachers as related to those of their cooperating teachers. *Educational Leadership Research Supplement*, 1973, 146–151.

Sorenson, G., & Halpert R. Stress in student teaching. *California Journal of Educational Research*, 1968, *19*, 28–33.

Sprinthall, L. *Supervision: An educative or miseducative process*. Mimeo. St. Cloud, Minnesota: St. Cloud State University, 1980.

Veldman, D. J. Pupil evaluation of student teachers and their supervisors. *Journal of Teacher Education*, 1970, *21*, 165–167.

Vroom, V. H., & Deci, E. L. The stability of past decision dissonance. *Organizational Behavior and Human Performance*, 1971, *6*, 36–49.

Yee, A. H. Do cooperating teachers influence the attitudes of student teachers? *Educational Psychology*, 1969, *60*, 327–332.

Zimpher, N. L. deVoss, G. G., & Nott, D. L. A closer look at the phenomenon of university student teacher supervision. *Journal of Teacher Education*, July/August, 1980, 11–15.

5

Basic Elements in Teacher Education Program Evaluation: Implications for Future Research and Development

James M. Cooper

University of Houston Central Campus

INTRODUCTION

Within the last 15 years, a new field of study has emerged within the social and behavioral sciences. This new field is evaluation, and education has enthusiastically embraced its methodology. Virtually every national and regional meeting of educators these days has a portion of the program that addresses evaluation issues. Accountability pressures, consumerism, and fiscal stringencies are some of the forces that have led to the demand to evaluate persons, products, and programs. In response to these demands, educational evaluation has blossomed as a field of study, attracting such scholars as Bloom, Scriven, Stufflebeam, Stake, and Tyler. The attraction of so many intellectually gifted individuals to the field of evaluation has contributed greatly to the conceptual development of this area in recent years.

Teacher education has not escaped the increased interest in evaluation. Pressures to evaluate our efforts in teacher education have come from many sources, including the National Council for Accreditation of Teacher Education (NCATE), the competency-based teacher education movement, state legislatures, public school officials, and the general public, who want to know why standardized test scores keep dropping. Teacher educators are beginning to respond seriously to the evaluation pressures, but face numerous obstacles in the process. While some progress has been made, we are a long way from where we need to be as Schalock has illustrated so well in his earlier chapter.

This chapter attempts to identify the current state of the scene regarding research and development efforts in teacher education *program evaluation*, suggest some possible implications for current practice, and identify needed research and development efforts.

CURRENT EFFORTS IN TEACHER EDUCATION PROGRAM EVALUATION

One impetus for program evaluation has historically come from the National Council for Accreditation of Teacher Education. NCATE has required teacher education programs seeking accreditation to conduct evaluation studies, particularly of their graduates. Standard 6 of the NCATE Standards states:

> Maintenance of acceptable teacher education programs demands a continuous process of evaluation of the graduates of existing programs, modification of existing programs, and long-range planning. The faculty and administrators in teacher education evaluate the results of their programs, not only through the assessment of graduates but also by seeking reactions from persons involved with the certification, employment, and supervision of its graduates. The findings of such evaluation are used in program modifications (*Standards*, 1981, pp. 10–11).

The old Standard 5.1 of the 1971 NCATE Standards required that the "institution conducts a well-defined plan for evaluating the teacher it prepares" (*Standards*, 1970, p. 12). Sandefur observed that evaluation teams visiting twelve different institutions raised more questions regarding Standard 5.1 than any other standard, prompting him to conclude, "It is evident that teacher education institutions have largely ignored the evaluation of their graduates. This failure has been due primarily to the profession's inability to determine what constitutes effective teaching, and partly to the lack of evaluative tools and techniques with which to measure effective teaching" (Sandefur, 1970, p. 2).

While Sandefur's comments were made in 1970, it is probably still true that the majority of preservice teacher education programs do not adequately satisfy the NCATE evaluation standard. Fortunately, however, there are some institutions where systematic program evaluations have been conducted.

Austin Colloquium

In 1978 a colloquium was convened in Austin, Texas, by the Research and Development Center for Teacher Education, under the sponsorship of the National Institute of Education, which was concerned with teacher education program evaluation studies. The colloquium brought together a group of educators who were engaged in conducting evaluations of the teacher education programs at their institutions. Participants from eight different institutions were present at the meeting (Ohio State University, Oregon College of Education, Tennessee Technological University, University of Houston, University of Oregon, Weber State University, Western Kentucky University, and the University of Texas at Austin).

As the evaluation efforts were presented, it became apparent that each institution had approached the evaluation question quite differently, even though there were a number of similarities, especially regarding the purpose of the evaluation. The major reason expressed by colloquium participants for conducting teacher education program evaluation studies was to collect, analyze, and disseminate information that would be useful for decision making regarding program improvement. Another reason mentioned for conducting the evaluation efforts was to meet NCATE standards. While this latter reason is a motivating factor for many institutions whose program evaluations seem to be limited to those years preceding an NCATE visit, this was not the case for the institutions attending the colloquium. Most of these institutions were engaged in longitudinal efforts that reflected a genuine concern for program improvement.

Two of the eight institutions attending the Austin Colloquium (Western Kentucky and Tennessee Tech) developed their evaluation efforts based on Sandefur's model for evaluating teacher education graduates. This model was built on generalizations from the research literature on effective teaching and suggested procedures and instrumentation for conducting an evaluation of teacher education program *graduates*. The model examines the program's effectiveness from a product perspective, that is, whether or not the graduates of the teacher education program manifest those behaviors and characteristics that the research literature indicates are attributes of effective teachers. If the graduates do demonstrate these attributes, then the program is deemed to be effective. As Medley states, "In program evaluation, teacher educators examine the relationships between the *training experiences* teachers have and the *performance competencies* they exhibit in the classroom. To the extent that the training experiences produce the competencies defined as objectives of the training program, the program is evaluated as effective" (Medley, 1977, p. 69).

The other institutions tended to employ what might be called a "goal-attainment" model. This approach examines the degree of congruency (or discrepancy) between what the program attempted to accomplish and what actually occurred. This type of evaluation requires that the teacher education program have specified its desired *processes* as well as its outcomes. Particular questions which guided the evaluation inquiry about the effectiveness of the programs were developed and these questions mirrored the goals and objectives of the programs.

This goal-attainment approach fits within a broader input-output model. The input-output model describes and measures the inputs to the teacher education program, including the trainees' knowledge and characteristics. The processes of the training system are described and measured to see if the various components of the system are operating according to their stated functions. The graduates, i.e., the products, are measured to see if they have acquired the knowledge, behaviors, and attitudes the program had as its goals. If discrepancies between what was intended and what actually occurred are detected, then that information can be used by program managers to make necessary adjustments in the program's operations.

Types of Data Collected. The types of data collected by the eight institutions can be grouped into at least six different categories: (1) teacher characteristics and demographic data; (2) teacher effectiveness; (3) program effectiveness; (4) program characteristics; (5) contextual variables; and (6) pupil outcomes.

Teacher Characteristics and Demographic Data. Most of the institutions collect data on teacher trainee characteristics and attitude. Instruments such as the Minnesota Teacher Attitude Inventory, National Teacher Examination, Career Base Line Data Questionnaire, California F-Scale, Rokeach Dogmatism Scale, Teacher Concerns Checklist, Adjective Self-Description, Bown Self-Report Inventory, and One-Word Sentence Completion, are administered at various phases of the teacher education programs. Individual teachers' specific learning needs have been assessed with the Profile of Learning Priorities. In many cases, these instruments provide pre- and postprogram data to determine how students have been affected by the program. Usually demographic data such as age, sex, marital status, academic performance, and ethnicity are collected to see if they correlate with various input and output measures.

Teacher Effectiveness. Data on program graduates' effectiveness as teachers are collected from principals, supervisors, teaching peers, pupils, and through self-assessments and observers. Principal means of collecting these data are questionnaires, rating scales, personal interviews, and observation instruments. Some sample instruments include the Ryans Classroom Observation Record, Tuckman Teacher Feedback Form, the Fuller Affective Interaction Record, Student Evaluation of Teaching, Principal's Questionnaire, Teacher Evaluation by Supervisor Form, modified Flanders Interaction Analysis Category System, Language of the Classroom system, Hall's Instrument for Analysis of Science teaching, informal observation instruments, and institutionally developed instruments.

Program Effectiveness. Perceptual data on the teacher education program's effectiveness are collected from program graduates, student teachers, currently enrolled students, supervising teachers, and principals. The primary means of collecting these data are questionnaires, rating scales, and personal interviews; examples include the Professional Plans and Affiliations Questionnaire, and the Exit Interview Questionnaire. In most instances, nonstandardized instruments were developed to reflect the characteristics and objectives of each program.

Program Characteristics. A few of the institutions, such as the University of Houston and Weber State, collect data based on an analysis of curriculum materials used in the program. Teams of faculty members analyze instructional modules used in the programs to see if they conform to certain prespecified characteristics that are deemed desirable.

Contextual Variables. In order to better interpret teacher effectiveness data, some programs, such as Ohio State and Oregon College of Education, have collected contextual data on the communities, schools, and classrooms where student teachers and program graduates are teaching. (See Schalock's discussion of specific context factors in Chapter 2.) There is a growing body of evidence that indicates that such contextual variables as class size and school settings affect the perceived competence of teachers. Knowledge of the teaching context must obviously be considered in making judgments about either teacher or program effectiveness.

Pupil Outcomes. While several programs include in their evaluation designs the collection of pupil outcome data, few data have actually been collected. Whereas accountability proponents argue that data on student achievement are needed to evaluate teacher education program effectiveness, this argument rests on several assumptions, as Borich has indicated:

> By focusing on pupil performance, the relative gain model measures behavior at least one step removed from the training program. The effect of training must register not only on teacher measures, but also on tests of pupil performance. The relative gain model rests on the assumption that teacher competencies can be translated directly into pupil competencies and that potentially confounding variables can be statistically controlled to an extent sufficient to allow the effects of teacher training to filter down to the pupil (Borich, 1978, p. 40–41).

Borich is more optimistic than some that these assumptions can be met. The collection of pupil achievement data to evaluate teacher effectiveness has not proven to be either an easy task or one largely successful to this point in time. To stretch the linkage one more step and use pupil achievement data to evaluate teacher education programs' effectiveness seems unrealistic and hardly worth the effort in most cases from this perspective.

Data Analyses. Data that are useful for internal program decision making are not necessarily useful for research purposes; for example, they may have been gathered without much concern for such issues as establishing validity and reliability estimates for instruments used to gather data. Furthermore, some institutions have chosen to focus on questions and problems that are unique to their particular programs. Thus, their evaluation data may not have generalizability beyond the decision-making processes of their own programs.

In contrast, other programs have taken care to use instruments whose estimates of validity and reliability are established, and have attempted to answer questions that are of general interest to teacher educators; i.e., they began to address the issue of external validity Schalock argues for. Western Kentucky University, for example, collects data on over 200 variables, and in many instances employs repeated measures. The evaluators at that institution conduct their analyses to answer such questions as: (1) What are factors related to perceived problems of first-year teachers? (2) Can any probable factors be identified related to teachers' entry into teaching and retention after three years of teaching? (3) Does teacher behavior change with experience?

Those programs that have been conducting evaluation efforts for several years are accumulating a data base with a significant number of subjects. For meaningful analyses to occur, it is essential that data be collected on a regular, ongoing basis. One-shot evaluation efforts every five or seven years will not yield very useful data for program decision making or for research findings.

The Austin colloquium proved valuable for several reasons. It offered the opportunity for teacher education program evaluators to meet together and share information about one another's evaluation programs. Different methods of conducting the evaluation process were discovered, and publication of the papers presented has provided an opportunity for sharing information outside the colloquium. Participants also were able to discuss common problems and to share ideas about how to improve evaluation procedures. And, perhaps most importantly, the colloquium provided moral support to the participants to continue their efforts.

There are many other institutions in addition to those attending the Austin colloquium that have conducted evaluations of their teacher education programs. The Austin participants are highlighted here because their evaluation projects are among the best known and documented. From their documentation and experiences many implications can be derived for current practice.

IMPLICATIONS FOR CURRENT TEACHER EDUCATION PROGRAM EVALUATION

Establish Goals for the Evaluation Process

The most critical step in the evaluation process is the clear explication of goals. Since evaluation is "the process of obtaining information and using it to form judgments which in turn are to be used in decision-making" (TenBrink, 1974, p. 8), the first step in the evaluation process is to specify the judgments and decisions that need to be made regarding the program's evaluation. How this process is accomplished will vary according to the programmatic decision-making process at each institution, but it must be accomplished.

If the major goal of the evaluation is to make judgments about the effectiveness of the teacher education program operation and, on the basis of those judgments, make decisions about program revision, then it seems that certain judgments are basic and essential. Among these are:

1. What is the effectiveness of our program's graduates: (a) initially, (b) over time, and (c) in different settings? (Again, recall the emphasis in Chapter 2 on time and context as critical moderating variables.)
2. To what extent and in what ways do the program's graduates attribute their effectiveness to experiences received during the training program? To other experiences?
3. What effect does the program have on the characteristics, knowledge, skills, and attitudes of trainees?
4. How long do graduates of the program stay in teaching? How does this compare with local, state, and national norms?
5. How do graduates of the program perceive it and its various components? Are they satisfied with their preparation?
6. How do significant others (supervising teachers, principals, personnel directors) perceive the program and its capabilities?
7. What is the congruency/discrepancy of what the program intends and what is actually occurring?
8. Does the program conduct its educative processes according to what research and theory indicate should be taking place?
9. What kinds of students with what attributes does the program attract?
10. What teaching behaviors or styles do our graduates manifest in the classroom?
11. What is the effectiveness of the program in terms of cost-benefit analyses?

While some educators strongly urge that another judgment be made as to whether graduates of the program make a difference with kids, for most teacher education programs this is an unrealistic expectation. Linkages between teacher behaviors, pupil behaviors, and pupil product outcomes desperately need to be made, but seem to be beyond the reach of most teacher education program evaluations. When these linkages have been discovered, then teacher education programs should be accountable for building them into the training programs. Until such time that this is feasible, however, this issue should remain in the domain of process-product researchers and not be imposed upon teacher education program evaluators.

Many other questions could be asked as part of the evaluation process, but these seem to be the major ones that are critical for adequately evaluating a program. Certainly many other questions concerning relationships between trainee characteristics and competency acquisition, for example, could be built into the evaluation design for research purposes.

Describe the Information Needed

After the evaluation decisions and judgments have been specified, program evaluators must identify the information needed to make the judgments. For example, in order to make a good judgment about what graduates think were the strong and weak points of the program, it is necessary to obtain information on this issue from the graduates. What specific information we obtain will depend on what particular judgments we want to make about the various components of the program. Do we want their opinions of specific courses? Specific objectives or competencies they were asked to meet? Advisement functions? The list could go on and on according to the nature of the specific program being evaluated. The major point to be made is that information should not be gathered for its own sake; it needs to be directly related to the goals of the evaluation process.

HOW WILL THE INFORMATION BE COLLECTED?

There are four major techniques or methods for obtaining evaluative information: observation, inquiry, analysis, and testing. Which technique to use depends on the kind of information required, the amount of time available, and the amount of accuracy needed. Using the same example as in the section above, inquiry would probably be the best technique to obtain graduates' opinions regarding strong and weak points of the program. On the other hand, if information were desired regarding what teaching skills a sample of graduates possessed, observing them teach would probably be the best way to obtain the information. (TenBrink's summary of the major characteristics of each of the four information-gathering techniques is shown in Table 5.1.)

TABLE 5.1   A Summary of the Major Characteristics of Each of the Four Information-gathering Techniques

	Inquiry	Observation	Analysis	Testing
Kind of Information Obtainable	Opinions Self-perceptions Subjective judgments Affective (especially attitudes) Social perceptions	Performance or the end products of some performance Affective (especially emotional reactions) Social interaction psychomotor skills Typical behavior	Learning outcomes during the learning process (intermediate goals) Cognitive and psychomotor skills Some affective outcomes	Attitude and achievement Terminal goals Cognitive outcomes Maximum performance
Objectivity	Least objective Highly subject to bias and error	Subjective but can be objective if care is taken in the construction and use of the instruments	Objective but not stable over time	Most objective and reliable
Cost	Inexpensive but can be time consuming	Inexpensive but very time consuming	Fairly inexpenisve Preparation time is somewhat lengthy but crucial	Most expensive but most information gained per unit of time

SOURCE: From *Evaluation: A Practical Guide for Teachers* by Terry D. TenBrink. Copyright © 1974 McGraw-Hill Book Company.

Identify Specific Instruments

Once appropriate techniques have been chosen to obtain particular information, specific instruments need to be selected or constructed. If one of the evaluation goals is to conduct research on program variables, then it would be wise to use instrumentation whose estimates of reliability and validity are known, if at all possible. There is also no need to go to the trouble and expense of constructing new instruments if existing instruments are appropriate for the information needs. If no existing instrument is suitable, then one must be developed. When development is necessary, pilot testing the instruments to ensure its adequacy is, of course, a wise procedure.

Collect and Analyze Data

This aspect of the evaluation process seems self-evident, but is full of pitfalls. When instruments have been selected or constructed, they need to be administered at the appropriate times and places. This phase needs considerable planning to ensure that data are collected in an appropriate manner. Aspects to consider include allowing time for reproduction of instruments, contacting the sample population, training observers, establishing data administration and collection procedures, and choosing data analysis techniques and personnel. Whether descriptive and/or statistical analyses are used will depend on the nature of the data and for whom they are intended. In any case, the data need to be analyzed and summarized.

Forming Judgments and Decisions

The last phase completes the circle by linking back to the first phase where it was specified what judgments and decisions needed to be made. Using appropriate data, each judgment and decision is made by the persons responsible for making them, and these judgments and decisions then should be reported to those who will be affected by them. Reporting the evaluation process and findings may take two forms. One form may be that of a technical report that is statistically oriented and contains data tabulations. This report may be used for research purposes or for use by program managers. Another form may be a summary of the data and major decisions and judgments that is readily understood by most of the faculty. It is important that the report be presented in a manner and form that will be useful to those for whom it is intended.

Lessons We Have Learned

Variety of Evaluation Designs. There exists a wide variety of evaluation designs, ranging from simple "Toyota" models to extremely complicated "Cadillacs." Each type will take you to your destination but will differ in terms of what each costs. For example, simple follow-up studies, using mailed questionnaires to program graduates, will yield perceptual data regarding strong and weak points of the program and measures of satisfaction with how the program prepared its trainees to teach. More complicated evaluation designs will yield descriptive data on how the program operates; observational data on teaching performance for selected samples of student teachers and program graduates; content analysis data on instructional modules and other materials; perceptual data from graduates, current students, affiliated public school personnel, and college faculty; and research data on relationships among input-process-output variables of the program. There are, of course, many variations beteeen these "Toyota" and "Cadillac" models. The goals of the evaluation process will determine how complicated a design is needed. Obviously, there is no one evaluation design that is appropriate for all institutions.

Program Personnel Involvement. If there is an expectation that faculty members will use the evaluation data to form judgments and make decisions about program modification, then faculty ownership must be developed in the initial study design stage. If the evaluation data are to be perceived by faculty members as being valid and persuasive then faculty must be involved in the formulation of the evaluation and research questions. Operationally, this principle implies that while small committees of faculty and/or evaluators may take the leadership in the evaluation design, the faculty as a whole needs to review, make modifications when deemed appropriate, and then approve the design.

Experience with the eight institutions represented at the Austin colloquium suggests that anything short of this type of faculty approval process will result in the faculty not accepting or using the data. As Ayers reports, "It is felt that the faculty of the teacher preparation programs have not made full use of the data collected. In turn, changes and improvements in the programs for the preparation of teachers have been slow in emerging" (Hord & Hall, 1979, p. 106). When the majority of the faculty have not been involved in the evaluation design they tend to perceive the whole evaluation effort as something that is being done *to* them rather than *for* them. When this perception occurs, the result is an evaluation report that produces some scholarly papers for a few individuals, but generally is ignored by the faculty responsible for implementing program changes.

Data Understandability. Another reason why many faculty don't use the data produced by program evaluation studies is the form in which data are presented. Cooper's law of evaluation, coined expressly for this occasion, states: "Faculty use of program evaluation data is inversely proportional to the sophistication of the statistical analysis." While complicated statistical analyses may be necessary for certain research aspects of the evaluation design, data which have implications for program revision need to be presented in a form whose practical applications are readily understood. Faculty also need to meet together to have the evaluation results interpreted and to discuss the implications of the data for program revision. Do not expect distribution of evaluation results to individual faculty members alone to produce program changes. Faculty need the opportunity to discuss the results with colleagues and decide what actions are implied by the data.

Data Management and Analysis. Program evaluation studies should produce data that are timely and credible. There is nothing more frustrating in the whole evaluation process than to experience an unreasonable time lag from data collection to analysis and reporting. Many factors may contribute to this problem, including computer programming problems, insufficient personnel, and competing task demands. Regardless of the problem, if data are perceived as "old" they will not be persuasive. Faculty members will discount the results, arguing that the program has moved beyond the point at which the data were collected and the data therefore are no longer valid.

There is also a credibility problem created when an inordinate time lag occurs between data collection and data analysis. Faculty begin to believe that all the time and effort spent in collecting the data were wasted because no results are forthcoming. Therefore, careful attention must be paid to this issue or all the effort might be spent in vain.

Cost of Evaluation Efforts. Returning to the "Toyota" and "Cadillac" analogy, costs will vary according to model selected. It is sometimes difficult to separate real costs, actual dollars expended, from costs that can be covered by reassigned duties of personnel already on the payroll. It is clear, however, that some new expenditure of funds is usually required. Evaluation studies that incorporate research questions are likely to be more expensive due to the more stringent data requirements.

Tennessee Technological University spends $15,000 per year for the development and implementation of its longitudinal study of graduates. Oregon College of Education spent $10,000 for its on-site observational study of a sample of 24 teachers, and $2,000 for a telephone-mail follow-up design for a similar number of teachers. The Univeristy of Oregon Secondary Teacher study, using on-site observations of 25 graduates, spent $3,500 in out-of-pocket expenses. The costs were kept at a minimum by using university supervisors to collect the data for the on-site visitations.

We have learned many do's and don'ts from the experiences of those who have taken teacher education program evaluation seriously, but much more is needed. The research and development needs of teacher education program evaluation is discussed next.

NEEDED RESEARCH AND DEVELOPMENT

As an underfunded, underconceptualized field, teacher education program evaluation has many research and development needs. Some of the most pressing and vital needs are described below.

Conceptual and Operational Models

Probably the most pressing need is the definition and establishment of parameters regarding what program evaluation entails. In other words, what questions can legitimately be asked regarding program evaluation, what variables are involved, what methodologies can be used to gather data, and what specific instrumentation is available to measure the different variables? Both *conceptual* and *operational* models for evaluating teacher education programs are needed.

There have been some attempts to define and apply parts of a conceptual framework to the evaluation of teacher education programs (Borich, 1978; Borich, 1977; Gage, 1972, Peck & Dingman, 1968; Sandefur, 1970). However, a comprehensive model spanning both preservice and inservice teacher education programs has yet to be developed.

The major elements in such a model have been outlined by Cooper, et al. (1980). These authors urge that the model provide: (1) a comprehensive framework useful to both preservice and inservice teacher education programs; (2) a comprehensive list of variables which can be empirically or theoretically related to the effectiveness of teacher education programs, including such variables as teacher trainee characteristics, relevant context variables, training process variables, and desired outcomes of each program; and (3) analytic models (sampling designs, measurement strategies, statistical procedures) which are appropriate to the size and nature of the evaluation questions to be answered in a given study.

These authors also recommend that an implementation manual and a catalog of research/evaluation instruments accompany the conceptual model. The implementation manual would describe how the model can be used, which variables seem to be most important, and what kinds of alternative designs are available, along with cost estimates for conducting the evaluation efforts. The catalog of research/evaluation instruments would identify instruments useful for measuring the important variables in the model. For each instrument information regarding availability, validity and reliability estimates, cost estimates, and programs where the instrument has been used could be reported. Examples of different types of studies, from simple to complex, could be discussed in the implementation manual, complete with illustrative variables, instruments, analytic designs, and a review of present informed opinion about practical implications. Table 5.2 outlines some of the variables that might be included in such a conceptual model.

Such a model, and its accompanying implementation manual and catalog of evaluation instruments, would go a long way in helping teacher education institutions conduct more effective and useful evaluation studies of their programs. Without such guidelines, the quality of evaluation efforts will continue to suffer.

Longitudinal Studies

One-shot evaluation studies conducted shortly before NCATE visits will yield only limited research information. Longitudinal studies such as those being conducted at Oregon College of Education, Tennessee Technological University, and Western Kentucky University are vitally needed. These institutions have been collecting evaluation follow-up data on their program graduates for years and, in the case of the Oregon College of Education, plans exist to follow a sample of its graduates over a

TABLE 5.2 Categories of Variables to Be Included in Conceptual Model

Context Variables	Instructor Input Variables	Trainee Input Variables	Training Process Variables	Program Outcomes Variables

1. Curricular characteristics
2. Design of program
3. Time allotted for training
4. Program objectives
5. Institutional characteristics
6. Constituency expectations
7. Etc.
	1. Instructor characteristics
	2. Knowledge of program's content and procedures
	3. Attitudes toward trainees, peers, administrators
	4. Etc.
		1. Trainee characteristics: knowledge, interests, attitudes, concerns, and other relevant personal characteristics	1. Observations of teaching-learning process
			  a. instructor behavior
			  b. trainee behavior
			2. Trainee interactions with curriculum materials
			3. Etc.
				1. Trainee characteristics
				  a. individual skills, concerns, etc.
				  b. efforts on pupils
				  c. knowledge
				  d. attitudes
				2. Program effects on instructors
				3. Program effects on institutional policies and practices
				4. Program effects on constituent groups
				5. Etc.

SOURCE: Cooper, et al. *Needed: Systematic evaluation of teacher education programs*. Houston: Texas, University of Houston, 1980, unpublished manuscript, p. 5.

nine-year time span. By continued sampling over long time periods, patterns may be identified. Moreover, replication of findings is most important when conducting research on teaching and teacher education, and longitudinal evaluation studies allow for the possibility of replication occurring.

Figure 5.1 illustrates another longitudinal study, Western Kentucky University's design for collecting data on program graduates. Participants are first observed as undergraduate student teachers, and again at the end of their first, third, and fifth years of teaching. Each year begins a new cycle of the evaluation, and each cycle consists of four phases. Phase 1 concentrates on evaluating student or preservice teachers, and subsequent phases evaluate the same participants as inservice teachers.

FIGURE 5.1 Cycle and Phase Arrangement for TPEP

	1972	1973	1974	1975	1976	1977	1978
CYCLE I	Phase 1	Phase 2		Phase 3		Phase 4	
CYCLE II		Phase 1	Phase 2		Phase 3		Phase 4
CYCLE III			Phase 1	Phase 2		Phase 3	
CYCLE IV				Phase 1	Phase 2		Phase 3
CYCLE V					Phase 1	Phase 2	
CYCLE VI						Phase 1	Phase 2
CYCLE VII							Phase 1

SOURCE: Adams, R. D. Western Kentucky University follow-up evaluation of teacher education graduates. In S. M. Hord & G. E. Hall (Ed.), *Teacher education program evaluation and follow-up studies: A collection of current efforts*. Austin, Texas: Research and Development Center for Teacher Education, The University of Texas at Austin, 1979, p. 11.

There are certain types of research questions on teaching and teacher education that evaluation data can help to answer. Schalock in the Chapter 2 has identified three types of studies which can be conducted within the context of operating teacher education programs: (1) policy-oriented studies, (2) practice-oriented studies, and (3) basic research studies. Within this framework, potential research questions can and should be developed. However, all teacher education programs are not equally worth studying, nor are they equally capable of conducting the needed type of evaluation efforts to produce good research. Selected institutions, along with specialists in evaluation and research on teacher education, need to be identified and funded to conduct research studies which attempt to answer critical questions.

Collaboration and Dissemination

The participants at the Austin colloquium discovered mutually beneficial results from sharing ideas and findings. As the papers presented at that meeting were disseminated, the organizers of the colloquium, Hall and Hord of the Research and Development Center for Teacher Education, The University of Texas at Austin, received many inquiries from individuals wishing to become part of a communication network on teacher education program evaluation. They have compiled such a list and are attempting to disseminate new findings among these individuals and to facilitate communication.

Evaluation and research efforts are likely to have much greater payoff if some coordination and collaboration occurs among the institutions conducting studies. For instance, institutions seeking the answers to similar questions might use the same instrumentation, thus facilitating the comparison of research findings. A network of institutions that are seriously engaged in program evaluation needs to be encouraged.

Comparative Studies

If a network of institutions can be developed, and if research questions and instrumentation can be coordinated, then comparative studies among different institutions will be facilitated. These comparative studies are needed to make normative judgments about the teaching effectiveness of program graduates. Also, the concern for utility and generalizability of research results requires that studies be replicated in a variety of educational contexts.

As in invariably the case, one of the greatest needs is financial support. Up to now almost all the funding support for program evaluation has come from resources within institutions. These funds have been relatively small in comparison to the money spent on the instructional functions of teacher education programs. If program evaluation efforts are to improve, it appears that institutions must commit a larger portion of their budgets to such efforts. Furthermore, if interinstitutional cooperation and mutual research efforts are to develop, funds from external sources need to be sought. Without such funding the major research and development needs identified in this paper are unlikely to be fulfilled.

SUMMARY

Despite the limited funding available, there have been a limited number of well-conceived attempts to evaluate teacher education programs and much can be learned from the experiences of these institutions. Beyond these "lighthouse" evaluation programs, however, exists a state of relative darkness. Most teacher education faculty have had little experience conceptualizing how one evaluates a teacher education program, what variables are involved, what data to gather, what instruments to use to collect the data, and how evaluation efforts may best be used to guide program improvement. Given existing presses to evaluate and conduct research on teacher education programs and the limited conceptual understanding of how to go about this process, teacher educators are placed in a real dilemma. This bind could well result in frustration, poorly done research, and the inability to respond adequately to accountability demands. Teacher education can ill afford these consequences.

Through properly designed and executed evaluation efforts, research questions can be identified and answered within the context of *operating* teacher education programs. *Collaborative* efforts facilitated by a communications network and guided by a conceptual framework could stimulate progress in research and provide opportunities for replication so necessary to the advancement of teacher education theory and practice. By following the latter course, those in teacher education will be able to better demonstrate accountability and at the same time improve the profession.

BIBLIOGRAPHY

Borich, G. D. *The appraisal of teaching.* Reading, Massachusetts: Addison-Wesley, 1977.

Borich, G. D. *Three school-based models for conducting follow-up studies of teacher education and training.* Austin, Texas: The University of Texas at Austin, 1978.

Cooper, J. M. *Improving teacher education program evaluation.* Paper presented to the national invitational conference entitled, "Exploring Issues in Teacher Education: Questions for Further Research." Sponsored by the Research and Development Center for Teacher Education, the University of Texas at Austin, and the National Institute of Education, January 10–12, 1979, 16 pgs.

Cooper, J. M., Felder, R. D., Hollis, L. Y., & Peck, R. F. *Needed: Systematic evaluation of teacher education programs.* Houston, Texas: University of Houston, 1980 unpublished manuscript, 12 pgs.

Gage, N. L. *Teacher effectiveness and teacher education.* Palo Alto, California: Pacific Book Publishers, 1972.

Hord, S. M., & Hall, G. E. (Eds.). *Teacher education program evaluation and follow-up studies: A collection of current efforts.* Austin, Texas: The Research and Development Center for Teacher Education, The University of Texas at Austin, 1979.

Implications of experience in teacher education program follow-up studies for future work. Symposium papers presented at the annual meeting of the American Educational Research Association, San Francisco, April, 1979. Austin, Texas: The Research and Development Center for Teacher Education, The University of Texas at Austin.

Medley, D. M. *Teacher competence and teacher effectiveness.* Washington, D.C.: American Association of Colleges for Teacher Education, 1977.

Peck, R. F., & Dingman, H. F. Some criterion problems in evaluation of teacher education. *Psychological Reports,* 1968, *23,* 300.

Sandefur, J. T. *An illustrated model for the evaluation of teacher education graduates.* Washington, D.C.: American Association of Colleges for Teacher Education, 1970.

Schalock, H. D. *Closing the knowledge gap: CBTE programs as a focus of and context for research in education.* Multi-State Consortium on Performance Based Teacher Education, Syracuse University, 1975.

Schalock, H. D. *Eating humble pie: Notes on methodology in teacher education research.* Paper presented to the national invitational conference entitled, "Exploring Issues in Teacher Education: Questions for Further Research." Sponsored by the Research and Development Center for Teacher Education, The University of Texas at Austin, and the National Institute of Education, January 10–12, 1979, 19 pgs.

Standards for accreditation of teacher education. Washington, D.C.: National Council for Accreditation of Teacher Education, 1970.

Standards for the accreditation of teacher education. The accreditation of basic and advanced preparation programs for professional school personnel. Washington, D.C.: National Council for Accreditation of Teacher Education, 1981.

TenBrink, T. D. *Evaluation: A practical guide for teachers.* New York: McGraw-Hill, 1974.

6

Research on the Beginning Teacher: Implications for Teacher Education

John M. Johnston

University of Wisconsin-Milwaukee

Kevin Ryan

Ohio State University

In the professional life span of teachers, few periods of time compare in impact and importance with the first year of teaching. The beginning of a teaching career for some may be charged with excitement, challenge, and exhilarating success. For others, the first year of teaching may seem to be confusing, uncontrollable, filled with unsolvable problems, and threatened by personal defeat and failure. For many, beginning to teach is a unique and more balanced mixture of success, problems, surprises, and satisfactions. For all engaged in the educational enterprise, the first year of teaching has come to be recognized as a unique and significant period in the professional and personal lives of teachers.

PROFESSIONAL LIVES OF BEGINNING TEACHERS

It is probably safe to assume that at no other time in their teaching career will teachers be so unsure of their own competence as during the first year of teaching. Beginning teachers are faced with difficult challenges to their professional self-confidence. In many instances they are uncertain about what they should actually do in the classroom. What course of action should be taken? What strategies should be used to meet the varying demands of the work of teaching? Also, first-year teachers are faced with gnawing doubts: Will students listen to me? Will they do the things I ask? Will I keep my job as enrollments decline?

The circumstances of beginning teachers are further complicated by administrators' and colleagues' lack of knowledge of the beginners' competence. For students, parents, other teachers, and principals, beginning teachers are a new and unknown entity. Beginning teachers are strangers to the school communities they enter. They bring no credible background of professional experience. They bring no reputation other than "beginner." At no other time in a teacher's professional career are others so unsure of the beginner's competence as during his or her first year of teaching.

First-year teachers are aliens in a strange world; a world that is both known and unknown to them. Though they have spent thousands of hours in schools watching teachers and involved in the schooling process, first-year teachers are not familiar with the specific school setting in which they begin to teach. Beginning teachers must learn the geography of their new community setting: the location of supplies, the music teacher's room, and the P.E. director's office. They are not familiar with the rules and regulations which govern the internal operation of the school community and the larger system in which they are teaching. For instance, procedures for field trips, accident reports, professional leave, and assigned duties may be neither clear nor readily available to beginning teachers.

Even more difficult to comprehend are the informal routines and customs of the school. Unless told, it might take the beginning teacher a while to realize that the principal always pulls fire drills during sixth period. A program set for Wednesday night by the beginning teacher might be in conflict with the local community's church attendance patterns. Such situations will likely prove troublesome for the first-year teacher who is not aware of the unwritten lore of the community.

Perhaps more important, first-year teachers do not know the other people in their work setting. Beginning teachers are not familiar with the names, faces, and personalities of those with whom they work. Beginners are outsiders entering an ongoing professional and social community. They bring to this community only a weak and embryonic sense of belonging to the profession of teaching. They have a more limited sense of belonging to the specific school community in which they are to teach.

PERSONAL LIVES OF BEGINNING TEACHERS

At the same time first-year teachers are facing an unfamiliar work setting, their personal lives are often undergoing reorientation and change as well

(Johnston, 1979b; Ryan et al., 1980). For many beginning teachers, life has been concerned with school, friends, and family. For most beginning teachers, completing college has been their primary endeavor. Their immediate and tangible goal has been graduation and finding a teaching position. Suddenly, over the short space of a summer or less, beginning teachers' lives are changed dramatically. They are no longer students. Now they are teachers. No longer can they rely on their knowledge, understanding, and experience of the student's role. They are now thrust into the role of teachers, a role they have observed countless times but only briefly tried out.

First-year teachers may face other changes in their lives as well. With their beginning teaching position—and initial paycheck—may come the first real financial independence in their lives. They must alter their life style to accommodate a new budget and to attend to other responsibilities incumbent upon their new status as teachers. Family relationships often must be altered to accommodate the change from student to full-time wage earner. Since they are often thrust into a new locale, suitable housing must be obtained and made livable. The beginning teacher must learn where to shop for his or her various needs, where to purchase car insurance, where to find doctors and dentists, and where to register to vote.

In this brief introduction to the problems of the beginning teacher we have sketched a few of the more obvious factors affecting their professional and personal lives. Our intent was to provide a backdrop that may be helpful in interpreting our knowledge about the induction of beginning teachers. We suggest, in the balance of this essay, that knowledge about the beginning teacher and the process of beginning to teach consists largely of intuition, personal wisdom, advice, and recollections. It is based on a limited foundation of thoughtful research and scholarship. We further suggest that what has been learned from teacher-induction research and is available to teacher educators and school practitioners is rarely put into practice.

LITERATURE ABOUT THE BEGINNING TEACHER

References to the beginning teacher in the literature are longstanding. In this brief section of the chapter we examine *nonresearch* professional literature published on the beginning teacher in the United States from 1930 to the present. Books, journal articles, and microfiche will be considered in terms of four overlapping categories proposed by Applegate et al. (1977): (1) reflective interpretations of beginning teachers' experiences, (2) advice about the first year of teaching, (3) scholarly essays about the beginning teacher and the process of beginning to teach, and (4) reports of beginning teachers' own experiences. Research on the beginning teacher will be considered separately in greater detail following this overview.

Reflective Interpretations of Beginning Teachers' Experiences

This category consists of accounts of beginning teachers, interpreted from the theoretical perspectives of anthropology, psychology, and sociology. Fuchs (1969) and Eddy (1969) were the first to bring theoretical perspectives from anthropology to the self-reports of beginning teachers. Eddy (1969), for example, using reports of 22 beginning teachers in inner-city schools, interprets their experiences through theories of transition. Ryan's (1970) interpretive essay is combined with accounts of three inner-city and three suburban beginning teachers. More recently, Ryan et al. (1980) offer accounts of 12 beginning teachers' experiences, each of which has been written by an observer after extensive classroom observation and interviews. These 12 accounts present fine-grained portraits which describe a range of experiences in the professional and personal lives of these 12 beginning teachers. These accounts provide a unique view of the reality of the first-year teaching experience since the participant's subjective, first-hand reports are complemented by the more objective perspective of the trained observer. These informed accounts needed insight into the ecological realities of the beginning teacher. Such description and interpretation represents a fundamental item in any research agenda into the study of beginning teachers.

Advice about Beginning to Teach

The most frequent type of professional literature about beginning to teach comprises this category (Johnston, 1978). Most often written by higher education faculty members, titles such as "Seven Touchstones for Beginning Teachers" (Krajewski & Shuman, 1976), or simply "Advice for Beginning Teachers" (Mangione, 1969) are commonplace. The advice frequently focuses on classroom management or discipline (Doyle, 1975; Reimer, 1970; Visor, 1973), planning for the first days (Coard, 1957; Dawson, 1960), or planning in general (Andrews, 1967; Bromberg, 1968). Such advice may be highly specific admonitions to beginning teachers in specific subject areas such as agriculture, business, typing, music, or speech. More frequently, however, advice is directed to all beginning teachers. The type of advice offered to beginning teachers also varies greatly. Applegate et al. (1977) noted that advice offered in one publication may actually contradict advice offered in another.

While advice *to* beginning teachers is most frequently represented in this category, advice *about* beginning teachers is also common. Such advice is usually written by college faculty or school administrators and is directed to other principals and supervisors (Brown, 1973; Brown & Williams, 1977; Marashio, 1971; Southwell, 1970; and Wofforo 1931). Such advice represents opinions about the nature of the support beginning teachers require and the sorts of problems which supervisory personnel should be watching for.

Scholarly Essays about Beginning to Teach

Analyses of specific aspects of beginning to teach comprise an important part of the literature about the beginning teacher. These papers address topics and issues such as anxiety (Jersild, 1966), early career experiences (Bush, 1965), socialization (Jackson, 1974), survival (Ryan, 1974), personal and professional development (Glassberg, 1979), induction (Howey & Bents, 1979; Rehage, 1968), and internships (Bents & Howey, 1979). In contrast to reflective interpretations of beginning teachers' experiences, these essays frequently examine a single aspect of the first-year experience in tightly focused analyses which combine relevant social science theory and research data with the writer's understanding of the world of beginning teachers. These essays thus provide a basis for understanding salient and specific facets of beginning to teach.

Reports of Beginning Teachers' Experiences

First-person reports by beginning teachers in the process of their beginning experience comprise this category (Banks, 1939; Leiberman, 1975; Milius, 1952; Smith, 1949; Spinning, 1960). Publication of beginning teachers' accounts of their experience are a common feature of the professional literature about beginning teachers. The usual format includes an account of unanticipated events, problems encountered and conquered, and satisfactions derived. A predictable feature of such accounts is their largely positive aura. Only one account with an overall negative tone was encountered in a recent analysis of professional periodical literature (Johnston, 1978).

RESEARCH ON THE BEGINNING TEACHER

In gathering material for this review, we were faced with the question: What constitutes a beginning teacher? Does enrollment in the first professional preservice teacher education course constitute beginning status as suggested by Gaede (1978)? Is beginning status earned at the start of the first field experience or student teaching (as Coates and Thorensen (1976) imply)? This lack of clarity when using the term "beginning teacher" can pose problems in interpretation and application of research findings (Tisher, Fyfield, & Taylor, 1978).

   In the present review, research was included if any of the subjects were described as first-year teachers *in their initial professional experience following graduation*. We have further limited the present review to studies of beginning teachers in this country, though acknowledging that considerable attention is being given to the induction process in other countries (Bolam, 1973, 1976; Tisher, 1978).

Throughout this chapter, the related terms *induction practices, induction programs*, and *induction strategies* are used to refer *to deliberate actions designed to provide entry-level support for beginning teachers.* These supportive efforts are designed to increase the likelihood that beginning teachers will be successful in their initial teaching experiences, and will continue in the profession. Typically, induction practices are not made available to "experienced" teachers. Reduction of teaching loads, extra time for preparation, and time off for observation of other teachers are but a few examples of common induction practices. Generally, induction practices are extended only to teachers during their first or second years of teaching.

In the remainder of this chapter, research on beginning teachers will be considered in five clusters: (1) the problems of beginning teachers, (2) the psychosocial aspects of beginning to teach, (3) evaluation of preservice and inservice induction efforts, (4) discipline and the beginning of school, and (5) qualitative studies of beginning to teach. Current induction efforts will also be considered in relation to this research. In the final section of this chapter an agenda for further research on beginning to teach will be proposed.

Research on Problems of Beginning Teachers

The most frequent type of research literature on beginning teachers in the past five decades has focused in one form or another on the problems of the beginning teacher—a fact precisely paralleled in the nonresearch literature. The orientation of this research has varied little in the past 50 years. Initial efforts were concerned primarily with the identification of problems in order to improve supervisory support or as the basis for preservice curriculum development. Efforts to validate or evaluate teacher education programs or induction support programs also spawned the problems type of research. Efforts to predict performance of beginning teachers in varied settings resulted in other problems studies (Turner, 1967). Efforts to link problems to particular personality traits or teacher characteristics gave rise to still other studies of the problems of beginning teachers (Cohen & Brawer, 1967; Ort, 1964; Turner, 1965).

Among the earlier investigations, Barr and Rudisill (1930) studied 120 first- and second-year teachers on the assumption that knowledge of the most frequent problems of beginning teachers would constitute the basis for improved supervision practices. For purposes of comparison, general statements about the difficulties of beginning teachers were also secured from principals. Discipline, motivation of students, and organization of work and teaching materials were persistent difficulties identified throughout the first two years. Discipline, planning and organization, and what to expect of students were characteristic difficulties during the first two weeks of teaching.

Johnson and Umstattd (1932) also sought to identify classroom difficulties of beginning teachers in order to improve teacher-training programs. Using a list of beginning teacher problems gleaned from the literature and from perceptions of administrators, 119 first-year teachers were asked to rate on scale from 1 (always) to 7 (never) the frequency with which they encountered each of the problems. The problems most frequently identified were remarkably similar to those identified by Barr and Rudisill (1930). Eliassen (1932) employed a procedure much like Johnson and Umstattd (1932), and also obtained similar results. Kyte's (1936) study of problems confronting 141 beginning rural teachers employed a similar methodology, The author developed a list of 175 problems and asked the teachers to check a problem once if it was "troublesome" and twice if it was "very difficult." The findings identify instructional problems and, though not unlike those reported in the studies above, were more specific to features of rural schools. McGill (1948), in a study of beginning business teachers, obtained his data by means of "discussion" and an undescribed "survey" of beginning teachers. Grading, motivation of students, and classroom management were identified as the most prevelant problems. Flesher's (1945) study of problems of beginning teachers asked both teachers and administrators to rate the frequency, difficulty, and degree of seriousness of problems. The majority of problems faced by beginning teachers were concerned with relationships between teacher and pupil. Discipline problems were reported with the greatest frequency by both teachers and supervisors.

During the 1950s there was a marked increase in the frequency of survey research on the problems of beginning teachers. Research methods changed little during this period, nor were any significantly new problems discovered. Most researchers derived examples of beginning teacher problems from professional literature, or asked principals or supervisors to list the problems they observed in beginning teachers. Given a list of problems, researchers surveyed beginning teachers asking them how frequently the problem occurred, how difficult a problem it was, whether they needed help with it, and whether they received that help. Rarely were beginning teachers themselves asked directly: What problems do you perceive you have in your teaching?

Again, the general intent of the beginning teacher problems studied in the 1950s was the improvement of supervision during the first year. The studies assumed that if frequent and significant problems could be identified, then appropriate intervention could be taken by principals, supervisors, and to a lesser extent, preservice teacher education programs. The beginning teacher problems studies of the 1950s supplied no new wealth of information about the difficulties encountered by beginning teachers. Wey's study (1951) is representative. Wey found that both student teachers and beginning teachers have these problems: (1) handling problems of pupil control and discipline, (2) adjusting to deficiencies in school equipment, physical condition, and materials, (3) adjusting to the teaching assignment, (4) adjusting to needs, interests, and abilities of pupils, and (5) motivating pupil interest and response. Readers should note the similarity of Wey's (1951) findings with those of Barr and Rudisill (1930) 20 years earlier.

The procedures and findings of other problems studies demonstrate little variation. Strickland (1956) explored beginning teachers' rankings of the severity of adjustment problems, and the extent to which they had received help with these problems. Teachers were asked to rank problem statements taken from a survey of professional literature. Wallace (1951) surveyed new, but experienced teachers, as well as beginning teachers. Again, the professional literature supplied the list of problems. Lambert (1956) examined the status as well as problems of beginning teachers. Tower (1956) surveyed beginning teachers with a list of problem statements gathered from beginning teachers, experienced teachers, principals, and supervisors. Cable (1956) summarized findings from five dissertations on the problems of beginning teachers, each of which essentially used the procedures described above. The collective results of these investigations differed little from those of Wey (1951) and other studies of problems of beginning teachers undertaken in the previous two decades.

In contrast, however, to the 1930-through-1950 focus on the improvement of preservice programs and inservice supervision practices, several studies during the next two decades explored relations between personality traits or characteristics of beginning teachers and problems experienced in beginning to teach. Smith (1950) suggests that problems can be viewed as attributes of teacher personality. Thus, Stout (1952) queried 80 administrators and supervisors about deficiencies of beginning teachers for whom they were responsible and discussed these from the perspective of beginning teacher "personality and character traits." Later studies examined relationships existing between selected personality characteristics of beginning teachers and supervisors' ratings of the beginners' abilities to meet the general demands of their position. Research by Cohen and Brawer (1967), Ort (1964), and Turner (1965) used measures of teacher personality characteristics such as "warmth" and "friendliness" in attempts to predict teaching success and to explore relationships between the diverse characteristics of teachers and the kind of teaching environment to which particular constellations of characteristics might be most adaptive.

Other variables were also considered relative to problems encountered. In 1963 Dropkin and Taylor used a questionnaire containing 70 items categorized into 7 professional problem areas. Seventy-eight elementary school teachers were asked to rate the difficulty of the problems they experienced. Two preservice variables were correlated with each problem area scored: grade-point average, and the total score on the American Council on Educational (ACE) Pyschological Examination.

The problems in descending order of difficulty were: (1) discipline, (2) relations with parents, (3) methods of teaching, (4) evaluation, (5) planning, (6) materials and resources, and (7) classroom routines. Problem areas (1), (5), (6) and (7) were significantly related in a negative direction to grade-point average, and area (6) was significantly related in a negative direction to the ACE Psychological Examination scores.

Studies by Cornett (1969) and Turner (1967) examined the relationship of principals' and supervisors' ratings of beginning teachers with preservice course grades and teacher characteristic scales. Turner summarized, "On the basis of the present data it would be unwise to contend that one can predict with surety the kinds of problems that beginning elementary school teachers will have" (p. 256). Turner's remarks, though directed to his own study, can be meaningfully applied to the general line of research on predicting beginning teacher problems from personality characteristics. This line of inquiry did extend the general problems type of research by identifying problems associated with certain teacher characteristics and is suggestive of variables for further study in aptitude-treatment-interaction designs (recall Chapter 3).

Study of problems of beginning teachers sometimes leads to changes in inservice and preservice programs and instructional alternatives. Broadbent and Cruickshank's (1967) efforts to identify and analyze the problems of first-year teachers led to the development of simulation materials for use in the preservice teacher education program (Broadbent & Cruickshank, 1967). Some preservice teacher education program follow-up and evaluation efforts (Fowers & Shearon, 1976; Vittetoe, 1977) are also examples of beginning teacher problems studies and suggest areas from which program reform could proceed.

Given the relatively long history and frequency of efforts to study the problems of beginning teachers, there has been only a limited contribution to understanding the process of beginning to teach. Most studies of the problems of beginning teachers have not aimed for a complete accounting of the complex events in the lives of beginning teachers and thus questions can be raised regarding the extent to which this line of inquiry has even adequately explored beginning teachers' problems. Why, for example, has there been little new understanding of problems of beginning teachers since studies from the early 1930s (cf. Barr & Rudisill, 1930; Dropkin & Taylor, 1963; Flesher, 1945; Wey, 1951)? The problems identified in these studies, with minor exceptions, have apparently remained the same. The suggestion here is that methodological shortcomings may account for some limitations of the knowledge generated from beginning teacher problems studies.

Pencil and paper questionnaires and descriptive surveys provide little usable knowledge of the realm of specific teacher behaviors in specific school and classroom environments. This type of research provides only the most basic knowledge as a necessary first step for providing help to beginning teachers. A more fundamental methodological weakness stems, however, from the source of many problem statements in these surveys. In many studies, the professional literature was the source of problem statements to which beginning teachers were asked to respond. In others, data was bounded by the perceptions of problems by those outside the classroom. Rarely, as indicated earlier, were first-year teachers themselves involved in framing questions which addressed the problems they were experiencing.

Johnston (1978) has observed that the bulk of all periodical literature about beginning teachers was written by experienced teachers, administrators, and supervisors. In other instances, researchers polled experienced teachers, administrators, and supervisors asking them for their perceptions of problems of beginning teachers. Thus, he suggests that it is not surprising that the findings of 50 years of beginning teacher problems research closely parallels the non-research professional literature. There has been little opportunity for beginning teachers to identify with some precision problems other than those which their professional colleagues and superiors think they encounter. The research findings do reinforce the logical and intuitively common sense understandings about the transition from student to practicing professional, and the more general difficulties facing most anyone who begins any new job for the first time. To this point in time, however, research on the problems of beginning teachers provides little knowledge of why beginning teachers have certain problems; of why some beginners experience problems and others do not; of why some problems occur in some situations and not in others; and what can be done to prevent problems. As a general line of inquiry, research on the problems of beginning teachers has failed to move beyond the basic question, "What problems do beginning teachers experience?" and the provision of general suggestions for addressing these. Comprehensive ecological descriptions of the "who, what, when, why, and where" in the lives of beginning teachers is clearly needed with the beginning teacher accorded a more central role in the inquiry process.

Psychosocial Research on Beginning Teachers

There is no scarcity of psychosocial perspectives on the environment and the work of teaching in general (Bidwell, 1973; Dreeben, 1970; Elsbree, 1939; Lortie, 1975; Waller, 1967). There are also more focused considerations of research on schools as organizations (Dreeben, 1970, 1973; Lortie, 1973, 1975), the school as a place to work (Dreeben, 1973), and teaching as work (Becker, 1952; Geer, 1966; Lortie, 1973). There is considerably less knowledge of the psychosocial aspects of beginning to teach.

Lortie (1975) has observed that beginning teachers do not ease into the role of teacher. They are students in June and teachers in August.

There is in fact but brief opportunity for beginning teachers to learn the role of teacher before entering the professional work world. The socialization process is made more difficult since they are typically isolated from more experienced teachers when they begin teaching.

The socialization of beginning teachers was a frequent research topic in the 1960s. Perspectives from psychology and sociology have provided four alternative explanations of beginning teacher socialization. Edgar and Warren (1969) studied the developing values of beginning teachers. They examined how the values of sanctioning colleagues affected beginning teachers' values. Edgar and Warren presented a view of socialization which involves pressure on beginning teachers to change in socially "desirable" ways. They observed that coworkers with sanctioning and evaluative power over beginning teachers are likely to cause beginners to drop previous patterns of behavior and accept new behavior norms which are held by significant others in the work setting. (Note Haberman's concerns in Chapter 4.)

Hoy, in a series of studies with student teachers (1967) and first- and second-year teachers (1968, 1969) examined how the "pupil control ideology" of beginning teachers was shaped. He was concerned with idealistic new teachers who were confronted with a relatively custodial or control orientation as they became a part of the organization. Hoy argued the importance of such concern since he found that in most school subcultures good teaching and good discipline were equated. Hoy's (1969) findings support the general hypothesis that interaction with colleagues socializes student and beginning teachers to adopt a more custodial pupil control ideology.

Haller (1967) took a different perspective. In an ingenious sociolinguistic study, Haller demonstrated that increased contact with children changed certain aspects of teacher speech toward the direction of more childlike, less adult patterns. Haller suggested that teachers are rewarded by certain pupil behavior which teachers interpret as task achievement. In the collegial isolation of the work of teaching, such immediate indications of effective role performance have considerable power to modify teacher behavior. In this case, it was hypothesized that primary and experienced elementary teachers would evidence decreased speech complexity in their adult interactions as length of teaching experience increased. The hypothesis was supported in the case of teachers' use of complex modes of speech. Haller's postulation of an operant conditioning mechanism in teacher socialization is intriguing and bears further exploration. Such a conceptualization of classroom reward mechanisms offers a fruitful theoretical framework for further research on beginning to teach. Moreover, teachers' speech represents a potentially rich data source which has yet to be fully explored.

Wright and Tuska (1966, 1967, 1968) have studied the socialization of beginning teachers from a psychoanalytic perspective. They suggest that teacher behavior is affected to a considerable extent by certain relationships with parents and significant teachers during early childhood. Wright and Tuska (1967) found that childhood identifications with mother, father, or teacher affect prospective teachers' choices to work with primary, middle, and high school students. They further suggest that an understanding of an individual teacher's personal orientations should be incorporated in their preservice and inservice training.

In a later study (1968), they report that at the end of the first year of teaching, beginning teachers rated themselves significantly less happy and less inspiring, and significantly higher on acting impulsively, controlling, and blaming others for their problems than they were at the beginning of the first year. They interpret these findings in relation to the failure of the student-teaching experience to correct the fantasy impressions about teaching which underlie the decision to become a teacher. This line of inquiry holds potential for understanding why many beginning teachers leave teaching at the end of their first or second year.

Beyond these few sociological and psychological perspectives on how beginning teachers become socialized in the teaching professions, there is little research about the beginning teacher in the psychosocial domain. Ligana (1970), using the Minnesota Teacher Attitude Inventory (MTAI), examined beginning teacher attitudes toward students. He described a "curve of disenchantment," a strong downward change in beginning teachers' attitudes toward students during the first four months of teaching. He reports that beginning teachers' MTAI scores during this period are actually lower than those of students just entering training. Following the initial four months of teaching experience, beginning teacher attitudes level out and begin a slight rise.

Gaede (1978) studied beginning preservice teacher education students just prior to student teaching, just after student teaching, at the end of their first year of teaching, and at the end of their third year of teaching. He demonstrated that knowledge of teaching, as measured by the Professional Training Readiness Inventory, *decreased* significantly by the end of the first year of teaching, while it rose in all other groups. Gaede's findings are generally consonant with those of Collea (1972), Wright and Tuska (1968) and others.

Unlike the problems research, which simply affirms and describes particular aspects of the experience of beginning teachers, psychosocial research on the beginning teacher, however sparse, presents explanations about the important socialization process in the lives of beginning teachers. This line of research has provided a variety of tentative explanations which should be further researched. We are fortunate to have multiple perspectives from which to launch further research as Haberman has suggested in Chapter 4.

Preservice and Induction Evaluation Research

A number of similar studies were accomplished in the late 1960s and 1970s to evaluate preservice teacher education programs or induction programs. Only a handful have been published. Others are available on ERIC microfiche. Typical is Handley and Shills' (1973) study of work values and job attitudes of beginning teachers in vocational education in Mississippi. Studies such as this one examine specific populations in specific regions and thus are limited in their contribution to a broad understanding of the process of beginning to teach (Bisbee, 1973; Costa, 1975; McCampbell, 1970; Moore & Bender, 1976).

There are a few studies of general classroom teachers. For example, Blackburn and Crandall (1975) and Blackburn (1977) have studied populations of K-12 beginning teachers. These studies report a pilot program for aiding beginning teachers with the responsibility shared among the teacher-training institution, the local education agency, and the state department of education. The program sought to identify both common and specific needs for members of the experimental group, and to meet those needs. Questionnaires were used to determine beginning teacher needs. Pre- and posttests were administered to determine the initial status and progress of teachers. Interviews and summative questionnaires were used to determine the most effective means of support for teachers in the program. Data from the second year showed significantly higher levels for teacher attitudes and principal ratings of teacher competencies in the experimental group. However, no significant differences were observed in student progress or attitudes in either the control or experimental group during the first and second years of teaching.

As the effect of NCATE Standard 6.1 calling for follow-up studies of preservice teacher education programs is felt, and as more states mandate internship programs (Bents & Howey, 1979), additional research of this sort will likely be forthcoming.

Discipline and Beginning School

The remaining quantitative studies reviewed here suggest the importance of the first days of school in establishing patterns of appropriate student discipline. In studies by Moskowitz and Hayman (1974, 1976) structured observations and field notes were collected on both junior high first-year teachers and experienced teachers judged as "best" by their students. Results appear to support the contention that the struggle for effective instruction is often won or lost at the very beginning of the school year. The first contact with students appeared to be crucial in this regard. Moskowitz and Hayman found that differences between first-year and experienced teachers rated as "best" at the start of the school year related to climate-setting behaviors. The experienced teachers used the first day to get students oriented. First-year teachers tended to begin content activities more quickly. The experienced teachers smiled at and joked with students more than first-year teachers, and dealt more with student feelings than did first-year teachers.

Recent studies of effective classroom management at the beginning of the year have been conducted at the elementary level (Emmer, Evertson, & Anderson, 1979) and at the junior high school level (Emmer & Evertson, 1980). These studies, outgrowths of the Correlates of Effective Teaching Program at the Texas Research and Development Center, include beginning teachers in the samples but do not report data in terms of teacher experience. Initial data does, however, generally support Moskowitz and Hayman's findings.

In the Elementary School Study (Emmer, Evertson, & Anderson, 1979), ratings of the degree of student engagement at task were used to rank teachers for comparison on emergent organizational strategies. Successful managers made clear presentations to students about rules, procedures, and assignments. These teachers followed up by pointing out to the students in detail what they were and were not doing that was appropriate. They were consistent in this attention to detail. Successful managers had thought about, established, and communicated rules to students before problems arose. Finally, they considered the teaching of these rules and procedures as a very important part of the first weeks of instruction. It was clear that successful classroom managers had carefully promulgated clear, realistic expectations and rules on important areas of classroom procedure before classes began. Also, when school began, successful teachers seriously took the time to teach rules and procedures to their students.

The results of both of these studies are presently being applied in a limited pilot study which is examining the effects of training relatively inexperienced teachers prior to the start of school. This pilot has produced encouraging preliminary findings which suggest that training in initial management strategies results in less off-task behavior and more students on task during academic activities (Evertson, 1980). Among other findings. teachers in the treatment groups did a better job of teaching their students rules and procedures, and presented directions and instructions more clearly.

The efforts of the researchers at the Texas Research and Development Center for Teacher Education are encouraging. Their work models the importance of carefully designed and executed descriptive research linked to a thoughtful program of experimental inquiry. Such efforts are rare indeed in our quest for understanding and helping the beginning teacher.

Qualitative Research on the Beginning Teacher

Inquiry into the process of beginning to teach using field research methods from anthropology and sociology is also a relatively rare and recent phenomenon. In an effort to develop a fine-grained portrait of the life space of the first-year teacher, 18 beginning teachers were studied intensively during their first year (Ryan et al., 1980). Five semistructured interviews were recorded, the first before school began, and the final interview at the end of the year. Classroom observations were made frequently throughout the entire year and narrative field notes were developed. Additional telephone contacts, social interactions, and conversations and interviews with school faculty, administrators, and students resulted in considerable data. Throughout the study, the research team tried to maintain an "inside-outside" perspective; with the beginning teacher as an inside participant and the researcher as the outside, nonparticipant.

Analysis of data from the beginning of the school year (Applegate et al., 1977) examined first-year teachers' changing perceptions and relationships with others. This analysis first describes the changes which first-year teachers perceived along six dimensions: (1) surprises, (2) satisfactions, (3) trouble sets, (4) perceptions of self in relation to students, (5) attitudes toward teacher preparation, and (6) career plans. For example, it was observed that beginning teachers' perceptions of satisfactions related to students underwent a subtle shift between preschool interviews and interviews conducted three or four weeks after school had begun. Being with students was the most frequently stated source of expected satisfaction in the August preschool interviews. These anticipated satisfactions would come from positive events, "when things go well." However, after three weeks of teaching, satisfactions were not expressed in a positive sense, but rather as the absence of the negative: "When an unruly kid was good." Descriptive findings of this nature can serve as a basis for more focused study and as an indication of needed support as teachers begin their professional careers.

Analysis of beginners' perceptions of their professional preparation was undertaken later in the year (Ryan et al. 1979). Two themes emerged: a realization of the limits of teacher preparation programs and a valuing of first-hand experiences. Beyond these two themes, however, there was little consistency from teacher to teacher in their judgments about adequacy of their preparation.

The data were also analyzed for findings about the personal concerns of first-year teachers (Johnston, 1979b). Two specific types of personal concerns were identified. Type I personal concerns focused on the developmental tasks of adulthood and were not expressed in direct relationship to the work of teaching. Two examples of Type I personal concerns are: (1) becoming established in the city and community where employed, and (2) beginning and ending romantic relationships. Type II personal concerns were those in which aspects of the work of teaching were perceived as being responsible for, or contributing to the concern. Type II personal concerns are: (1) justifying to spouse the need and desire to work, and (2) time demands of the teaching job which interfere with social life.

At the end of the school year the complete data set was analyzed for first-year teachers' perceptions of changes (Johnston, 1979a). The Applegate et al. (1977) analysis demonstrated that beginning teachers varied greatly in their perceptions of changes early in the school year. However, by the close of school in this study, the similarity of response was so great among teachers that many of them used identical words and phrases to describe the ways they had changed. The beginning teachers' perceptions of how they had changed focused on their primary responsibility: the act of instruction. Beginning teachers found they were no longer strangers in their schools; that they had developed legitimate professional identities of their own. Most importantly, they expressed a growing sense of confidence in themselves as mature, capable professionals.

Newberry (1977), in an interesting study of environmental features of the beginning teacher's world, examined what teachers knew about what was happening in other classrooms, and how they acquired this knowledge. She discovered that beginning teachers were making use of subtle and indirect means to gather information about goings-on in other classrooms: nonverbal responses of others to their comments, observation of events and records, materials being carried by experienced teachers, and the like. Newberry also noted factors affecting whom beginning teachers would ask for help and whom they would not.

Though descriptive and primarily hypothesis-generating, qualitative examination of the lives of beginning teachers is of considerable value. Such studies are essential to a broader, more comprehensive understanding of the beginning teacher and of the process of beginning to teach.

In summary, the past five decades of research on the beginning teacher and the process of beginning to teach, though neither rich nor varied, do nonetheless provide us with guidance for current induction practices. From the accumulated findings of fewer than a hundred studies, the profession now has some degree of empirical validation for many of its beliefs about the process of beginning to teach. There is an extensive, though somewhat shallow, description of specific professional problems encountered by beginning teachers during the first year of teaching. Problems of discipline and classroom management typically have been reported. Research on problems of beginning teachers conducted during the past 50 years has also reliably identified other common problem areas: (1) planning and organization, (2) evaluation of students' work, (3) motivation of students, and (4) adjustment to the teaching environment. Multiple perspectives have also been identified from which to view the professional socialization of beginning teachers. There is an emerging though sketchy image of the professional and personal lives of beginning teachers. There are also better indications of what particular knowledge of teaching may be most useful to teachers as they begin their first year.

Training beginning teachers to establish, clarify, and teach to students certain classroom management or "going to school skills" is one example of this.

INDUCTION: RESEARCH AND CURRENT PRACTICE

The relationship between our research-based knowledge and current practices of induction of beginning teachers is a straightforward one. It is not unlike the beleaguered East Tennessee farmer's response during the Great Depression to the naive, young TVA agent's advice about innovative cultivation practices: "Son, I already know more about farming than I'm able to do." Simply stated, while we have much yet to learn it appears that the education profession knows more about the induction of beginning teachers than is employed in practice. For a variety of reasons outlined below, knowledge about the induction of beginning teachers is outrunning our ability to put that knowledge into practice. There is research-based support for many induction practices which have long been advocated on an intuitive basis or practiced in a limited fashion. Reduced load and released time for first-year teachers are but two such practices. Present research-based knowledge does not suggest radically different induction practices but supports practices that have been practiced on a limited scale for the past half century.

The National Association of Secondary School Principals' project on the induction of beginning teachers (Hunt, 1968) is generally representative of the type of support needed. The NASSP project contains several features which are supported by research findings. Included in the NASSP project were four common elements: (1) a teaching load reduced by one class period for the beginning teacher during the first year of employment; (2) a teaching load reduced by one class period for an experienced teacher who would advise and counsel the beginning teachers who were in the project; (3) assistance for beginners in finding and using good instructional materials; and (4) provision of special information on the character of the community and of the student body, and information on school policies. The NASSP project also attended to the timing and sequence of each of the component parts. The project began the moment the new teacher was hired. Information provided for the beginning teacher was paced and limited to the essentials necessary for the work at that particular time.

In another similar induction project, more specific emphasis was given to instruction and classroom management (McGinnis, 1968). Other programs focused on learning to organize time and activities, grouping students, achieving self-confidence, and developing a professional attitude (Noda, 1968). Others have stressed cooperation among universities and school systems (Blackburn, 1977). One has featured community involvement in the orientation of beginning teachers (Brown, 1973). In the 1930s and 1940s, considerable attention was paid to helping beginning teachers find suitable housing and become a part of the community (Edmonson, 1944; Hale, 1931), though this is not common today. These and many other induction practices suggested or described in the literature can derive support from the research on beginning teachers.

However, beginning teacher induction programs such as the NASSP project are indeed the exception. Induction practices are uncommon, let alone induction practices that appear to have research-based support of a comprehensive nature. Implementation of research knowledge into practical programs appears further hampered by poor dissemination. Interest in induction programs has tended to be evanescent and dependent upon the economy and scarcity of teachers. The result is that most initial induction efforts have tended to be short-lived.

The question remains: What needs to be done in order to improve present induction practices? As is all too typical in education, the answers are not easy ones. First, there must be at all levels of the educational enterprise a recognition that the first year of teaching is to some degree problematic for all beginners. The profession itself must resolutely affirm the difficult nature of becoming a teacher, and work to educate the public about the importance of careful induction of beginning teachers. If significant change is to occur, all segments of the profession and the public must come to realize that entrance into teaching is a unique period in a beginning teacher's personal and professional life—a time of special significance which demands special attention and resources.

Secondly, genuinely collaborative programs for induction of beginning teachers must be mounted by universities, local school systems, and state departments of education. While recognizing that colleges of education, and universities in general, are suffering from very tight budgets which do not allow for costly new initiatives, teacher education institutions can take greater responsibility for the induction of beginning teachers. One of the more visible effects of the declining need for teachers and the concomitant decline in teacher education program enrollments is that teacher education personnel are available for involvement in new educational ventures. For example, universities might offer transition courses during summer months. Such summer courses might well be joint ventures between teacher preparation programs and surrounding school districts. Highly focused workshops or short courses could be offered on topics of particular relevance to beginning teachers. Findings regarding starting to teach in the fall (Evertson, 1980) could be the focus of one such short course. School districts might sponsor such workshops in order to explicate specific program materials unique to the district. School service centers, local teacher centers, or administrative school study councils could each be useful vehicles for increased assistance to beginning teachers.

In a time of scarce resources, the lack of public commitment to substantive, meaningful programs of induction represents the most serious deterrent to improved induction practices. As Howey has indicated in his overview, the belief that the first year of teaching can only be a trial by fire, or sink-or-swim experience is not uncommon. The first year of teaching is seen as a teacher's professional birth, a natural and unavoidable part in the professional life of teachers. Some pain or discomfort is to be expected, with one being considered fortunate if it is absent.

Obviously a professional commitment to the induction of beginning teachers is required first. Increasing governmental involvement in the initiation and development of intern or induction programs will require increased professional awareness and activity. Lack of commitment by the education professors may take the matter out of the hands of teacher educators. Florida and Arizona have already developed such programs (Bents & Howey, 1979) and Oklahoma has recently created an "Entry-Year Assistance Program," involving the beginning teacher, a teacher consultant appointed by the school system to work directly with and supervise the beginner, and an entry year committee made up of the school principal, a higher education instructor, and the teacher consultant. This committee will work with the beginning teacher and make recommendations regarding permanent certification.

A RESEARCH AGENDA

While we have learned enough about the beginning teacher to clearly support better induction practices, this is not to say more research is not needed. Existing research on the process of beginning to teach has neglected many important topics, while others—problems of beginning teachers, for example—have been an apparent siren to investigators and are overworked. Since so little of the territory has been explored, finding new areas for inquiry is easy. Establishing a research *agenda*, however, is more difficult.

Underlying the agenda sketched below is the belief that future research on the beginning teacher and the process of beginning to teach should place a high priority on description. Hinely and Ponder (1979) suggest that an emerging function of theory is the description of practice. Like Koehler (1979), they see the purpose of such description to provide understanding of what events occur in classrooms, why certain events occur, and of the meaning of these events in the classroom context. It is precisely this sort of systematic investigation which should be given strong emphasis in efforts to better understand the events in the lives of beginning teachers.

Another underlying tenet of this research agenda is the need to better pull together the accumulated knowledge about beginning to teach. In the above overview of nonresearch literature about beginning to teach, we have tried to suggest that the reflective interpretations of beginning teachers' experiences, advice to and about beginning teachers, scholarly essays about specific aspects of beginning to teach, and the first-hand reports of beginning teachers represent a great mass of knowledge and data about beginning teachers and the process of beginning to teach. There is a need, however, to produce coherent syntheses and comprehensive overviews of the knowledge about beginning to teach. For example, Howey and Bents (1979) have recently offered an overview of selected facets of beginning to teach. Such efforts to tie together the many complicated pieces of beginning to teach provide much needed focus and direction for further study.

Other aspects of beginning to teach are also in need of scholarly analysis and synthesis. For example, intervention and induction program effects have not been explored with any concerted effort. In 1978, NIE awarded a large research contract to the Educational Testing Service to conduct a study of the nature and effectiveness of programs designed to aid beginning teachers. This study is now available from NIE (*Study of Induction Programs for Beginning Teachers: Executive Summary*, NIE, 1982, Contract No. 400–78–0069, Frederic J. MacDonald, Patricia Elias) and provides further direction in developing a beginning teacher research agenda.

With an aim toward more comprehensive, descriptive research, high priority should be assigned to exploring the beginning teachers' world from their perspective of important experiences. Newberry's (1977) study of what environmental features furnish information to beginning teachers about activities in other teachers' classrooms is but one example of where a small in-depth descriptive study is particularly appropriate. The first-year teacher study (Ryan et al., 1980) represents a recent effort to provide a comprehensive description of a broad range of beginning teacher experiences. Rather than foucs on one or two aspects of beginning to teach, the first-year teacher study sought to explore events in the lives of 18 different first-year teachers in different settings. The study described the context of a particular beginning teacher, and that teacher's perceptions and construction of the reality of that context. Such understandings can provide an informed basis for induction efforts, and can provide additional direction for needed inquiry.

Knowledge and research from other professional fields and academic disciplines may also inform our own efforts. Professional socialization, induction, and the beginning year are not concerns unique to teaching. In business, architecture, and nursing, for example, neophytes must somehow enter their respective professional worlds. Do they have similar problems, and what is known of these problems? Research on beginning nurses, for example (Kramer, McDonnell, & Reed, 1972; Kramer, 1974; Tenbrink, 1968), suggests findings similar to research on beginning teachers (cf. Fox, 1977; Kramer, 1974). Utility of induction schemes developed for other professionals should not be ignored by those concerned with induction of beginning teachers. Role comparison research within the teaching occupation might also prove fruitful. One instance of such research, a study exploring the experience of beginning college professors, is currently in progress at Syracuse University (Mager, 1980).

Knowledge and research from academic disciplines such as psychology, anthropology, and sociology should be incorporated into our understanding of beginning to teach. For example, four different perspectives on the socialization of teachers have been advanced (Edgar & Warren, 1969; Haller, 1967; Hoy, 1967, 1968, 1969; Wright & Tuska, 1966, 1967, 1968). Undoubtedly there are other explanations for such a complex process. Further, the fundamental importance of the socialization process in the professional career of teachers demands continued exploration from a variety of perspectives using a variety of research methods.

As Vaughn (1979) and Glassberg (1979) have suggested, another potentially rich and important field of inquiry concerns knowledge of adult development as it relates to the training and induction of beginning teachers. Sprinthall and Theis-Sprinthall comment further on this in Chapter 3.

The basis for programs designed to support teachers as they enter the teacher profession must be based on the knowledge of what affects the beginning teachers when. Research by Applegate et al. (1977), Gaede (1978), Johnston (1979a), Ligana (1970) and others suggest the importance of particular periods and experiences as teachers begin their professional careers. The precise timing and nature of support needed is not well known. Moreover, little is known of how various presage, context, and process variables interact to affect the beginning teacher and the nature of induction support required. Careful description of how beginning teachers change is essential for the development of effective induction programs. When used in conjunction with what is currently known about the problems of beginning teachers, such knowledge can provide a basis for induction efforts. One example is the work on classroom management and the beginning days of school, currently in progress at the Texas R and D Center (Evertson, 1980).

The research agenda sketched above is modest though appropriate to the present level of professional knowledge and practice. Of central importance is the need to seek knowledge which will provide a sound descriptive theoretical base for further inquiry. Equally important is the need to employ research strategies appropriate to such ecological description. Present research knowledge of the beginning teacher, as in much of teacher education, does not provide an answer to the question posed by Fuller and Brown: "The appropriate question at this state of our knowledge is not 'Are we right?' but only 'What is out there?' " (1975, p. 52).

BIBLIOGRAPHY

Andrews, F. M. Guideposts for beginning teachers. *Music Educators Journal*, 1967, *54*, 37–38.

Applegate, J. H., Flora, V. R., Johnston, J. M., Lasley, T. J., Mager, G. M., Newman, K. K., & Ryan, K. *The first year teacher study*. Columbus, Ohio: The Ohio State University, 1977. (ERIC Document ED 135 766).

Banks, N. A career begins—I hope. *Peabody Journal of Education*, 1939, *16*, 368.

Barr, A. S., & Rudisill, M. Inexperienced teachers who fail—and why. *The Nation's Schools*, 1930, *5*, 30–34.

Becker, H. S. The career of the Chicago Public School teacher. *American Journal and Sociology*, 1952, *57*, 470–477.

Bents, R. H., & Howey, K. R. A historical perspective. In K. R. Howey & R. H. Bentx (Eds.), *Toward meeting the needs of the beginning teacher*. Minneapolis: Midwest Teacher Corps Project and University of Minnesota St. Paul Schools Teacher Corps Project, 1979.

Bidwell, C. E. The school as a formal organization. In J. G. March (Ed.), *Second handbook of research on teaching*. Chicago: Rand McNally, 1973.

Bisbee, K. K. *The interpersonal values and role perceptions of beginning vocational education teachers in Missouri*. August 1973. ERIC Document ED 085 476.

Blackburn, J. *The first year teacher: Perceived needs, intervention strategeis, and results*. Paper presented at the meeting of the American Educational Research Association, New York, April, 1977. ERIC Document ED 135 768.

Blackburn, J. D., & Crandall, J. *Preliminary results of a first year teacher pilot program: Data analysis, interpretation, and projections*. April, 1975. ERIC Document ED 104 805.

Bolam, R. *Induction programmes for probationary teachers*. The University of Bristol, 1973.

Bolam, R., & Baker, K. Helping new teachers: The induction year. *DES Reports on Education*. No. 86; March, 1976.

Broadbent, F. W., & Cruickshank, D. R. *The identification and analysis of problems of first year teachers*. Brockport, New York: New York State University College, 1965. ERIC Document ED 013 786.

Broadbent, F. W., & Cruickshank, D. R. Simulating problems of beginning teachers. *Elementary School Journal*, 1967, *68*, 39–43.

Bromberg, S. L. A beginning teacher works with parents. *Young Children*, 1968, *24*, 75–80.

Brown, M. H., & Williams, A. L. Lifeboat ethics and the first year teacher. *Clearinghouse*, 1977, *51*, 73–75.

Brown, R. E. Community involvement in staff orientation and inservice. *The Bulletin of the National Association of Secondary School Principals*, 1973, *57*, 26–30.

Bush, R. N. First few years. *Pennsylvania School Journal*, 1965, *114*, 8+.

Cable, P. E. Problems of new teachers. *Educational Administration and Supervision*. 1956, *42*, 170–177.

Coard, R. K. That first September. *Peabody Journal of Education*, 1957, *35*, 41–45.

Coates, T. J., & Thorensen, C. E. Teacher anxiety: A review with recommendations. *Review of Educational Research*, 1976, *42*, 159–184.

Cohen, A. M., & Brawer, F. B. Adaptive potential and first year teaching success. *Journal of Teacher Education*, 1967, *18*, 179–185.

Collea, F. P. First year science teacher: A study of his intentions, perceptions, and verbal behavior. *School Science and Math*, 1972, *72*, 159–164.

Cornett, J. D. Effectiveness of three selective admission criteria in predicting performance of first year teachers. *Journal of Educational Research*, 1969, *62*, 247–250.

Costa, C. *A comparative study of Career Opportunities Program (COP) graduates as first year teachers*. November, 1975. (ERIC Document ED 117 042.)

Dawson, E. First days for the beginning teacher. *Instructor*, 1960, *70*, 24+.

Doyle, W. Helping beginning teachers manage classrooms. *National Association of Secondary School Principals Bulletin*, 1975, *59*, 38–41.

Dreeben, R. *The nature of teaching*. Glenview, Ill.: Scott, Foresman, 1970.

Dreeben, R. The school as a workplace. In R. M. W. Travers (Ed.), *Second handbook of research on teaching*. Chicago: Rand McNally, 1973.

Dropkin, S., & Taylor, M. Perceived problems of beginning teachers and related factors. *Journal of Teacher Education*, 1963, *14*, 384–390.

Eddy, E. M. *Becoming a teacher: The passage to professional status*. New York: Teachers College Press, 1969.

Edgar, D. E., & Warren, R. Power and autonomy in teacher socialization. *Sociology of Education*, 1969, *42*, 386–399.

Edmonson, J. B. Give the new teacher a chance. *The Nation's Schools*, 1944, *34*, 21.

Education reforms proposed in Oklahoma. *Legislative Briefs*, 1980, *6*, 7.

Eliassen, R. H. Classroom problems of recent teaching graduates. *Educational Research Bulletin*, 1932, *11*, 370–372.

Elsbree, W. S. *The American teacher*. New York: Greenwood Press, 1939.

Emmer, E. T., & Evertson, C. M. *Effective management at the beginning of the year in junior high school classrooms*. Paper presented at the meeting of the American Educational Research Association, Boston, April, 1980.

Emmer, E. T., Evertson, C. M., & Anderson, L. M. *Effective classroom management at the beginning of the school year* (R and D Rep. No. 6005). Austin, Texas: Research and Development Center for Teacher Education, November, 1979.

Evertson, C. M. Personal communication, March 25, 1980.

Flesher, W. R. The beginning teacher. *Educational Research Bulletin*, 1945, *24*, 14–18.

Flowers, J. D., & Shearon, G. F. CBTE graduates show superiority in personal development. *Phi Delta Kappan*, 1976, *58*, 280.

Fox, T. *The dynamic nature of teacher professional development*. Paper presented at the meeting of the American Educational Research Association, New York, April, 1977.

Fuchs, E. *Teachers talk: View from inside city schools*. New York: Doubleday & Company, 1969.

Fuller, F. F., & Brown, O. Becoming a teacher. In K. Ryan (Ed.), *Teacher education: The seventy-fourth yearbook of the National Society for the Study of Education* (Part 2). Chicago: University of Chicago Press, 1975.

Gaede, O. F. Reality shock: A problem among first year teachers. *Clearinghouse*, *1978, 51*, 405–409.

Geer, B. Occupational commitment and the teaching profession. *School Review*, 1966, *74*, 31–47.

Glassberg, S. A developmental model for the beginning teacher. In K. R. Howey & R. H. Bents (Eds.), *Toward meeting the needs of the beginning teacher*. Minneapolis: Midwest ·Teacher Corps Project and University of Minnesota/ St. Paul Schools Teacher Corps Project, 1979.

Hale, F. M. New teacher's first days. *Grade Teacher*, 1931, *49*, 16+.

Haller, E. J. Pupils' influences in teacher socialization: A sociolinguistic study. *Sociology of Education*, 1967, *40*, 316–333.

Handley, H. M., & Shills, J. F. Work values and job attitudes held by new teachers in vocational education in Mississippi. 1973. ERIC Document ED 096 451.

Hinely, R., & Ponder, G. Theory, practice, and classroom research. *Theory Into Practice*, 1979, *18*, 135–137.

Howey, K. R., & Bents, R. H. (Eds.). *Toward meeting the needs of the beginning teacher*. Minneapolis: Midwest Teacher Corps Project and University of Minnesota/St. Paul Schools Teacher Corps Project, 1979.

Hoy, W. K. Organizational socialization: The student teacher and pupil control ideology. *Journal of Education Research*, 1967, *61*, 153–155.

Hoy, W. K. The influence of experience on the beginning teacher. *School Review*, 1968, *76*, 312–323.

Hoy, W. K. Pupil control ideology and organizational socialization: A further examination of the influence of experience on the beginning teacher. *School Review*, 1969, *77*, 257–265.

Hunt, D. W. Teacher induction: An opportunity and a responsibility. *The Bulletin of the National Association of Secondary School Principals*, 1968, *52* (330), 130–135.

Hunt, D., & Sprinthall, N. Psychological and moral development for teacher education. *Journal of Moral Education*, 1976, *6*.

Jackson, P. W. On becoming a teacher. *Today's Education*, 1974, *63*, 37–38+.

Jersild, A. T. Behold the beginner. National Commission on Teacher Education and Professional Standards, *The real world of the beginning teacher: Report of the nineteenth national TEPS conference*. New York, 1966. ERIC Document ED 030 616.

Johnston, J. M. Conceptions of the first year of teaching: An analysis of periodical professional literature (Doctoral dissertation, Ohio State University, 1978). *Dissertation Abstracts International*, 1979, *39*, 4882A.

Johnston, J. M. *First year teachers' perceptions of changes*. Paper presented at the meeting of the American Educational Research Association, San Francisco, April, 1979(a).

Johnston, J. M. *Personal concerns of first year teachers*. Paper presented at the meeting of the American Association of Colleges for Teacher Education, Chicago, February, 1979(b).

Johnson, P. O., & Umstattd, J. G. Classroom difficulties of beginning teachers. *School Review*, 1932, *40*, 682–686.

Koehler, V. *Methodology for research on teaching training*. Paper presented at the conference on Exploring Issues in Teacher Education: Questions for Future

Research, Research and Development Center for Teacher Education. Austin, Texas, 1979.

Krajewski, R. J., & Shuman, R. B. Seven touchstones for beginning teachers. *contemporary Education*, 1976, *47*, 96–100.

Kramer, J. *Reality shock: Why nurses leave nursing.* St. Louis: C. V. Mosby, 1974.

Kramer, M., McDonnell, C., & Reed, J. L. Self-actualization and role adaptation of baccalaureate degree nurses. *Nursing Research*, 1972, *21*(2), 111–123.

Kyte, G. C. Problems which confront rural school teachers. *Educational Method*, 1936, *15*, 227.

Lambert, S. M. Beginning teachers and their education. *Journal of Teacher Education*, 1956, *7*, 347–351.

Lieberman, A. May the best frog win. *Teacher*, 1975, *93*, 71+.

Ligana, J. *What happens to the attitudes of beginning teachers.* Danville, Ill.: Interstate Printers and Publishers, 1970.

Lortie, D. C. Observations on teaching as work. In R. M. W. Travers (Ed.), *Second handbook of research on teaching.* Chicago: Rand McNally, 1973.

Lortie, D. C. *School-teacher: A sociological study.* Chicago: University of Chicago Press, 1975.

Mager, G. Personal communication, April 2, 1980.

Mangione, A. R. Advice for beginning teachers. *Clearinghouse*, 1969, *44*, 41–42.

Marashio, P. A proposal for helping the beginning teacher. *Clearinghouse*, 1971, *45*, 419–421.

McCampbell, J. F. *A comparative study of three Illinois MAT of English programs. Interim report.* 1970. (ERIC Document ED 039 239).

McGill, E. C. Problems of the beginning business teacher. *Journal of Business Education*, 1948, *24*, 11–12.

McGinnis, C. Beginning teacher project in New York State. *The Bulletin of the National Association of Secondary School Principals*, 1968, *52*(330), 62–72.

Milius, J. We begin to teach. *Pennsylvania School Journal*, 1952, *101*, 41.

Moore, G. E., & Bender, R. E. *Teaching effectiveness of two groups of beginning teachers of vocational agriculture.* 1976. ERIC Document ED 131 188.

Moskowitz, G., & Hayman, J. L., Jr. Interaction patterns of first-year, typical, and "best" teachers in inner-city schools. *The Journal of Educational Research*, 1974, *67*, 224–226.

Moskowitz, G., & Hayman, J. L., Jr. Success strategies of inner city teachers: A year long study. *The Journal of Educational Research*, 1976, *69*, 283–289.

Newberry, J. M. *The first year of experience: Influence on beginning teachers.* Paper presented at the meeting of the American Education Research Association, New York, April, 1977. ERIC Document ED 137 299.

Noda, D. S. Beginning teacher development in Hawaii. *The Bulletin of the National Association of Secondary School Principals*, 1968, *52*(330), 62–72.

Ort, V. K. A study of some techniques used for predicting the success of teachers. *Journal of Teacher Education*, 1964, *15*, 67–71.

Rehage, K. J. Induction: When student becomes teacher. *The Bulletin of the National Association of Secondary School Principals*, 1968, *52*(330), 144–155.

Reimer, S. J. Beginning teacher's guide to a disastrous first year. *Pennsylvania School Journal*, 1970, *119*, 74–75.

Ryan, K. *Don't smile until Christmas.* Chicago: University of Chicago Press, 1970.

————. *Survival is not good enough: Overcoming the problems of beginning teachers.* Washington, D.C.: The American Federation of Teachers, 1974.

Ryan, K., Applegate, J., Flora, R. V., Johnston, J., Lasley, T., Mager, G., & Newman, K. "My teacher education program? Well . . .": First year teachers reflect and react. *Peabody Journal of Education,* 1979, *56,* 267–271.

Ryan, K., Newman, K., Mager, G., Applegate, J., Lasley, T., Flora, R., & Johnston, J. *Biting the apple: Accounts of first year teachers.* New York: Longman, 1980.

Smith, H. P. Study of the problems of beginning teachers. *Educational Administration and Supervision,* 1950, *36,* 257–264.

Smith, L. E. My first year. *National Education Association Journal,* 1949, *38,* 656–658.

Southwell, J. L. Teacher aids teacher: Beginners prefer help from their experienced colleagues. *Clearinghouse,* 1970, *45,* 104–106.

Spinning, J. M. The first day of teaching 47 years ago—and now. *Nation's Schools,* 1960, *66,* 72–73.

Sprinthall, N., & Bernier, J. Moral and cognitive development of teachers. *New Catholic World, 221,* 1978.

Stout, J. B. Deficiencies of beginning teachers. *Journal of Teacher Education,* 1952, *3,* 43–46.

Strickland, E. C. Orientation programs for new teachers in Ohio Schools. *Educational Research Bulletin,* 1956, *35,* 169.

Tenbrink, C. L. The process of socialization into a new role; the professional nurse. *Nursing Forum,* 1968, *7*(2), 146–160.

Tisher, R. P. *Teacher induction: An aspect of the education in professional development of teachers.* Paper presented at the conference on Exploring Issues in Teacher Education: Questions for Future Research, Research and Development Center for Teacher Education. Austin, Texas, 1979.

Tisher, R. P., Fyfield, J. A., & Taylor, S. M. *Beginning to teach: The induction of teachers: A bibliography and description of activities in Australia and the U.K.* (Educational Research and Development Committee Report No. 15). Canberra, Australia: Government Publishing Service, 1978.

Tower, M. M. Study of problems of beginning teachers in the Indianapolis public schools. *Educational Administration and Supervision,* 1956, *42,* 261–273.

Turner, R. L. Characteristics of beginning teachers: Their differential linkage with school systems. *School Review,* 1965, *73,* 48–58.

Turner, R. L. Some predictors of problems of beginning teachers. *Elementary School Journal,* 1967, *67,* 251–256.

Vaughn, J. The interaction of context with teachers and teacher education: An emphasis on the beginning years. In K. R. Howery & R. H. Bents (Eds.), *Toward meeting the needs of the beginning teacher.* Minneapolis: Midwest Teacher Corps Project and University of Minnesota/St. Paul Schools Teacher Corps Project, 1979.

Visor, A. L. Classroom discipline. *School and Community,* 1973, *59,* 22.

Vittetoe, J. O. Why first year teachers fail. *Phi Delta Kappan,* 1977, *58,* 429–430.

Wallace, M. S. Problems experienced by 136 new teachers during their induction into service. *North Central Association Quarterly,* 1951, *25,* 291–309.

Waller, W. *The sociology of teaching.* New York: Wiley, 1967. (Originally published, 1932.)

Wey, H. H. Difficulties of beginning teachers. *School Review*, 1951, *59*, 32–37.

Wofford, K. V. The beginning teachers and the supervisor. *Educational Method*, 1931, *11*, 153–155.

Wright, B. D., & Tuska, S. A. *Student and first year teachers' attitudes toward self and others*. Cooperative Research Project No. 1503, University of Chicago, 1966.

————. The childhood romance theory of teacher development. *School Review*. 1967, *75*, 123–154.

————. From dream to life in the psychology of becoming a teacher. *School Review*, 1968, *76*, 253–293.

7

Toward Solving the Dilemmas of Research on Inservice Teacher Education

Sam J. Yarger

Syracuse University

Gary R. Galluzzo

Glassboro State College

INTRODUCTION

At a recent meeting between a group of practitioners and a researcher, one of the practitioners noted, "When I put together a training activity and want elementary teachers to come, I call it a workshop. When I want secondary teachers to come, I call it a seminar," When quizzed by the researcher concerning the difference, the practitioner chuckled and noted that those types of distinctions may be important to researchers, but program developers are just trying to find ways to motivate teachers to become involved.

The above anecdote is not apocryphal. Although it hints at some of the dilemmas implied in the title of this chapter, it does not address the many problems facing those who choose to do research in the area of inservice education. Simply stated, the language of inservice teacher education is so vague as to be almost unusable for research purposes. Those who try to make common meaning from this language area, in fact, grabbing at mirages. It logically follows that if the language in the field is fuzzy, the research will be equally unclear. In fact, it appears that research on inservice education has no standards for comparison and no accepted methodologies.

Inservice teacher education, because it actually does occur, obviously has form, operates within some structure(s), and delivers some content. Few would dispute that. The problem of understanding inservice education, however, is quite different. Because of the language problem, it would appear that the only "safe" unit for analysis is the individual program event or single activity. Attempts to aggregate data across many programs, program events, and program activities are likely to run headlong into the language problem, thus creating a situation where the analyst is grabbing at mirages. A brief look at the limited number of reviews of research in this area will illustrate this problem more clearly.

Three reviews have been selected because the authors had clear purpose for their work. Lawrence (1974) was attempting to sort out the important factors in differentiating between effective and ineffective inservice teacher education. Nicholson and Joyce (1976) were attempting to identify data needs and major issues in inservice teacher education. Joyce and Showers (1977) were looking for the effects of training efforts that have involved teachers at all levels (K through postsecondary). Each review represents a different perspective, and will be subjected to a brief critical analysis consistent with the goals of this chapter.

Lawrence used the existence of quantified data directly related to a summary judgment of the inservice program or program activity in question as a criterion for inclusion in his review. Lawrence's review is more a review of evaluation than research per se. His findings focused on client satisfaction (e.g., client involvement in planning, ease of participation, and client-determined evaluation). This is not surprising because the majority of evaluations cited by Lawrence are, in fact, client perceptions of a variety of inservice activities, each using a different form of inquiry. Additionally, Lawrence accepted nomenclature-type labels at face value. Thus, when a workshop was described in one evaluation, it would be considered the same as a workshop in another, unrelated report. Such a practice is not only risky but probably misleading. Although much can be learned from this review, particularly in the area of client opinions of successful inservice program activities, serious questions can be raised about the application of his synthesis beyond this domain. The liberal standards for inclusion in the review, as well as the standardization of linguistic meaning constitute marked limitations.

Nicholson and Joyce did not set out to review research, though they did not ignore it either. Rather, they accepted the enormous task of surveying the literature on inservice education from 1957 through 1976. They do not explicitly state the criteria employed for inclusion or exclusion of a particular piece of work. However, since they included slightly over 2,000 citations, one must assume that they omitted a great many. The organizing concepts for their reviews included varieties of inservice education, collaboration, values regarding inservice education, and various definitions of inservice education. They noted that "important questions are clouded by rhetoric, vague and redundant language, and, above all, by the lack of a general analytical process which separates fact from ideology, issue and concept" (p. 3). They also make clear in their document that the existence of credible research studies on inservice education is, indeed, limited. Thus it appears that the Nicholson and Joyce work is plagued by the same problems that affected Lawrence—the problems of language and standards. One is left with the option of accepting the creative, intellectual, and analytical judgments of the authors—in this instance not a difficult choice to make—or with going to the original sources.

The Joyce and Showers work is probably the most helpful review of the three. The reason is that the authors of this paper focused quite directly on "more than 200 studies in which researchers investigated the effectiveness of various kinds of training methods" (p. 1). Although the authors do not cite the types of study, certain comments lead the reader to believe that the majority of them were quasi-experimental, if not truly so. In their words,

> Nearly all the research either compares specific methods with a "traditional" method or with no treatment or placebo treatment. The "traditional" method usually refers to a lecture-discussion sometimes followed by coaching on site. The experimental method usually has the advantage of focus. That is the criterion measure and experimental method usually concentrate on specific behaviors while the traditional method is more diffuse. The specific methods almost always have greater effects than the more diffuse ones (p. 15).

Joyce and Showers were selective in the research they reviewed to the extent that they included "only investigations in which there were pre- and post-measures of teacher behavior and in which the objective was some kind of change in teacher performance" (p. 14). Interestingly, they add, "also, we stressed that the review is *selective*. There are several hundred pertinent investigations which we have not reported here" (p. 14). At any rate, the Joyce and Showers work does deal with the problem of standards for inclusion, and avoids the language problem mentioned earlier in that the focus was on studies where language is typically quite precise. Although many studies were admittedly omitted, and even though the subject of inquiry in this review is quite limited, this review comes closer to what the authors believe constitutes an acceptable standard for reviewing research on inservice education.

Succinctly, Joyce and Showers investigated the areas in research on training that they labelled feedback, micro-teaching and mini-courses—teaching skills, modeling, micro-teaching—models of teaching, self-instructional methods, simulation, and curriculum implementation. Although they emphasized the difficulties in using these studies, they did suggest that teachers can utilize feedback and training to achieve both simple and complex teaching skills and strategies and to implement curricula. They further state that teachers appear to have the ability to respond to external and self-instructional methodologies quite rapidly. Finally, the researchers call for more work in the inservice domain pointing out that a good deal of their research used preservice teachers as subjects.

The purpose of discussing these reviews was to note the problems encountered as one attempts to aggregate information in an effort to learn about the phenomenon of inservice education. There simply is no language that allows us to communicate with the necessary precision. Additionally, there is a lack of methodology that will allow for comparison of different investigations. The unit of analysis is probably at the heart of this problem, i.e., it is typically impossible to differentiate an integrated, long-term program from a group of short-term program activities or even a single event. Finally, this situation has led to a recognition of the absence of criteria for selecting works to be compared. This lack of standards mitigates against any attempt to aggregate information in order to learn about inservice teacher education. Thus far, the only solution to this problem has been to narrow the focus of the review and to limit the studies to those of a single type, e.g., quasi-experimental studies in the Joyce and Showers paper. Although this approach may be helpful, it tends to fragment the field, and to extend the period of time it takes to develop a thorough understanding of inservice teacher education in all its complexity.

None of the problems cited above can be totally overcome, at least on the short range. Rather, these problems will be solved not only with time, but also with a great deal of serious work and collaboration by teacher educators and researchers. Nonetheless, the solution to the issues presented above constitutes lofty goals that must be addressed. Regardless of the fact that they cannot be solved quickly, and particularly in a single chapter, the desire to achieve these goals has clearly influenced us in the organization, selection of material, and style of writing found in this chapter.

In order to limit, at least to reasonable bounds, the area to be covered in this chapter, both inservice teacher education and research on inservice teacher education will be defined. Subsequently, a matrix will be presented which includes five research types and their relationship to inservice education. In addition, there are four major question areas that have been, are being, and need to be addressed, Then, we will present examples of the state of knowledge vis-à-vis each of the research types, as well as an estimate of the gaps that exist in that knowledge. A partial synthesis of the works selected for this chapter will appear next. The authors believe high-quality research is so limited that a full and powerful synthesis simply is not possible at this time. Finally, utilizing the estimate of gaps in knowledge presented earlier, an attempt will be made to construct an agenda or research on inservice teacher education.

NECESSARY DEFINITIONS

Defining terms and explicating concepts is a risky business in education. On the one hand, if one defines terms precisely, there are those who will argue that the "unnecessary" limitations on the ideas inhibit creativity and also impede the potential for learning about important aspects of the topic because they have been eliminated by definition. On the other hand, if terms and concepts are not clearly defined, the substantive focus of the topic at hand remains unclear, and meanings are left to vary from reader to reader.

Faced with this dilemma, the authors decided to "gum the bullet," and to provide at least two important definitions. It was decided that it would be impossible to talk clearly about research on inservice education if both research on inservice and inservice education itself were not defined.

Inservice Education

In recent years, describing and defining of inservice education and its possible elements has become a popular sport. New words and terms have been introduced but few have had acceptance. In the absence of general agreement, we have adopted Hass' (1957) definition:

> Broadly conceived, inservice education includes all activities engaged in by the professional personnel during their service and designed to contribute to improvement on the job (p. 13).

Although at first reading this definition appears to be very broad, it does, nonetheless, provide some useful constraints. It includes all categories of professional personnel, but only includes those who are employed. Likewise, all types of inservice activity can be included, but only if they are intended to "contribute to improvement on the job." This definition eliminates some aspects of programs that many would not wish eliminated. For example, an inservice program that was designed to help teachers learn modern dance would not be considered an example of inservice education, unless the clear intent of the program was to prepare teachers to help children learn about it as well. A program designed to introduce people to new educational concepts because they had not taught for many years would not be considered inservice education, because the participants are not actively employed. Thus, although the Hass definition is broad in many respects, it does contain some very important and useful characteristics.

Research on Inservice Education

Defining research on inservice education is a more difficult task because a research area can be defined along several different dimensions, including but not restricted to research methodology, substance of research, and subjects. The research methodology dimension will be dealt with in the next section of this chapter. At this point, the question of the subjects employed and the substance of the research are important.

In many cases, the subjects form the only characteristic that differentiates research on inservice education from what one might call research on professional teacher education. One can certainly ask whether or not the subjects alone are an important distinction, particularly if the substance of the research is the same, i.e., if research on how preservice and inservice teachers learn to use specific models of teaching or teaching strategies in the classroom could be labeled as research on professional teacher education. The only distinction is the difference between preservice and inservice. A question then arises concerning the importance, for definitional purposes, of the level of subjects involved in research as a necessary distinguishing characteristic. The question is made more interesting when one considers that research on student teaching and on teacher education programs have historically, and correctly, been labeled research on preservice teacher education.

The authors concluded that the distinction is, in fact, important. Thus, research on inservice education in this chapter will include only studies where the subjects are professional educators, employed actively in their profession, and participating in programs that are designed to contribute to improvement on the job.

One must also establish a general definition of research on inservice education that will accommodate the field. The issue here is that most of the contemporary definitions of research in education are derived from the field of psychology where research methodology is embedded in a history of affiliation with the natural sciences. Unfortunately, this definition limits the inquiry that can be made, and is probably necessary in such a diffuse field as inservice teacher education. Thus, in this chapter, research on inservice education is defined as *studious investigation aimed at discovering and interpreting facts about some aspect of the field*. Although research should strive to employ accepted research methodologies, as will be seen later in this chapter, that is not always possible. Clearly, one should accept only work where there is an obvious attempt at truthfulness and objectivity, yet in some cases that "funny feeling in the pit of the stomach" will be the only criterion for making judgments. Finally, while many take the position that only work which can be replicated should be considered research, it will be noted in the next section of this chapter that capability for replication will characterize only some of the research types presented.

In summary, research on inservice education is defined as studious investigation aimed at discovering and interpreting facts about the field. Subjects for this research will consist of practicing professionals who are involved in programs designed to improve their performance on the job while they are actively employed. These "generally specific" definitions will undergird both the selection of studies to be presented in this chapter and the recommendations for future research.

THE RESEARCH TYPE AND QUESTION MATRIX

There are two purposes for presenting the matrix on research type and questions about research on inservice education. First, the matrix will serve as an advance organizer for the presentation of studies as well as the generation of a research agenda. The reader will be better able to understand our thinking by first encountering the scheme that guided the work. Secondly, the matrix is a conceptual model in that there is a goal of reducing complexity. As has been previously discussed, research in inservice education suffers from a lack of communicable language, and an absence of convention and methodology. This matrix will provide a beginning point for rendering these phenomena more understandable.

The Matrix

The matrix for exploring research on inservice teacher education is presented in Figure 7.1. The matrix consists of research types in inservice education and questions that are appropriate about the enterprise. The research types are the rows, and the research question areas are the columns. Because the authors have accepted a very broad definition of research on inservice education, some studies will be included that might

FIGURE 7.1   A Matrix for Exploring Research in Inservice Teacher Education

Questions Research Types	What Exists?	What is Appropriate?	What is Feasible?	What is Effective?
Program Descriptions				
Case Studies				
Surveys				
Correlational Studies				
Experiments				

not be included by those who are more conservative in their understanding of research.

The Research Types. The five research types are viewed as hierarchical in nature, with the most unsophisticated type listed first, and the most complex and confirming listed fifth. One's conception of research must be stretched considerably in order to accommodate the lower two types. We deem this appropriate because research on inservice education is at the starting point, and the field needs the benefit of information and guidance that typically would be considered to transcend traditional notions of research.

Program descriptions. Program descriptions are the most basic kind of "research" on inservice education. Although many scholars would not include descriptions of programs as research, the reason we include them is simple—they are the source of many good ideas concerning what is happening in inservice education. A program description can be defined as an account of the genesis, initiation, development, implementation, and/or evaluation of an inservice program or program activity, or of some part therein. A program description follows no particular format and is not bound to offer evidence of any type concerning the veracity of the statements that are included. Typically, program descriptions are personalized accounts written by participants or primary actors in the inservice activity. Program descriptions can be problematic in that they are rarely written to do anything but promote the success of a program. Thus, they are likely to be "gilded" in some respects. No claims are made in program descriptions for validity, reliability of observations, or anything else. They are simply the perceptually bound accounts of some person(s) concerning a specific inservice teacher education program or program activity.

Case studies. Case studies differ from program descriptions in that they tend to be more organized, and are typically written for a purpose other than to promote the program itself. Case studies usually offer some glimpse of the methodology employed, and claims are often made for objectivity, if not for validity and reliability. Ofttimes, special emphasis is placed on aspects of the program that may be generalizable; however, no "hard" evidence is necessary in support of the potential generalizability. Case studies, like program descriptions, can focus on the genesis, initiation, development, implementation, and/or evaluation of an inservice program or program activity, or some part therein.

Surveys. Surveys are usually intended to sample large populations concerning topics that are pervasive and relevant to large populations. Although survey data may be low in inference and generalizability, they tend to cover topics that are fairly broad and abstract. Pseudo surveys are often used to gather information about program clients' attitudes, opinions, and beliefs about inservice programs or program activities. However, in inservice education, these "evaluations" often take little note of the issues of sampling, instrument design, return rates, response rates, social acceptance issues, and a host of other important technicalities. Thus, the existence of true survey research in inservice education is quite limited.

Correlation studies. Although correlational studies appear to be nonexistent in inservice teacher education, they are an important type for future consideration. A correlational study is defined as an attempt to establish relationships between two or more variables deemed important to an inservice program or program activity. Correlational studies can grow from surveys, or they can involve the actual observation of clients and instructors in inservice education. When appropriately designed, correlational studies can be extended to include the prediction of one variable from another, though causal relationships require more sophisticated methodology.

Experimental studies. Experimental studies represent the most sophisticated order of research in inservice education, and are almost impossible to implement successfully in the field. In an experimental study, not only are variables controlled, but sampling is performed appropriately, subjects are assigned to treatment, and a true experimental manipulation of a variable is required. Due to the fact that most inservice teacher education programs cannot be controlled sufficiently to accommodate experimental studies, true experiments most likely will occur only in a laboratory setting either in a research center or on a campus. One, then, must consider the problems of generalizability, and the relationship of the experimental treatment to the world under investigation.

Questions about Research on Inservice Education. In any discussion of research on inservice education, one must wrestle with the problem of what questions are to be asked. Although it would go beyond the scope of this paper to attempt to delineate every possible and important question, there do seem to be question areas that are more important than others. One point that emerged from the three reviews on inservice education cited earlier was that four areas seem to be the most frequent object of focus. These four areas constitute the questions about research on teacher education and will be explained more fully:

What exists? This question is attempting to document systematically the state of the scene in inservice education. Not only will one be interested in the content but there will also be an interest in delivery systems, governance structures, costs, instructors, and so on. Addressing this question will, in many cases, require the use of what would typically be considered "messy" data. It is in the answer to this question that one will encounter the unit of analysis problem. Frequently, it is difficult to understand whether information one has relates to integrated long-term programs, degree programs, certification programs, program activities, single events, or something else. Although no clearcut answer is evident, it is likely that most of the information and data refers to program activities, single events, or at best, loose confederations of program activities.

What is appropriate? The *zeitgeist* in inservice education is for appropriateness to be defined almost exclusively from a client perspective, i.e., teachers. This position has emerged from a teacher advocate point of view, and is not entirely illegitimate. Thus, it is important to define appropriateness in terms of credibility with the client. However, one must also consider the perceptions of education professionals other than classroom teachers, e.g., school administrators, policy makers, professors. This entire area can be referred to as *perceived appropriateness*, and is typically the result of what in inservice education is called needs assessment. One can also define appropriateness in terms of information that is embedded in substance. In this case, substance can be defined as concrete information from a neutral source that can withstand a variety of analyses. For example, if reading test scores in a school district are dropping, a variety of different professionals can analyze those scores and hypothesize reasons for their occurrence. Thus, *substantive appropriateness* is embedded in data, and is neutral with regard to its meaning. Finally, appropriateness can be defined in terms of the manner in which it flows from the political process. *Policy appropriateness* can emanate from local, state, or national political bodies. It can, in fact, be totally consistent with perceived or substantive appropriateness though that is not necessary. For example, the appropriateness of training for teachers to help children learn basic skills can, in some cases, be linked directly to the growing movement in American education for competency tests.

What is feasible? Although the question of feasibility is related to the question of appropriateness (content), it is more generally related to the area of political conditions, economics, and motivation of clients. Examples of questions that may be encountered under this question area are: What can school districts stand in terms of available delivery systems? What is it possible for schools and colleges of education to deliver? What will state departments approve? Who will pay for the activity? What's the role of the federal government? Feasibility questions can often be framed in such a way that information from "special" programs and program activities can be helpful in arriving at possible answers. A paraphrasing of the question of what is feasible might be, "Given the worst of all worlds, the best of all worlds, and the world we live in, what factors operate that will either inhibit or facilitate program developers and clients from doing exactly what they might want to do in terms of inservice education?"

What is effective? This question addresses outcomes of inservice education. It is possible to look for attitude and knowledge outcomes in inservice education clients. One can go farther and look for behavioral changes on the part of teachers as a result of the inservice education in which they participated. Finally, it is possible to deal with the question of student outcomes, i.e., the influence of the teacher who has learned skills on the behavior of children. This is a complex question, and must be handled with great care, or incorrect and misleading generalizations are likely to occur. Perceptual evaluations focusing on whether or not clients liked particular inservice program activities would not be considered, as they do not relate to specific outcomes.

THE "GOODNESS OF FIT" BETWEEN RESEARCH TYPES AND QUESTIONS ABOUT INSERVICE EDUCATION

"Goodness of fit" is a statistical term that relates to the appropriateness of specific statistical tests for data of different types. This notion can be used to think about the relationship of research types to the question areas presented above.

As one thinks about the research types and the questions, it becomes clear that not all question areas can be dealt with equally well by all research types. Thus, some selection is necessary. Although the "goodness of fit" between research type and question requires the exercise of judgment, it is neither a capricious nor arbitrary activity. An estimate of the "goodness of fit" for research types and questions about research on teacher education is presented in Figure 7.2.

FIGURE 7.2   An Estimate of the "Goodness of Fit" for Research Types and Questions about Research on Inservice Teacher Education

Questions / Research Types	What Exists?	What is Appropriate?	What is Feasible?	What is Effective?
Program Descriptions				
Case Studies				
Surveys				
Correlational Studies				
Experiments				

Succinctly, the first three questions (existence, appropriateness, and feasibility) can best be addressed by the lower-level research types. That is the reason for the inclusion of the program description and case study research types in the matrix. The question of appropriateness, often referred to as needs, is typically addressed, in the best instance of the word, by well-executed surveys. However, as one reads a variety of program descriptions and case studies, there are very likely to be statements concerning either perceived, substantive, or policy needs. One might have to extend the notion of program description or case study to include reports issued by political agencies where one is likely to find policy-appropriate needs embedded. However, one would not expect to find the question of appropriate needs addressed in correlational studies, or experiments. Rather, these research types will generally be found to deal with aspects of inservice education that have already been found appropriate at one level or another.

In general, the questions of existence and feasibility can be addressed using the same research types as the question of appropriateness. It is possible, however, to extend these two questions to include correlational studies. In this instance, variables or characteristics can be identified through correlational studies that were not known to exist previously. The feasibility issue would deal with the logistic aspects of feasibility with program descriptions, case studies and surveys, and with the substantive characteristics in correlational studies. Thus, one might address a question like, "What, if anything, is the relationship between nondirective instructor behavior and client achievement in an inservice program through a correlational study?"

Finally, the question of effectiveness can best be addressed by experiments and, in some cases, surveys and correlational studies. It should be pointed out here that the term experiments or experimental studies in inservice education will nearly always mean quasi-experimental methodologies. As we noted earlier, the real world of inservice education typically does not allow for the rigid control necessary for the implementation of true experiments. Research devoted to addressing the question "What is effective?" will nearly always focus on the attitudinal, cognitive, or behavioral outcomes, thus the assumption of independent and dependent variables is implied. On those occasions where student outcomes are the dependent variables of interest, one would have to assume that the teachers have already demonstrated the ability to exhibit effective outcomes from inservice education. Unfortunately, that is not always the case. No study of student outcomes as it relates to the success of inservice education can be justified unless the prior question of teacher behavior has been successfully addressed and answered.

The "goodness of fit" notion presented in Figure 7.2 will guide the selection of the studies to be presented. Additionally, the authors will operate within this concept in proposing the need for future research.

Although it is possible that a question area could be or has been addressed using a research type contrary to the matrix presented in Figure 7.2, the judgment of the authors is that this will occur rarely, and when it does occur, the lack of fit between research type and question alone should raise serious questions.

Regardless of the care taken to explain the terms in any analysis of research, one must continually wrestle with the problems of the quality of the work that is to be included. This is particularly the case when dealing with program descriptions and case studies, as these types of "research" offer little to justify their quality. In most cases, one must deal with this type of work based on one's own experience in the field, knowledge of clients and delivery systems, as well as knowledge of the content that is typically offered in inservice programs. One is often reduced to using that "funny feeling in the pit of the stomach" as a criterion as to whether a particular program description or case study rings true.

In considering the higher-order research types, there are the typical characteristics of good research that can be used to assess the quality of any particular piece. In this chapter, the authors have included only those works that exhibit high quality within a research type. However, it is accepted that even in this instance, gradients of quality are debatable. It appears that one cannot escape the necessity of knowing the judge as well as the judgment. Regardless, from the perspective of the authors, only "good" surveys, correlational studies, and quasi-experiments are included.

SELECTIVE REVIEW OF RESEARCH ON INSERVICE EDUCATION

Program Description

Far and away the most prevalent literature on inservice teacher education is the program description variety; there are literally thousands of such descriptions. Lacking in generalizability, they are most often discussions and reports of a wide range of local, state, or national inservice programs. There are definitional problems. An inservice program may be a one-day workshop, a leadership training institute for team leaders, a school-based, college-offered course or curriculum, a total-school staff development project aimed at curriculum revision, a summer institute, or a model purporting to identify the interrelationships among the components of a continuing education program for teachers. The value of program descriptions is the provision of a rich array of ideas concerning the field of inservice education. At their best they are informative works which aim to promote a program. The five selected for inclusion in this paper typify the wide and varied topics that comprise this largest of the research types.

Goodlad (1972) offers almost a model program description. In describing the staff development model developed by the Research Division of the Institute for the Development of Educational Activities, Inc., he includes an informative discussion of an inservice education program designed to facilitate teacher identification of needs and appropriate actions. The model is the work of the League of Cooperating Schools, a collaboration of 18 public schools and UCLA. Programs can be designed and delivered at the building or the individual teacher level. Regardless, teachers participate in the decision making at all levels. From this program description, the reader gains insight into the delivery mechanism and the consortial arrangement which guides program development.

Another variation on the program description theme is a report of a typical collaborative arrangement between a college of education and a local school district. Project MERGE (1975), the combined effort of Bowling Green State University and the Toledo Public Schools, is a competency-based preservice program which has a concurrent inservice program for cooperating teachers. Teams of university faculty are in the schools providing instruction and reinforcement of skills taught on campus to preservice teachers. These same faculty members develop similar programs for cooperating teachers. The purpose of these programs is three-pronged; an inservice program for the enhancement of skills, improving the skills of cooperating teachers, and the provision of a continuing education system for both preservice and inservice teachers.

As noted earlier, the term "program" means different things to different people. One less common meaning is characterized by *The Urban/ Rural Process: Views of the Participants* (1977). A larger effort than the previously cited program descriptions, the authors of this volume capture the essence of a federally funded project aimed at improving instruction to students by actively involving the community in the inservice education of teachers. Included in this monograph are the perceptions of the participants on such issues as the organization of the School-Community Councils, the governance bodies, the Urban/Rural program, and the inservice training activities. This is only one of five reports that have been published. A perusal of the entire set will provide a very complete analysis of a client-centered federal program.

Snow (1972) offers another approach to program descriptions. He describes the derivation and development of an inservice systems model created by the Stanford Center for Research and Development in Teaching. Entitled the Model Teacher Training System, its goal is to enhance the general skills of teachers in a variety of content areas. The seven components of the model follow from selection and diagnosis through training, assessment, and system revision.

There are a growing number of monographs and books which include a series of descriptions of inservice efforts (Devaney, 1979; Pipes, 1978). These volumes locate practitioners who can offer insight into their local programs and who can describe the relationship among the role groups on such topics as finance, delivery, incentive, governance, and the daily operation of teacher centers or other inservice agencies. These publications are an excellent source, and allow the reader to compare and contrast many program ideas.

When one considers the purpose for which program descriptions are written, and takes into account the great variety in format and comprehensiveness, it is not possible to attempt a meaningful synthesis. As we have stated throughout, the inclusion in this work of program descriptions is based on the fact that there just are so many, and to ignore them would omit a generous portion of the literature on inservice education. We find their value to be in the breadth of topics covered and ideas offered to the field both for research and for practice.

Case Studies

Case studies are becoming more available to the education community. As documentation and evaluation efforts increase in teacher education, no doubt there will be a marked increase in the number of case studies of inservice programs.

One such study is the evaluation of an inservice program focusing on science instruction (Bracht et al., 1973). A portrayal analysis of a portal school program, this highly descriptive report is summative in nature, and provides a wealth of data. Its strength rests in the completeness of the report about this program which helped teachers learn to implement science methods in their classrooms. Included are discussions regarding the genesis of the portal schools, the leadership training institute, the collaborative efforts between the schools and the local university, delivery systems and options, incentives, and participant satisfaction.

McDonald (1980) offers possibly the most complete case study of an inservice program. He reports on the training of teacher specialists in the New York City Teacher Center. McDonald discusses in great depth the selection and training processes of this cadre of specialists who are available to assist the classroom teacher in organizing and managing instruction. The value of this work is that McDonald has captured the development and processes of this inservice program as it is happening. By doing so, he discusses both the successes and problems encountered in the organization of an inservice agency.

Zigarmi, Goldstein, and Rutherford (1978) report a case study of a building level staff development program. As the research component of a Teacher Corps project, the authors examined the effectiveness of an inservice program designed to change the discipline techniques used in a junior high school. The focus is on the role(s) which the change agent must assume and the importance of considering the sequence of events. Teachers in groups were the clients and it is on this point that the authors suggest the importance of focusing on individuals in future staff development efforts.

Oja (1979) designed a program aimed at enhancing the psychological and personal growth of teachers. The teachers experienced a seminar/ practicum which emphasized action and reflection regarding new teaching skills. They were also asked to maintain journals, and to make judgments about the efficacy of their inservice activities. Showing positive results in demonstrating that teachers could adapt research findings from educational psychology, Oja observes that inservice programs should exist in a supportive atmosphere if teachers are expected to attempt innovations in their classrooms.

Encouraging results can be found from these case studies. All of the authors reviewed here report that teachers who participated did show changes in their styles in the expected directions. Among the observations drawn from case studies are that inservice programs should:

- provide time and support for change
- operate in a warm supportive environment
- focus on the individual

Unfortunately, there are very few case studies of program activities; thus, there are few reports accurately describing the "how to" of inservice education.

Surveys

Once again, the literature on surveys in inservice education is thin. There are few surveys in which the samples allow for generalization to a broader population. Typical of these surveys are needs assessments of teachers within a particular topic area in a particular state or substate area (e.g., social studies teachers in Smith County). We were impressed, however, with the quality of information we found in three surveys.

Ingersoll (1976) tested an instrument designed to assess the needs of classroom teachers. A factor analysis of the results yielded seven categories in which teachers expressed need for further education. These were individualized instruction, classroom management, developing pupil self-assessment, discipline, developing personal self-assessment, interpersonal communication, and administration.

Byrd (1979) compared the perceptions of teachers, administrators, and teacher educators on the need for teacher inservice education. He found remarkable similarities among these three role groups as to what they perceive teachers need. However, he also found higher rankings and a closer relationship between administrators and teacher educators. He suggested that program development should come, not so much from the outside in or from the top down, but from a collaborative endeavor involving all three groups.

In a larger survey of perceptions about inservice education, Yarger, Howey, and Joyce (1980) asked teachers, professors, and community members to respond to items concerning such areas as development, delivery, content, and participation in inservice activities. As well, they surveyed the views of these groups on issues pertaining to governance, the role of the states and the community, and the cost of inservice education. Among their findings are the following:

- teachers do not want complete control over inservice education;
- higher education faculty who train teachers want to be a part of the governance system;
- the community would like greater involvement in decision making regarding inservice teacher education;
- there is not much inservice and that which does occur lacks quality;
- inservice education appears to be based on a very narrow view of the teacher;
- there is a need for better instructors, although there are enough instructors presently available;
- tangible rewards are less an incentive than is typically thought.

Correlational Studies

We have included in our research types the correlational method for research on inservice education. However, we could locate no studies which met the criteria. Thus, correlational studies constitute the "null set" in this review.

Experimental Studies

Studies that use experimental designs comprise another small portion of research on inservice education. As we stated earlier, it is difficult to control the many intervening variables in the field setting (e.g., administration, colleagues, building atmosphere, and the capabilities of the students). Given that each study attempted to control for different extraneous variables, it is obvious that there are no grand conclusions to draw from the studies we have selected for this review. There is, however, some common ground for comparison. Among the commonalities is the focus of the training program on the dependent variable. Each of the studies measures the effect of a training program on some aspect of teacher performance, e.g., verbal behavior, skill acquisition, or modification in teaching style.

Experimental designs are most heavily used with the Flanders Interaction Analysis System. Many studies have examined changes in teacher verbal behavior via a training program that is derived from the Flanders system. Carline's study (1970) represents a well-conceived effort to measure such effects. Using elementary school teachers, Carline provided 14 hours of instruction based on the Flanders system. Teachers were trained to code and interpret the results of interaction patterns in their classrooms. Posttraining analysis revealed that the teachers in the experimental group increased in five areas of verbal behavior, including praise, accepting, extended clarification, praise following pupil-talk, and encouragement. The researcher called the training program a success.

In another study conducted by Dangel, Conard, and Hopkins (1978), verbal behavior was once again the focus. The researchers studied the effectiveness of an inservice program both immediately after and up to 26 weeks after the termination of the program. The purpose of the training program was to increase teacher praise and to help teachers learn to re-focus attention to the class as a whole and to those students who need to interact more with the class. Reinforcement for practicing these new skills was placed with the building principal, thereby making it important at the total school level. Dangel, Conard, and Hopkins conclude that the train-ing was successful. The subjects demonstrated altered teaching style by increasing praise and by redirecting interaction. Further, they found in-consistent results when the principal was the observer, therefore conclud-ing that only some teachers profit from such reinforcement. Once again, though, the program to alter verbal behavior in specific ways was successful.

Teacher verbal behavior was also the focus of a study conducted by Good and Brophy (1974). The purpose of their study was to change teaching behavior by making the teachers more aware of their teaching style. Using extensive observations and interviews with each teacher, along with another series of observations, the researchers found en-couraging results. The interview, which presented teachers with data on style, was effective on two fronts. Once the teachers were made aware of how they interacted with their students, a follow-up set of observations showed an increase, not only in the quantity of interactions with low-participation students but also in the quality of these interactions, includ-ing level of difficulty of questions, praise, and feedback.

The methods employed in these three studies were quite different, yet all three report that their treatments were effective in changing the verbal behavior of teachers. This leads to the conclusion that teacher ver-bal behavior can be altered by a variety of inservice activities.

A study by Moore and Schaut (1976) demonstrates the need for con-sidering the receptiveness of the teacher. They collected data on the re-sponsiveness of teachers to inservice training as it related to stability of teaching behavior, grade level taught, years of experience, and sex. The teachers participated in a six-week program intended to increase their ability to reduce learner inattention. They found that both groups were responsive to the training as measured by use, but that the "unstable" teachers were more receptive. No other differences were found.

In two studies using protocol materials, Borg (1977) and Borg and Ascione (1979) evaluated the effect of protocol materials for enhancing classroom management skills and promoting student self-concept. Borg (1977) trained two groups of randomly assigned elementary school teachers in one of the two sets of behaviors. He demonstrated positive change in teacher behavior. Those teachers trained in the classroom management behaviors demonstrated significant increases on 7 of the 13 behaviors. Those receiving training in enhancing student self-concept had significantly greater frequencies in 11 of the 12 behaviors. Although Borg's purpose was materials validations, one must be encouraged by the demonstrated changes in teacher performance after the training. In a related study, Borg and Ascione (1979) found quite similar results. The subjects could demonstrate about half of the classroom management behaviors. It appears that use of these new behaviors was person related, i.e., some experimental group teachers adopted all of these behaviors while others did not adopt any.

McDonald and Davis (1978) also found mixed results in a training program designed to train teachers to teach reading. Teachers could demonstrate teaching reading via skill "A" without much difficulty. The same teachers were then trained to teach reading using skill "B." They found that the teachers tended to drop skill "A" in favor of skill "B," leading the researchers to report that skills can only be acquired one at a time and the complementary use of skills is far from easy.

The consistently positive findings discussed earlier regarding teacher verbal behavior are not matched by these few studies of skill development. The knowledge about effective training in skill areas is far less conclusive and confusing than the knowledge relating to acquiring verbal skills. Generally it appears that:

- teacher verbal behavior and to a lesser extent more complicated skills can be changed via inservice education
- there appear to be a wide variety of processes and techniques that can be used to change behavior
- effects of some training are not lasting, and integration of new skills into existing teaching style is irregular
- inservice aimed at skill development needs to consider other intervening variables

Although inservice programs appear effective in showing short-term change, most studies fail to look at change beyond the termination of the training program. One wonders if program effects are maintained once the reinforcing agent is removed. Only the Dangel et al. study supplied reinforcement after the inservice activity ended, and their results were less than conclusive.

A TRIP THROUGH THE QUESTIONS

It would appear that the questions cited earlier provide an appropriate framework for identifying intelligent directions for future work. The statements in this section made concerning the existing state of knowledge in research on inservice education not only can be linked directly to the studies that have been cited, but can go beyond those studies in a reasoned way. Clearly, judgments have been made, and perhaps some mildly risky intuitive leaps have been made. Nonetheless, statements concerning what is known from the research will appear quite skimpy to most readers—reflective of the level at which research has occurred.

What Exists?

Turning to the research literature to answer the question "What exists in inservice education?" is a very messy procedure at best. There are program descriptions by the basketful, with lesser numbers of case studies and minimal numbers of comprehensive surveys. Yet, from within the plethora of program descriptions, one obtains a definite impression that either a good deal is occurring in inservice education or writers on inservice education are excellent novelists.

Typically, program descriptions focus on comprehensive accounts of large and widespread programmatic efforts. Additionally, they are usually written with a tinge of evangelical flair. Regardless, one can find program descriptions replete with ideas concerning needs identification, models for delivering inservice education, collaboration and governance models, specific teacher education orientations (e.g., CBE), and more.

When one considers case studies, there are limited but more accurate accounts of the problems encountered and the processes employed in the development of inservice education. Case studies tend to focus on more discrete units of analysis for inservice education programs, because they are typically more thorough and involve the use of more documentation in support of their efforts. It is in the case study literature that the professional desiring to learn from the research can find quite detailed accounts of how the program developed as opposed to descriptions about that which was developed—the hallmark of program descriptions. The McDonald study on the training of teacher specialists in the New York City Teacher Center is an excellent example.

Information gleaned from the rather skimpy productivity of generalizable survey data is important. The evidence suggests that not only are teachers deeply interested in quality inservice education, but so are teacher educators and even school administrators. Thus, there exists what appears to be a solid base of support for quality inservice programs to develop. Additionally, there exists considerable data about the types of problems that teachers view as important, the types of programs they have received in comparison with those programs they would like to receive, and information about many other aspects of the endeavor. While program descriptions and case studies offer evidence about the existence of a variety of actual programs and program activities, the survey data suggest what exists in terms of perceptions of experience, beliefs, and desires for the future.

What is Appropriate?

The appropriateness of inservice education programs has been described as (1) a result of the perceptions of clients and others, (2) the examination of neutral data which could be impacted by inservice programs, and (3) an examination of the directives of educational policy groups who have as their responsibility the guidance and direction of educational activities in the country. The latter two types of appropriateness are not addressed in the research literature on inservice education. The former (perceived appropriateness) is addressed most commonly in case studies and surveys, and to a lesser extent in program descriptions.

If one reads the program description literature, one can obtain a sense that just about anything is appropriate if the clients view it to be helpful in their assigned responsibilities. Going beyond that, however, it would appear that much of the perceived appropriateness documented in the research focuses on the conditions surrounding inservice education rather than the specific content of the programs. In this case we find that clients want inservice education that is accompanied by the time and support for implementing that which is learned. Additionally, appropriate inservice should operate in a supportive environment, and focus on the individual rather than on large groups. Clients prefer inservice that is focused on individualized instruction, classroom management, learning assessment, and a variety of other topics that involve the personal development of both adults and children.

It has been noted in the literature that appropriate inservice need not be completely controlled by teachers. Additionally, clients report that appropriate inservice could operate within much wider boundaries vis-à-vis helping teachers operate more successfully in classrooms; i.e., inservice programs could take a much broader view of the role of teachers and still provide many appropriate experiences. By implication from program descriptions, it is evident that many traditional and a few specialized topics form what most clients would perceive to be appropriate inservice. For example, the basic skills of reading, mathematics, language arts, and oral communication are generously represented in the program description literature . One can assume from inference that clients perceive these to be appropriate. Embedded in this same data source one can find many programs focusing on classroom management, discipline, specific instructional management skills, and other topics of that genre. It appears that nearly anything that directly relates to the instruction of children in class-rooms will be considered appropriate at one level or another.

The authors could find no examples in any of the literature where the appropriateness of the programmatic efforts related to substantive data concerning the needs of children or of schools. It is inappropriate to state flatly that programs of this type do not exist, but if they do, they are not reported in the literature. Finally, and primarily because it fell beyond the purview of this chapter, the policy literature on education was not sur-veyed; thus, it is not possible to provide examples of appropriate inservice programs growing from policy-related appropriateness.

What Is Feasible?

As previously mentioned, the authors consider feasibility to be a compan-ion question to appropriatness. The primary difference is that the ques-tion of feasibility is nested in economics, politics, and client motivation. One would look toward case studies and surveys, and to a lesser extent to program descriptions to make statements concerning the work that has been done that relates to the question of feasibility in inservice education.

The program descriptions and the case studies present several exam-ples of institutional arrangements where unique and different delivery systems have been implemented. Project MERGE as well as the teacher specialist training program in New York City are good examples of that. It is interesting to note that a great deal of the program description and case study data focus on such nontraditional institutional and personnel arrangements. It appears that once one leaves the standard university or school district inservice course format, there are a great number of in-novative, yet feasible arrangements for delivering inservice programs.

What does not exist in the literature is evidence concerning the cost effectiveness or cost benefits of different institutional and personnel arrangements, as well as the effects these might have on such things as morale, and the ability of people to maintain them. In fact, one must go a long way, further than the authors are willing to do in this case, to ex-plore cost effectiveness. About the only way to make judgments (and they would be high-inference judgments) of the cost benefit or cost effec-tiveness of inservice would be to look at the productivity of externally funded programs vis-à-vis the budgets that were offered in support of those programs. Unfortunately these data are usually not available, as program practitioners consider the issue to be one of high political sensitivity.

The domains of personal economics and motivation have been ex-plored minimally in the survey literature. Succinctly, clients are willing to pay their share for professional staff development, except where it relates to skills that are required by the school system directly and necessary for continued job productivity. Desires to encounter inservice education that leads to new roles, to personal growth, or to learning about educationally related topics that cannot be directly applied to classrooms, are areas where clients are willing to pay part if not all of the costs. Motivationally, it appears that clients view as feasible programs that relate to their work, have sufficient support systems to ensure an opportunity to implement them, and are offered at times that are not only convenient but also conducive to a more leisure state of learning than one normally encounters.

A notable void in the studies on feasibility in inservice education falls in the political domain. There has been virtually no research focusing on members of boards of education, state boards or boards of regents, high-level bureaucrats, and other policy makers concerning what the perceptions of those who represent policy bodies view as feasible. One can make inferences about these topics from a review of legislation, program regulations, and other documents that form the currencies of exchange for policy bodies. These do not constitute, however, research on inservice education, and have not been included in this chapter.

What Is Effective?

In general, research on inservice education that addresses the question of what is effective is more definitive, and also tends to be more focused. Questions of effectiveness have typically been researched using quasi-experimental designs, thus narrowing the scope of the study. Furthermore, the bulk of this research focuses on specific practices that might occur within inservice programs rather than on comprehensive programs themselves. That is, one could tell whether or not a specific training device embedded within a large inservice program worked, but it would be difficult to make statements concerning the total program.

There are some data from surveys which focus on the perceived effectiveness of inservice education. These would be attitudes and beliefs, not related to either teacher or child outcome. For example, teachers perceive inservice that is either embedded in their workday world or directly related to it as more effective. Thus, one could suggest the need to develop inservice programs that operate in schools during the time when children are there. If that were not possible, it would be important to ensure that inservice programs relate directly to what teachers do in school and that they contain sufficient plans for in-classroom follow-up so that there is a likelihood that the skills will be learned in a usable fashion.

The experimental literature has demonstrated many things concerning effectiveness. For example, teacher verbal behavior and skill development can be changed through inservice program activities. Also, there appear to be a variety of methods that can be used to achieve these changes. One notes, however, that the changes are often of fairly small magnitude suggesting that there are many other unperceived, unknown, and/or unmeasured variables that affect the studied outcomes. Finally, there is little evidence to suggest that most of the inservice training that does occur is integrated well into a teacher's repertoire of teaching behaviors, or is even long lasting. This suggests the need to explore more closely tha environment in which skills are used, as well as the personalogical variables of the learners.

The preceding paragraphs have attempted to offer a mini-synthesis of what is known concerning the existence, appropriateness, feasibility, and effectiveness of inservice education drawn from the research literature. Any picture that has emerged must be considered not only fuzzy, but also painted with very broad strokes. It would appear that inservice education operates at a point where not enough is known, but probably what is known is not used effectively in program initiation and development.

WHAT IS NEEDED IN RESEARCH
ON INSERVICE EDUCATION

One could take the position that there are more gaps than there is substance in the research on inservice teacher education. Whether or not that is the case, there is work that needs to be done, and the recent "Trip through the Questions" revealed notable gaps in our knowledge. The authors take the position that research on inservice teacher education is a new phenomenon in the area of educational research and believe that no apologies are necessary for the rather sketchy knowledge that is currently available.

In relation to the question "What exists?" there is probably no dearth of creative ideas about inservice education. By reading the program descriptions, one can obtain almost unending lists of content areas, delivery systems, unique collaborative arrangements, and other such things. It is likely, in fact, that program descriptions will continue to be prevalent in the literature, as they are written for reasons that go far beyond the need to generate knowledge about the field.

Program descriptions, however, display some glaring program weaknesses. When one moves to the limited number of case studies that are available, the "how to" or process aspect of developing inservice programs becomes more evident. Clear descriptions of the processes involved and the problems encountered are rare indeed. Certainly one aspect of research on inservice education that needs a great deal of work is the accurate and objective description of how one goes about developing a program that is believed to be a contribution to the field.

Even if a more comprehensive and understandable base of data is built focusing on descriptions of inservice programs, there is also a need for a more thorough knowledge concerning the beliefs, attitudes, and perceptions of experience that a variety of education professionals bring to the endeavor. Data from the limited number of generalizable surveys suggest that much of the conventional wisdom that currently undergirds inservice program development can, and probably should be, challenged. For example, Yarger, Howey, and Joyce discovered that in specific kinds of inservice education programs, professors are by far the most valued instructors. By nearly any analysis, this challenges the common belief encountered in the literature. Additionally, even though teachers prefer to have their colleagues work with them in the classroom, there is a distinct reluctance on the part of teachers to become helpers of their fellow teachers. It would seem that a research agenda on inservice teacher education should include the solicitation of information that can be combined with baseline data on programs, thus providing a "psychological" underpinning for future efforts.

Several gaps are evident in the literature on appropriateness. There is practically no research on the development and implementation of policy in inservice education. Perhaps there has been no policy, yet it is apparent from observations of the contemporary scene that policies are in fact being developed and will be developed in the future. There is even a paucity of speculative and hortatory literature concerning policy on inservice education. There can be little doubt that there is a need for policy studies that will allow both researchers and practitioners in inservice teacher education to move ahead with some certainty that they are moving in an appropriate direction.

As previously stated, there is no shortage of creative ideas about unique options for planning and developing inservice education programs. Rather, there is a distinct lack of data concerning how these unique options work, and whether or not they are appropriate. For example, one might have an inservice teacher education program that brings children together for a six- to eight-week period of time in conjunction with master teachers and teacher clients—the latter there to learn new skills, have the opportunity to practice them, and to receive feedback from "experts" and from their colleagues. When these types of programs occur, and they appear very good on the surface, typically there are no data presented that would allow one to view with certainty their appropriateness, let alone their feasibility or effectiveness.

Finally, there is little research that links substantive "appropriateness" to client acceptance. That is, the program descriptions and case studies rarely point out that the content of their program was derived from substantive needs. And, when that does occur, there are few attempts to relate the substantive need for inservice training with client acceptance or perceptions of appropriateness. This need is important, because there is a strong belief that teacher perceived needs are very different from "real" needs. Although there is no research to justify that perception, by the same token there is no research to challenge it. When considering the feasibility question, several areas of importance should be mentioned. Teacher education in general and inservice education in particular have not benefitted from either cost effectiveness or cost-benefit studies, and it is well known that the documentation of cost in teacher education is difficult. Programs move ahead, and it is likely that professionals "fill in" when cost becomes a factor. Additionally, teacher education has a long history of being able to "make do" with inadequate resources. If teacher education ever desires to become recognized as an important professional field, then the question of cost benefit and cost effectiveness must be addressed.

There is also a need for "feasibility" research that attempts to assess the strengths and weaknesses of institutional and personnel arrangements that involve variations from normal expectations. By this, we mean that if a university is going to allocate resources for working within public schools, what are the consequences for the university? By the same token, if a school district is going to invest a good deal of energy and resources into improved inservice training programs, what does that mean for the district? The question can be carried even further—what does it mean for a professor to spend the greater part of an academic year working with teachers in classrooms with children? What does it mean for a school principal to devote a good deal of his or her effort to facilitating staff development programs within the building? The list of questions could go on—the point is that although unique programs that involve different roles for institutions and personnel do occur sporadically and usually on a short-term basis, there is no research that attempts to explore the feasibility of the new roles and functions that are undertaken.

Finally, there is a paucity of research examining client motivation regarding involvement in inservice education. There is no paucity of conventional wisdom, but most of it is not wise. Perhaps because of the visibility of the teacher advocates, it is not uncommonly believed that teachers' primary motivation for involvement in staff development programs are the trinkets of credit, stipend, release time, and so on. Certain data from survey research, however, challenge this notion. Clearly, a more thorough and better understanding of these phenomena is needed.

In the area of "What is effective?", where the most clear information is available, gaps are still evident. First, there appears to be a need for a conception of effectiveness that encompasses a broader perspective. Although no one will deny the importance of measuring teacher outcomes from specifically defined inservice activities, the results are difficult to aggregate, and the field tends to become fragmented. Rather, we must look at effects on individual teachers that transcend the ability to develop language or behavioral skills. We must look at the effects on the climate of the school that will augur for long-term involvement or lack of involvement. We must look for perceptions, attitudes, and beliefs that are related to inservice teacher education programs. The need to expand in a legitimate way the concept of what is effective cannot be denied for the long-term future, or those who are to be served by programs may become less supportive of effectiveness research than they already are.

By the same token, there is a definite need to develop coordinated efforts to research effectiveness that are long term in nature. The great bulk of the effectiveness literature focuses on short-term events, and even focuses on preservice teachers rather than experienced professionals. There are hints in the literature that although inservice training programs can have significant and positive short-term effects, that long-term effects are much more difficult to achieve, as well as to measure. Probably the single greatest factor in achieving this goal would be the development of a five- or ten-year research agenda, one that is able to go beyond the whimsy of the fiscal year and the shifting priorities of those who support research.

Finally, and this almost goes without saying, there is a need for more research on the effectiveness of inservice teacher education. Lest the reader be misled, the fact that the research in this area is the most concise and focused does not mean that there is much. There are between two and three million teachers in America, and between 100,000 and 200,000 professionals who in some way teach in inservice programs, which only underscores the extremely limited base of research on the effectiveness of inservice education that exists. The number of studies that actually examine the effectiveness of inservice teacher education programs is very small by comparison.

A FINAL WORD

The purpose of this paper has been to explore what should become the bona fide field of research on inservice teacher education. Bluntly stated, the authors believe that at this point in our educational history, the field does not, in reality, exist. In an effort to initiate this exploration, this chapter has attempted to highlight the problem of imprecise language as being at the base. Also, two definitions were offered and an attempt was made to develop a matrix of research types in inservice teacher education and important question areas for this research to address.

Although the scope of this paper did not allow for an exhaustive review of all of the research on inservice education, an attempt was made to select exemplars of the "best" research within the various types presented. This led to an exploration of what can safely be said concerning research on inservice teacher education, and finally led to an initiation of the construction of a research agenda for the field.

If the reader is left with the feeling that the chapter is markedly incomplete, then the reader agrees with the authors. Although we do not consider this fact lamentable, we do believe it is a challenge to begin the development of a coherent and sensible research agenda on inservice teacher education. Further, we hope that by adding some structure to thinking about the topic, that the agenda can be legitimately and wisely constructed.

BIBLIOGRAPHY

Borg, W. Changing teacher and pupil performance with protocols. *Journal of Experimental Education*, 1977, *45*(3), 9–18.

Borg, W., & Ascione, F. R. Changing on-task, off-task and disruptive pupil behavior in elementary mainstreaming classrooms. *Journal of Education Research*, 1979, *72*(5), 243–252.

Bracht, G. H., et al. *Evaluation of the portal school program*, University of Minnesota, 1973, ERIC Document 148–640.

Byrd, D. M. *A summary of teachers', administrators', and professors' perceptions of the need for teacher inservice education*. Unpublished doctoral dissertation, Syracuse University, 1979.

Carline, J. Inservice training—re-examined. *Journal of Research and Development in Education*, 1970, *4*(2), 103–115.

Dangel, R. F., Conard, F. J., & Hopkins, B. Follow-up on inservice teacher training programs: Can the principal do it? *Journal of Educational Research*, 1978, *72*(2), 94–103.

Devaney, K. (Ed.). *Building a teachers' center*. San Francisco: Far West Laboratory for Educational Research and Development, 1979.

Good, T. L., & Brophy, J. E. Changing teacher and student behavior: An empirical investigation. *Journal of Educational Psychology*, 1974, *66*(3), 390–405.

Goodlad, J. I. Staff development: The league model. *Theory Into Practice*, 1972, *11*(4), 207–214.

Hass, C. G. Inservice education today. In *Inservice education for teachers, supervisors and administrators*, the Fifty-sixth Yearbook of the National Society for the Study of Education, Chicago: University of Chicago Press, 1957.

Ingersoll, G. M. Assessing inservice needs through teacher responses. *Journal of Teacher Education*, 1976, *26*(2), 169–173.

Joyce, B., & Showers, B. Training ourselves: What we have learned about our ability to learn. Unpublished manuscript, 1977. (For a published adaptation, see Joyce, B., & Showers, B., Improving inservice training: The messages of research. *Educational Leadership*, 1980, *37*(5), 379–385.

Lawrence, G. *Patterns of effective inservice education*. Tallahassee: Florida Department of Education, 1974.

McDonald, F. J. *The New York City teacher center, year one: Description, research and evaluation*, Vol. 3. The Teacher Specialists: Their Training and Its Effects. Princeton, New Jersey: Educational Testing Service, 1980.

McDonald, F. J., & Davis, E. L. *The effects of an in-service training program on teacher performance and pupil learning*. Princeton, New Jersey: Educational Testing Service, 1978.

Moore, J. W., & Schaut, J. A. Stability of teaching behavior, responsiveness to training and teaching effectiveness. *Journal of Educational Research*, 1976, *69*(10), 360–363.

Nicholson, A. M., & Joyce, B. R. with others. ISTE Report III: *The literature on inservice teacher education: An analytic review*. Palo Alto, California: Stanford Center for Research and Development in Teaching, 1976.

Oja, S. N. Adapting research findings in psychological education: A case study. In L. Morris, G. A. Sather, G. J. Pine, R.C. Richey, W. Cole, A. Wheeler,

W. Quirk, J. Walthew, S. Scull, *Adapting educational research: Staff development approaches.* Norman, Oklahoma: Teacher Corps Research Adaptation Cluster, 1979.

Pipes, L. Collaboration for inservice teacher education: Case studies. Washington, D.C.: ERIC Clearinghouse on Teacher Education, 1978. ERIC Document ED 151 327.

Project MERGE 1975. Bowling Green State University, Ohio College of Education, and Toledo Public Schools, Ohio, 1975. ERIC Document ED 098 201.

Snow, R. E. *A model teacher training system: An overview.* Palo Alto: Stanford Center for Research and Development in Teaching, Report #RD–92, 1972. ERIC Document ED 066 437.

The Urban/Rural Process: Views of the Participants. The Urban/Rural Leadership Training Institute Staff. Palo Alto: Stanford Center for Research and Development in Teaching, 1977.

Yarger, S. J., Howey, K. R., & Joyce B. R. *Inservice teacher education.* Palo Alto: Booksend Laboratories, 1980.

Zigarmi, P., Goldstein, M., & Rutherford, W. Implementing a new approach to discipline in a junior high school: A two-year study of interventions in a Teacher Corps project. *Journal of Classroom Interaction,* 1978, *14*(1), 19–27.

8

A Final Note: Synthesis and Reflection

William E. Gardner

University of Minnesota

Students of the theater note that the villains who used to inhabit the 19th century melodramas played an important role because they provided a personification of evil on which all other characters could focus their misfortunes. Without villains the other characters would be forced to share responsibility for their misfortunes. Indeed, when the villains disappeared, drama made a quantum leap forward; dramatic characters took on depth and breadth because they no longer could enjoy the childish pleasure of blaming everything on the villain.

In some respects the process of teacher education plays a villain's role. With the public schools, departments, schools, and colleges of education are seen by many not only as major deterrents to progress but also as major causes of difficulty in education. This culpability straddles the full range of educational problems, from the fiscal management of schools through declining test scores to drug use among fifth graders. If teacher education is not considered to be totally responsible for all these problems, it most certainly is thought of as a major contributing cause.

In view of the incipient villain's role for teacher education, it's somewhat surprising to find that, while commentary on the process has been rife, research has been sadly lacking. As a number of writers in this volume note, research on the process of teacher education could be characterized as both meager and diverse, a conclusion which is consistent with that of most other writers. In his review of teacher education research, for instance, Turner (1975) concludes that it lacks utility in that it has been directed toward the wrong ends. Also, in the bicentennial volume of the American Association of Colleges for Teacher Education intended to comment on the status of teacher education reform, Howsam and his colleagues (1976) make several dozen recommendations without reference to anything more than a few descriptive statistics. Their volume, designed to propel teaching into professional status, drew its major intellectual strength from logical and historical arguments rather than from research findings. Indeed, most of the authors in this volume note both the paucity of research bearing on teacher education and the need for additional work.

Our authors go much farther, however, than merely viewing with alarm this lack of research and noting with anticipation the beneficial outcomes of following their suggestions. Indeed, several of them (Yarger, Johnston & Ryan, Haberman, and Schalock) argue explicitly or implicitly that the current research base for teacher education exceeds our capacity to use it (that is, we know far more than we are using at present). Each of our authors presents a solid review of the research areas they were asked to examine. The conclusions they reach are consistent with the research findings, their chapters are uniformly comprehensive and thoughtful. They have presented us with excellent models of how informed scholars can help us understand and attack complex problems. I am hopeful that their work, together with other similar efforts, can nudge all of us into a view of the teacher education process which is less reminiscent of the melodrama's villain.

This chapter evolves largely from the work of these authors because it is intended to synthesize the issues they raised so that we all can get a better sense of the prospects of teacher education and the directions it should move in the future. There are several ways in which this purpose could be fulfilled. Each of the chapters could be dissected, summarized, and critiqued individually. Or, I could develop and discuss a taxonomy based on the several dozen issues and recommendations made by the group of researchers. Instead of these, or other more elaborate possibilities, I prefer simply to list a number of the strongest impressions developed or conclusions reached in my careful reading of these chapters. I am convinced that readers are as capable of summarizing and critiquing as I am, and, hence, need no help to do so. I am equally convinced that readers will develop their own taxonomies for research in the field. They will also be able to develop their own impressions and conclusions, but I thought that a unique contribution might be to write down my reactions and invite others to do the same.

It will be obvious early on that most of my impressions have been more deeply impacted by the policy questions, which involve economics, sociology, and political science, than by questions of educational strategy, which would involve psychology and social psychology. This is true only because most of my current activities are focused one way or another on the policy issues affecting teacher education. Also, I think the authors in this volume have chosen to deal only tangentially with policy matters, and, before striking our tents and quitting the field, we should examine at least some of the basic policy questions.

These, then, are my major impressions, the issues I see and the conclusions reached.

1. The first of these is one of those questions handled tangentially in the volume—the issue of who should be allowed to teach or who should be recruited for the profession; in short, the whole issue of selection.

My impression is that this is one of the least studied and researched issues in the field. Our authors do not treat it comprehensively. Schalock does comment on the question obliquely in his chapter, and several other authors note that criteria for selection are too low and that this may be a variable to consider. For the most part, however, none of our authors (except for my coeditor) regards the topic as having central importance.

My own view is that no topic is of more current importance than this one and that we should spend far more time researching it. There are several reasons for my belief. First, pitifully little is known about the intellectual and psychological capabilities of the total teaching cadre. We do have the current rhetoric fed by stories of plummeting SATs and ACTs which denigrates the beginning teacher's intellectual abilities. Weaver's studies of the talent pool in teacher education are suspected by some because his data base involves *prospective*, not *actual* teachers, but even allowing for substantial distortions in his data, the picture he presents is disheartening. Equally disheartening is the fact that we can say virtually nothing about how many intellectual arrows the prospective teacher's quiver *should* contain; we can only say that they appear to have fewer than before. As Howey notes in the overview to this volume, the available research is skimpy in quantity but has powerful implications for the future.

Second, although we know a fair amount about the sociology of teachers (e.g., their demography, social class), we have virtually no information as to its effects on schooling. For example, Lortie (1975) concludes that teachers are lower-middle class, first generation college-goers, upwardly mobile, and, above all, conservative in social and political outlooks. This is useful as description, but one would examine the research in teacher education in vain for information as to whether this set of characteristics differentiates teachers from people in other professions or whether teachers with other characteristics (some, after all, come from upper-middle-class backgrounds) differ in any important way in their abilities to teach.

Third, the lack of careful and rigorous selection processes tends to throw tremendous responsibility on the conscientious teacher educator to produce *after entry* to the program important characteristics which are absent *upon* entry. All too frequently, teacher educators readily assume the responsibility of making silk purses from sows' ears. I submit that remediation of this sort not only is time consuming and risky but enormously expensive—so much so as to raise serious questions about whether admission standards should be substantially revised with the eye toward choosing students who already possess desired characteristics. I advocate this because we know considerably more about the characteristics of persons we prefer to have teach than are reflected in current criteria which are limited largely to cumulative grade point averages.

The easiest illustration of this situation is the recurring discussion I have with teacher educators interested in developmental psychology. Uniformly, they advocate that all prospective teachers need to demonstrate their ability to perform at one or another level on the various tests of psychological or cognitive development. If the student cannot do so, they claim, educational experiences should be provided to help them attain the desired level. My argument is simply that if a certain level of development is either necessary or highly desirable, we can assure that level among our students in two ways: we can select those people who already have attained it, or we can seek to develop it through coursework or other required experiences. The former technique may be far more effective and far less expensive in *time* and *money* than the latter. The same point can be made in connection with other capabilities—the ability to do critical thinking, computer literacy, academic achievement as revealed by the SAT, to name only a few. I am not really advocating a wholesale shift to tests of abilities across the range of human competence. The point is, though, that for each of these a judgment needs to be made in terms of to what degree the specific ability level *should be a precondition* for entry to a program or to what degree the program should be geared to develop it. Further research is needed which examines the relationship between specific characteristics and specific indices of effectiveness teaching. (A good illustration is contained in the chapter by Sprinthall and Theis-Sprinthall in this volume.) For example, we need to know much more about the various developmental levels of experienced teachers and patterns of their classroom behavior over time.

The critical element in all this is obviously that the schools will not be viewed by the general public as bastions (or even foxholes) of intellectual endeavor if teachers continue to be viewed as less able than other college graduates. It may be that the SATs, ACTs, the Loevinger or Kohlberg scales are all irrelevant to the act of good teaching, but *something must serve as an appropriate indication of the intellectual character of teachers* and, further, *must symbolize to the general public the school system's commitment to intellectuality*. While intellectual power and curiosity alone may not define the effective teacher, they are core attributes, and it appears that a priority of the first order is to examine the standards of academic ability and psychological maturity which should be a precondition of entry into the profession.

2. Another very serious issue I would raise from my study of the preceding chapters is the extent to which the research described supports

the apparent trends and developments in the field. Trend setters in teacher education purport to be moving the process forward, to be leading the profession in preferred directions. It is instructive to ask whether these directions are consistent with research findings.

At the risk of substantial oversimplification, I would describe the major trends and directions in teacher education as follows. A rather substantial group of education deans and professors currently recommend that programs be "extended" (made longer) and that they be "field based" (conducted more extensively in elementary or secondary schools).* Proponents of these trends discuss them in terms of the need to "professionalize" the field of teaching, such professionalization to be aided substantially if not totally accomplished through appropriate changes in training programs. The need to move toward professional status (and, hence, change teacher education programs) is particularly timely now, the argument goes, because of both Federal and State mandates regarding equal opportunity for the handicapped. With the increased responsibility imposed by new legal mandates (e.g., PL 94–142), new teachers especially need a broader array of teaching techniques and different attitudes. Further, it is argued, those new techniques and attitudes are best acquired through an additional period of formal learning. Finally, the argument concludes that the whole process needs a fuller and deeper connection with "where it's at"; hence, the programs should be field based.

One of the problems with understanding and assessing these trends is that the terms are not clearly defined. The concept of "extended programs," for example, seems to cover programs ranging from five- (or even six-) year initial preparation programs which include 1½ to 2 years of "professional" work (e.g., coursework in education) to those programs responding to a legal requirement that the first teaching certificate be classified as "temporary" until such time as a person satisfactorily completes one or two years of successful teaching. The field-based character of these proposals ranges from the requirement that students "do more student teaching" to the carefully articulated programs requiring extended tutelage under competent supervision such as those recommended recently by B. O. Smith (1980) and earlier by Robert Schaeffer (1967). And these observers talk only in general terms about specific types of experiences. Haberman, Johnston and Ryan, and Sprinthall and Theis-Sprinthall all review research which provides specific directions both about the types of *experiences* and the types of *conditions* which would promote teacher

---

* In making these points, I am relying on and summarizing briefly the writings of Howsam et al. (1976), Monahan (1977), Reynolds (1979) and Denemark (1979). It should be noted that their comments seek both to describe what they see happening in the field and to prescribe a preferred scenario for teacher education programs.

growth. It seems the call for more experiences by many has been sounded without attention to *what* may be needed *when*. There is an evolving data base which has been largely ignored that provides clues to answering these questions.

The picture is made more cloudy by the fact that there is a lack of agreement on what the outcome characteristics of entering teachers should be. Some of the proposals for extended programs (cf. Reynolds) attempt to identify a "common body" of practice for teachers, but they have not been adopted or recognized as legitimate by the field. Certainly, there is no research finding which supports a five- or six-year over a four-year program on the time variable alone. For all these reasons, it seems that Turner's conclusion of several years back is still largely valid—the amount of dependable information in teacher education compared to what is needed to formulate more effective policies is miniscule. Of course, there is no research base indicating that a four-year program is preferable over a shorter time period either, and it's unlikely that we will ever have research to prove that point. The four-year requirement re-sulted from a political, not a research, process. Regardless, the question of how much cannot be divorced from the requisite question of what ex-periences are necessary and when they should take place.

This point illustrates one of the several dilemmas in planning a re-search program in teacher education. The major policy issues in the field will continue to be resolved in the political arena on the basis of economic and social considerations rather than on the basis of research results. The question of extended programs will be addressed within the states; and in all likelihood, states where small but strong liberal arts schools have traditionally supported teacher education will move more slowly to require programs of longer duration. The extended program development will also be deeply affected by government policy on loans and scho-larships for college students, as well as by the general economic position, which, I assume, will continue to affect teacher salaries as it has in the past. In the face of all of this, one is tempted to conclude that it's just as well that the question of extended programs has not been extensively stud-ied because if, in fact, the results supported more extensive preparation, they could not affect policy anyway. It is more likely that future changes in school experiences will occur because of new political alliances.

Although research cannot be said to be responsible for any wide-spread practice in clinical experiences, it sheds some light on both quanti-ty and quality issues related to the typical experiences the prospective teacher currently has in schools. The survey studies by Joyce, Howey, and Yarger, for example, reveal that the quantity of the clinical experiences of prospective teachers is ludicriously low, on the average substantially less than that required by other professional schools and by most of the pro-grams that train people for the semi-professions. The research raises questions about general quality as well; unless the students are extremely bright or the experiences extremely powerful, not much can be learned, nor can much truly *professional* socialization go on in so short a period of time.

But there are other reasons to suspect the quality of the experience. One of these centers on what I think should be a central question in teacher education generally—is it/should it be designed to prepare professionals who monitor their own behavior or to facilitate the learning of accepted technical behaviors? The rhetoric of the field clearly suggests that the former is appropriate but there is great need for studies of a philosophical nature into this question, and, as Haberman points out, for studies indicating what kinds of practice teaching tends to create a professional as opposed to a technician. At present, we know very little about this.

3. An issue closely related to those of quantity and quality in clinical experiences is the recurring question of how and where teachers are and should be socialized into their roles. This is the old questions of whether universities can in fact prepare the self-renewing type of teacher desired by many teachers or whether the effects of socializing experiences in the schools during practice teaching or the first year of teaching are so strong as to wash out the effects of a university.

As noted in a review of recent literature (Zeichner & Tabachnick, 1981), the prevailing view is that the university/college environment and training program has a liberalizing influence over beginning teachers which is lessened or obliterated when the students hit the schools. This conclusion has frequently been cited as rationale for continuing to locate teacher education programs on university campuses, for while university-based programs could not guarantee the persistence of the liberalizing influence, they could at least constitute an important leavening to the conservative influences of the school. The review cited earlier raises the important question of to what extent and whether the school is the only source of the "illiberalization" of new teachers and whether the university is not an active party to this process.

Our authors did not really examine this point, although it is full of significance. Except for Haberman who reviewed the literature describing relative influence of university and classroom supervisors, the authors generally ignored questions of the staying power of programs of pre- and inservice education. I take this omission to be an indication that very little has been done to examine questions of context and socialization; hence, there is nothing to review.

It strikes me that of all the unexamined issues in teacher education this, together with the selection issue, is one of the most significant. One of the general principles of teaching (and learning) centers is that linkages between observation, demonstration, practice, and criticism have to be made. In medical training, this problem is addressed through the internship which is spent in a teaching hospital. The context for the training has some tie with the more formal classroom enterprise which precedes it. The fact that this tie is often poorly conceptualized is for the moment immaterial; a structure which permits an integrated, developmental program is present in medical education. Not only are training programs in education lacking this important structural characteristic, but the coursework and the practice parts of the program are diffused to the point where the effects of one may cancel out the other.

This situation is very disappointing because the question of where training should go on is a most important policy issue. My guess is that for the forseeable future, training programs will stay under the control of universities, simply because no one else has the time, money, or energy to mount a challenge. It seems clear to me that a major way to improve teacher education is for universities to seek to develop training sites which are compatible with the concept of teaching hospitals. A useful model for these teaching schools is the idea advanced by Schaeffer in his book, *The School as a Center of Inquiry*. His model would provide more than a training site; it would be a meeting place for university professors as well as teachers and students. His model, and similar ones, should be developed and tested because they contain a potential answer to a very difficult problem.

4. Of particular interest to me (and, I think, of general significance as well) is Schalock's statement of the need for a "paradigm shift" in teacher education research. As I understand his argument, it is as follows. One of the major reasons for the ineffectiveness of research in teacher education has to do with external validity—it is extremely difficult to generalize research findings to contexts other than those which are greatly similar to the ones in which the research was conducted. To overcome these difficulties, Schalock calls for a "methodological shift," the development of a new design which would focus on sampling of educational environments (rather than people), studying a set of complex variables (rather than isolated ones), and articulating studies through time and theory (instead of one-shot research efforts).

These ideas are at once both invigorating and frustrating. The invigoration stems from the premise that researchers have at last achieved sufficient sophistication to make possible a true paradigm shift. The use of longitudinal designs using an ethnographic orientation, multiple measures of variables, and new modes of analysis would provide immensely exciting and useful studies. The frustration, of course, flows from the complexity of it all. In my mind, the studies proposed by Schalock, for example, imply the existence of a number of research labs which provide the superstructure for broad-gauge research studies, for centers of inquiry which would stimulate the generation of new sites for the conduct of research (e.g., "laboratory" schools) as well as the development of new and challenging hypotheses. Agencies such as these are not in existence in large number, and we must ask how they could be created. Here, sadly, is the issue of future funding for research in education. It is extremely unlikely that the paradigm shift will take place without rather substantial federal or major foundation support over a sustained period of time. The tasks perceived for the research effort would demand a research apparatus similar in concept, if not in scope, to the federal involvement in agriculture. We are all too keenly aware that the major problem in the years just ahead will be to protect the pitifully small investment in education research generally, let alone decide how to lobby Congress to adopt new initiatives. Schalock, although hardly oblivious to many problems, does seem to assume rather tacitly that the shift he sees taking place will continue to do so without a change in the support structure. I take a dimmer view; the policy decisions made in the early days of the Reagan administration will greatly lessen the chances of the "paradigm shift." And, those decisions are not likely to be reversed in the near future.

Finally, I should like to make two concluding comments. The first of these deals with the application of research findings to the major policy questions in the field. The authors included here accept as a basic premise that teacher education can be substantially improved through more and better research. The ways to develop superior programs, to find the optimum sequence for instruction, to evaluate the results of the process—all can be accomplished or greatly aided through research. A cautionary note is needed here. While an improved research base is necessary for improvement, it is not sufficient, for a great many of the basic issues cannot be resolved through research means. These issues are the ones concerned with politics (who is going to control entry into the profession in the future), economics (how teacher education can be financed in the face of increased competition from roads, sewers, and bombers, as well as from other schools), and sociology (from what socioeconomic strata or academic ability groups the teaching cadre will be drawn in the future.)

I do not want to fuel the notion that research has no utility in the drive to improve teacher education nor in helping to answer political, economic, and social questions. That clearly is not my meaning. It is really a case of recognizing that improvements in the teacher education system must be approached on several fronts, and that formal research, even the very broad type recommended by Schalock, is only one of these.

A second point is closely related. Little, if any, formal policy analysis has been done on the teacher education process or on proposals for improving it. Far more attention needs to be paid to analysis of consequences of proposed changes, for we do have a tendency to support change for the sake of change with the result that we risk defeating our purpose.

As an illustration, let me return once more to the matter of extended programs. The idea of longer initial programs is generally accepted as a good thing, but the acceptance is premised on the fact that a longer period of study will yield better performance. This premise can and should be tested through research such as that recommended in this book. But an approach which stops there ignores questions like these: Will a requirement for a longer period of study attract more or less able students into a teacher education program? Will extended and, hence, more expensive programs rule out the possibility that young men and women of modest means can choose teaching simply because they cannot afford to stay in school? Will states provide the new resources necessary to support longer programs? If not, can they be done on the cheap? Will graduates of an extended program compete successfully for jobs with those with less training who can be hired for less?

These are significant and difficult questions to answer, and I do not pretend that something called "policy analysis" will either resolve them or make them go away. But I do think that far more attention must be paid to the consequences of changes in teacher education. There are people who can do consequence analysis, examine documents, do opinion surveys, and develop scenarios based on assumptions. We could and should make use of these types of analysis in teacher education. It would provide a most useful adjunct to the formal research recommended in this volume.

BIBLIOGRAPHY

Denemark, G. W. *The case for extended programs of initial teacher preparation*. Mimeo. Arlington, Virginia, 1979.

Howsam, R. B., Corrigan, D. C., Denemark, G. W., & Nash, R. J. *Educating a profession*. Report of the Bicentennial Commission on Education for the Profession of Teaching of the American Association of Colleges for Teacher Education. Washington, D.C.: AACTE, 1976.

Joyce, B., Howey, K., Yarger, S. J. *Preservice teacher education*. Mimeo. Palo Alto, California.

Lortie, D. C. *Schoolteacher: A sociological study*. Chicago: The University of Chicago Press, 1975.

Monahan, W. G. Some straight-talk about teacher preparation. *Educational Leadership*, 1977, 202–204.

Reynolds, M. (Ed.). *A common body of practice for teachers: The challenge of PL. 94–142 to teacher education*. Minneapolis, Minnesota: The National Support System Project, 1979.

Schaeffer, R. J. *The school as a center of inquiry*. New York: Harper and Row, 1967.

Smith, B. O. *A design for a school of pedagogy*. Washington, D.C.: U.S. Department of Education, 1980.

Turner, R. L. An overview of research in teacher education. In *Teacher education: The seventy-fourth yearbook of the National Society for the Study of Education*, Part II. Chicago: University of Chicago Press, 1975.

Weaver, W. T. The talent pool in teacher education. *Journal of Teacher Education*, 1981, *22*(3), 32–36.

Zeichner, K. M., & Tabachnick, B. R. Are the effects of university teacher education 'washed out' by the school experience? *Journal of Teacher Education*, 1981, *32*(3), 7–13.

Index